BYGONE BRITAIN

ON HOLIDAY

1900–1970

LONDON: HMSO

Researched and prepared by Publishing Services, Central Office of Information

© Selection and introduction Crown copyright 1996

Applications for reproduction should be made to:

HMSO, The Copyright Unit, St Clements House, 2-16 Colegate, Norwich NR3 1BQ

ISBN 0 11 701898 8

Published by HMSO and available from:

HMSO Publications Centre
(Mail, fax and telephone orders only)
PO Box 276, London SW8 5DT
Telephone orders 0171 873 9090
General enquiries 0171 873 0011
(queuing system in operation for both numbers)
Fax orders 0171 873 8200

HMSO Bookshops
49 High Holborn, London WC1V 6HB
(counter service only)
0171 873 0011 Fax 0171 831 1326
68-69 Bull Street, Birmingham B4 6AD
0121 236 9696 Fax 0121 236 9699
33 Wine Street, Bristol BS1 2BQ
0117 9264306 Fax 0117 9294515
9-21 Princess Street, Manchester M60 8AS
0161 834 7201 Fax 0161 833 0634
16 Arthur Street, Belfast BT1 4GD
01232 238451 Fax 01232 235401
71 Lothian Road, Edinburgh EH3 9AZ
0131 228 4181 Fax 0131 229 2734
The HMSO Oriel Bookshop
The Friary, Cardiff CF1 4AA
01222 395548 Fax 01222 384347

HMSO's Accredited Agents
(see Yellow Pages)
and through good booksellers

Acknowledgments

We would like to thank the staff of the British Library Newspaper Library at Colindale for their ready and cheerful assistance and co-operation, and for their expertise in problem-solving. The staff at the British Library at Bloomsbury have also helped in turning up rare and distant journals. We are also indebted to the following, who so kindly allowed us access to their archives: the National Magazine Company (*Queen, Harper's Bazaar,* and *Good Housekeeping* magazines), the Thomas Cook Travel Archive, Erna Low Consultants, Swan Hellenic Cruises, Butlin's Limited, and Trade and Travel Publications Ltd (*South American Handbook*).

We stress that copyright in the extracts quoted belongs to the newspapers, magazines or organisations concerned, or to their successors in business. Present owners have been most kind in granting permission to quote. These include Times Newspapers Limited, Express Group Newspapers Ltd, Associated Newspapers, Mirror Group Newspapers Ltd, News Group Newspapers Ltd, The *Observer*, the Daily Telegraph plc and Ewan MacNaughton Associates, IPC Magazines Ltd, Punch Publications Ltd, BBC Worldwide, and the Condé Nast Publications Ltd.

In spite of all our efforts, it has not been possible to trace all present copyright owners in some of the extracts quoted. If we have in any way offended, we invite those concerned to get in touch with us.

We would like to thank our colleagues in COI Pictures Section for helping us to choose the photographs for this book. The top photograph on page 148 is reproduced by courtesy of the Press Association.

The centre cover illustration is by courtesy of the Thomas Cook Travel Archive; that on the left shows a Girl Guide camp (Cheshire Guides), c 1910; that on the right shows the beach at Broadstairs in Kent in 1970, and is a Fox Photo original.

PREFACE

By Sir Harry Secombe

There's nothing quite like coming across a 50-year-old newspaper or magazine – when you're moving house, perhaps, or having a particularly vigorous spring-clean. The shape and size of their yellowing pages may look familiar, but their contents seem to come from another world.

The Bygone Britain series explores our past through the pages of these old newspapers and magazines, which were only ever meant to be bought, read for a day or so and thrown away, but often end up lining people's drawers or wrapped round their crockery.

I find them endlessly fascinating. On the one hand here are events familiar through the reasoned analysis of history – battles, political upheavals – reported with vivid immediacy. Yet news items such as Chamberlain's successful appeasement mission to Berlin can only be viewed through the lens of hindsight. There are also the news stories that took a long time to happen: the earliest of many items about the Channel Tunnel in Bygone Britain is dated 1907!

Quite unselfconsciously, the articles, letters and advertisements reveal completely different priorities from our own. It is quite shocking that a small and ostensibly sentimental item about the discovery of an abandoned baby finishes with the casual disclosure that the infant was then consigned to the workhouse. Conversely, the behaviour of these aliens from another age has the power to amuse us in a way that would make them quite indignant: the excruciating niceties of visiting cards are surely no laughing matter, and what on earth is wrong with attempting to banish grey hair with radium? Likewise, in these knowledgeable days of niche marketing and core business, we find it absurd to see an advertisement urging hairdressers to sell the odd bicycle on the side.

But there are many hints that the people who populate these pages are not such strangers to us after all. Get-rich-quick schemes and dubious books already feature prominently in the small ads, and the slimming advertisements seem as widespread as in our own press. Some of the ideas voiced in the articles are ones that we thought our own generation had come up with: domestic science as a subject for boys, the dangers of too much exposure to the sun. And, needless to say, affairs of the heart loom large across the pages, whatever the decade.

The things that we can recall ourselves exert their own particular attraction. Coverage of events we remember, pictures of celebrities, advertisements for objects we coveted excite a warm glow of recognition and affection. Other pictures may arouse quite opposite emotions: horror and self-loathing to think that we ever went around with lapels like that! Our reactions to our memories are as much a gauge of how we as individuals have changed as of how society has changed.

So what conclusions can we draw from leafing through the pages of the Bygone Britain books? The increasing pace of technological change is evident, as is the growing informality – in manners, in language, and in address to the readers. The problem page letters confirm this. Early in the century, the letters themselves do not appear; all we see are the replies, addressed to a mysterious correspondent with a fanciful name: Heart's Ease or Sapphire. Fifty years later many writers think nothing of revealing their true identities along with their troubles. (In passing, let us be thankful for the demise of the enterprising service offered by the *Hairdressers and Toilet Requisites Gazette*, whereby people sent in samples of falling hair – and worse – for trichological analysis.)

Does the very different look of the articles in the 1900s and those of the 1960s – tiny, dense text with small headlines giving way to more spacious type with *Sun*-style screamers – mean that our powers of concentration are declining? That papers and magazines have to try harder to wrest our attention from television is obvious, but modern technology, availability of newsprint, and more widespread literacy have all played their part in shaping our contemporary press.

Whether you have a serious interest in British history and society, or you're an avid consumer of trivia; whether you can remember most of the first seventy years of this century, or you weren't even born, you will find plenty to wonder at, to mourn and to laugh about in the Bygone Britain series.

INTRODUCTION

'We're all going on a summer holiday,
No more working for a week or two'

sang Cliff Richard in his 1962 film *Summer Holiday*, a film that featured prominently all
the ingredients of a 'Continental' holiday: sun, sea and romance (definitely romance rather
than sex, since Club 18–30 had not yet been invented).

Yet the words of the song make one assumption that would not have been possible at the
turn of the century: paid holidays. In 1938 the Holidays with Pay Act established paid
holidays for all. Up until then these had been available to many office workers but not to
manual workers. The correspondence to the *Birmingham Mail* in 1934 (p. 69) shows how
hotly the issue of holiday pay for manual workers was debated. When it finally came in,
it made a world of difference: for the first time all workers would feel able to enjoy a break
from work rather than endure a period of enforced penury.

It is perhaps at this point that the term 'holiday' began to expand from its original
meaning of 'holy day' – a single day for rest and recreation – to include a longer stint
devoted to leisure. A notice placed in *Reynolds Newspaper* in 1907 by the Post Office
advising readers of their reduced services on Christmas Day (no collections but one
delivery) and Boxing Day (one delivery and one collection) gives an indication of how
many people then might have been at work, even on recognised bank holidays.

Until 1938, the scarcity of holidays for most people ensured that they made the most of
those they did get: in 1904 *Chic* magazine described the August Bank Holiday crowds
availing themselves of the 'admirable facilities offered by the Great Central Railway
Company from Marylebone to Stratford upon Avon . . . Cleethorpes, Scarborough and
Bridlington, and other renowned resorts.' It is interesting to note that on this occasion
'numerous special express trains were run to accommodate this holiday traffic, in addition
to many of the ordinary trains being duplicated.'

Trains had opened up the possibility of enjoying a change of scene as a break from work.
In 1900 Mr A. E. Wynn inaugurated the first long-distance bus service with his
motor-wagonette trips between London and Leeds. A cutting from a 1926 edition of
Holidays, Tours and Travel gives an early account of caravanning. Cruising is perennially
popular, and holiday travel reaches its apotheosis, of course, in the cheap package holiday
of the 1960s: 15 days in Majorca for £39.50.

Despite this, holidays in Britain retained their attraction, whether for reasons of economy,
the mistrust of foreigners, or the avoidance of strange food 'swimming in oil'. As early as
1912 Mrs Frances Campbell – a widow of a relative of the Duke of Argyll, no less –
complained in the *News of the World* that the food on her Mediterranean trip was 'inferior,
badly cooked and badly served', which gave her ptomaine poisoning. And the mistrust
seems not to have been misplaced, in the case of one unfortunate visitor to Calais in 1900,
who wrote to the *Evening Standard* to warn travellers that they might, like him, end up
being pelted with rotten lemons.

In fact, the British holiday, particularly the British seaside holiday, has acquired a mythology
all of its own: Blackpool landladies (Mrs Billington advertises her 'tap basins and electric all
bedrooms; sep. tables'), the mystery man of the seaside carnival (Lobby Lud challenges us to
identify him and claim £20 at the Littlehampton and Bognor Regis carnivals, p.155), and
the always thorny problem of undressing on the beach (should ladies be allowed extra time –
or would this encourage exhibitionism? See p. 22). There was a palpable sense of shock in
Clacton in 1964 when this idyll was shattered by rioting Mods and Rockers (p. 138).

No account of the British on holiday would be complete without a mention of the holiday camp, so don't miss Butlin's jolly head chef at Skegness and the enticing entertainments on offer at Prestatyn Holiday Camp throughout the 1970 season: Paper Bouquet Competition in the Sun Lounge and Glamorous Grandmother Competition in the Ballroom.

'Let me tell you about the very rich. They are different from you and me,' said F. Scott Fitzgerald. On the evidence of *On Holiday* it certainly seems so. The very rich float serenely around the globe and across the decades, apparently impervious to wars, austerity and currency restrictions. See them wintering in Rapallo in 1908, or considering whether to book a tour in Japan and the Philippines in 1917 (1917!), or perhaps weighing up the merits of buying a plot in the Bahamas (1963). 'Surely you are coming to Cairo as usual this winter?' inquires the National Hotel in the pages of Thomas Cook's *Traveller's Gazette* (1928), as if to do anything else were unthinkable. Throughout, the *South American Handbook* was indeed on hand, to advise on a range of topics, from choosing the perfect mule to precautions against typhoid and malaria.

The pages of *On Holiday* offer infinite variety. So whether your idea of a perfect holiday is a stout pair of boots and a rugged landscape, tinkling ice cubes and Bahamian breezes, or strolling along the prom to survey the floral clock, you will find it reflected here.

Verity Ridgman
COI
March 1996

1900 ▆ 1909

BURLESQUE CRICKET.

DAN LENO AND MISS KATIE SEYMOUR AT THE WICKETS.

Charity took on a motley garb at East Molesey Cricket Ground yesterday.

For the benefit of the local cottage hospital Dan Leno, Miss Katie Seymour, and a strong following of equally distinguished members of "the profession" provided entertainment for fully 1,000 visitors from the immediate neighbouring vicinity and London.

The proceedings consisted mainly of a costume cricket match, in which a variety of grotesque "make-ups" served to introduce Mr. Fred Wright, Mr. Harry Grattan, the MacNaughtons, Mr. Lionel Mackinder, and other humorists of fame.

Dan Leno's arrival, attired as a huntsman with excruciating whiskers and a nose of vermilion, literally sent the company into fits of laughter.

In the middle of the match he fired off a revolver, and the whole team fell as if mortally wounded, and when he went in with a stuffed "property" bat everybody clung on to the garden furniture in paroxysms of merriment.

Nor was the great philosopher of the music halls alone in his humour, for Miss Katie Seymour having, in a vain attempt to cut Mr. Edward Lauri, upset her wicket, flatly refused to go out, and playfully smote the umpire on the nose. "Arrest that woman," shouted the injured umpire, and presently the astonished spectators saw Miss Seymour flying before a burly policeman and gaining every stride until she sprang into a coach full of wounded soldiers and defied arrest.

To the exuberant happiness of the afternoon the "poor fighting men broke in our wars" supplied a note of pathos. They came upon the ground in brakes from "The Gables," the residence of Mr. Cooper at Surbiton. Those who could walk hobbled about the ground and showed the bullets that had sent them home.

After the cricket, or the burlesque of it, was over, there were visits to the tents of "The Mermaid," "The Human Love Bird," and other freaks. There were also an "all fiasco" concert, bicycle polo, and a dozen other side-shows, all ingeniously designed for the swelling of the fund, which, it is satisfactory to learn, benefited handsomely.

Daily Mail 1900

No. 3069.

No. 3068.

Mother's Help and Little Dressmaker 1900

SCOTT ADIE, The Royal Scotch Warehouse,

115, 115a, REGENT ST., LONDON, W.

FOR

Homespun and Scotch Cheviot
Travelling Coats and Suits,
Cycling Gowns and Golf Capes.

Cheviot Rugs
21/-

Steamer Rugs... ... from 18/6

Carriage Rugs... ... ,, 15/6

Carriage Rugs
50/-

Scotch Shawls ... ,, 15/6

Scotch Jewellery,

Hand Knit Stockings,

Reversible
Rugs from
22/6

Tartans, Silks, and Ribbons.

SCOTCH TWEED
WATERPROOF COAT.

TELEGRAMS:—"SCOTT ADIE, LONDON."

Silk Plush Rugs
84/-

Cook's Excursionist and Tourist Advertiser 1901

Regular motor car trips between London and Leeds and other places are now the order of the day. During the past week or so a number of passengers have travelled in Mr. A. E. Wynn's motor-wagonette on its way to Leeds, and only a highwayman or two, a turnpike-gate, and a change of horses were needed to make the whole far-away reminiscence complete. The idea of Mr. Wynn, who is a Leeds man, is to run a service of petroleum-driven coaches from London to Leeds, and if London is willing he means to go to Brighton, to Cornwall, to Worcester, to all corners of her Majesty's home dominions. The beginning of the new movement was in the Upper Street, Islington. There Mr. Wynn set out on a passenger-seeking journey through Hatfield and Hitchin and Biggleswade and the ninety miles of territory between London and Stamford. A halt was made at night at Stamford for rest, and next day the car went on through Grantham and Doncaster and Pontefract to Leeds. That is Mr. Wynn's trip, and he means to traverse it every week until the end of this month.

The Road 1900

ENGLISH VISITORS TO CALAIS.

"An Englishman" writes:—May I be allowed to put English visitors on their guard who are intending to visit Calais? A few weeks ago I paid the town a short visit with a friend. We had not been long on shore before we heard the most insulting shouts after us because we were English. Yesterday I had occasion to re-visit Calais. I was walking along with my umbrella up, as it was raining, when suddenly my umbrella was struck with heavy blows. I found that rotten lemons had been thrown at me. I make no comment on these proceedings; I merely record facts.

Evening Standard 1900

The charges for solid and liquid refreshments are prominently displayed in every car, but vary considerably according to the Country through which the train is passing. In every case, however, are the figures reasonable, as shown by the following extract:—

Light Breakfast (Tea, Coffee, or Chocolate, with Bread and Butter)	... ...	10d. to 1/8
Lunch	... ...	2/6 to 4/-
Dinner	... ...	3/6 to 6/-

Liquid refreshments of the best quality, which are not included in this tariff, are supplied at reasonable charges.

Cook's Excursionist
and Tourist Advertiser
1901

Queen **1900**

Lord Chelsea.	Mrs A. James.	Lady Chelsea.	Lady G. Curzon.
Lord St. Oswald.	Capt. the Hon. H. Lambton.	Mrs W. James.	Major the Hon. W. Lambton.

MR AND MR   WILLIE JAMES'S HOUSE PARTY AT WEST DEAN PARK, FOR GOODWOOD

PAPER PATTERN.

HOLIDAY COSTUME.

A good coat and skirt is a necessity where holidays are in contemplation, and the above model can hardly be improved upon. The skirt is an excellent shape for walking, and is perfectly plain at the back, where the placket is hidden beneath a stitched mitred strap.

The coat is the familiar semi-sacque, slightly falling into the figure at the back, and double-breasted in front.

Paper pattern of either coat or skirt, price 1s. 1d., the costume complete, 2s. 2d., from *Queen* Office, Bream's Buildings, E.C. By post only.

Queen 1901

CONDENSED ITINERARY OF TOUR No. 1.

The Conductor leaves Edinburgh on Wednesdays, *via* the Forth Bridge, for STIRLING and ABERFOYLE, whence coach is taken for the TROSSACHS, the route embracing two fine coach drives, and two lovely steamer trips on LOCH KATRINE and LOCH LOMOND. Glasgow is reached about 7·0 p.m. (*Windsor Hotel*). Thursday will be spent in Glasgow, carriages being provided for visiting the

THE TROSSACHS.

most interesting sights, including the International Exhibition. On Friday the voyage to Oban is made by the "Columba" to Ardrishaig, thence by the "Linnet" through the Crinan Canal, and by the "Chevalier" to the gay little capital of the Western Highlands. Oban is picturesquely situated on a land-locked bay, and from the heights above the town the view embraced is magnificent. After breakfast at the hotel (*Marine*) on Saturday, members will make the famous and delightful trip round the Island of Mull to STAFFA and IONA, one of the most popular day excursions from Oban. Sunday will be spent at Oban. Dunstaffnage Castle, about three miles distant, is well worth a visit, and there are other endless attractive walks in the neighbourhood. Monday and Tuesday are devoted to the journey to Inverness, *via* the Caledonian Canal, proceeding on Monday as far as BANAVIE (*Lochiel Arms Hotel*), breaking the journey at Ballachulish for a coach drive through the sublime scenery of GLENCOE, past the scene of the massacre, and back (18 miles). After breakfast on Tuesday, the "Gondolier" is taken on the Caledonian Canal. Few steamer trips in Scotland can compare with this for splendid combination of mountain and loch scenery. The entire length from Banavie to Inverness is 60½ miles, 23 only of which are canal, the rest consisting of the beautiful lochs—Lochy, Oich, and Ness. From Banavie, Ben Nevis looks glorious.

INVERNESS is reached about 5·30 p.m. (*Station Hotel*). On Wednesday train is taken to FORRES (*Royal Station Hotel*). A delightful carriage excursion will be made to the banks of the FINDHORN, which are admitted to present the most striking and beautiful combination of rock, wood, and water scenery in the United Kingdom. After dinner a pleasant hour may be spent inspecting the sights of Forres, including the Cluny Hills and the Trafalgar Tower. After breakfast on Thursday, train is taken to DUNKELD (*Birnam Hotel*). After inspecting the charming grounds of the Dowager Duchess of Athole on Friday, and visiting the Rumbling Bridge and Hermitage Waterfalls, the most lovely in the Perthshire Highlands, train will be taken in the afternoon for PERTH and EDINBURGH, completing a matchless tour of about 700 miles.

BRITISH LINER ASHORE.

ALL PASSENGERS SAVED.

PANIC ON BOARD.

ST. JOHN'S, Wednesday.

The liner Lusitania, from Liverpool to Montreal, commanded by Captain McKay, ran ashore before daybreak this morning at Seal Cove, twenty-five miles north of Cape Race, having mistaken the course in a thick fog. Her 500 passengers have been landed. The weather is fine, and there has been no loss of life.

Three steamers have gone from here to the assistance of the Lusitania. The agents of Messrs. Elder Dempster, at Montreal, have arranged with Messrs. Bowring Brothers, of St. John's, to look after the passengers and see that they are sent to their several destinations.

The scene of the wreck is miles from the nearest telegraph station, and up to now only meagre details are to hand. According to the latest information, the Lusitania ran over a reef, and is now hanging against the cliff, but it is expected that her cargo will be salvaged.

It is said that when she struck the passengers were seized with panic, and were only with difficulty got under control by the officers and crew, some of the rougher element having recourse to their knives. The women and children were landed first, and the men followed, while the crew stood by the ship. A heavy sea was running at the time.—Reuter.

ST. JOHN'S, Wednesday (Later).

Latest accounts state that the Lusitania is breaking up, her forehold being full of water. Her cargo is being salved. Altogether six steamers are now en route for the scene of the wreck, and it is expected that the sailors and passengers will be brought here to-night.

According to narratives given by the passengers, they had a terrible experience. They first became aware of the disaster through the rasping of the ship over the rocks hurling them from their berths, many of them sustaining bruises. They hurried on deck in their night clothes, and some, even, of the male passengers lost all control of themselves. Others, more cool-headed, retained their calm, and assisted the crew in getting out the boats.

One of the boats was upset and its occupants immersed, and some fears are now entertained that some of these may have been lost, but owing to the confusion prevailing at the time it has been impossible to obtain any trustworthy statement on the point. It has, however, now been definitely ascertained that one boat, with twenty on board, has not been reported, and it is thought that she is adrift in the fog. A rumour circulating here that twenty lives had been lost is supposed to have its origin in this fact.

The women and children when brought ashore were almost naked, and were drenched with the spray. They had to be literally pulled up the cliffs by the coast people. Some of the boats were demolished in the surf, their half-drowned occupants clinging on to the rocks, shivering and cold, until they were rescued. The passengers, after waiting for hours for the dawn on the bare hill-top, wet through and chilled to the bone, tramped for miles to the houses of some fishermen, where they are now sheltered. All night long there was a heavy sea, and it rained furiously.

The Lusitania struck near the spot where the Scottish King was wrecked.—Reuter.

ST. JOHN'S, Wednesday (3.30 p.m.).

It is now confirmed that all the passengers of the Lusitania have escaped, though several were injured. The missing boat has come to land safely. The Lusitania has now listed over, and is half-full of water.—Reuter.

Daily Telegraph 1901

WORDSWORTH, we are reminded, is adequately celebrated at Grasmere by the preservation of Dove Cottage. The official catalogue of the contents of Dove Cottage, Grasmere, Wordsworth's home from 1799 to 1808, and afterwards De Quincey's residence, is issued by Mr. George Middleton, of Ambleside, as a neat paper-covered booklet. It is a little distressing, perhaps, to read, among the rules for admission—

III. No pic-nic parties are allowed within the grounds.
IV. Visitors are forbidden to deface, injure, or remove any flower, plant shrub, or tree within the grounds of the cottage; or any relic of the Poet, or of others, placed within it.

But, alas, such memorials become sacred to the few long before they do to the many. Even for the few this important rule has been framed—

No extract, in writing or by photograph, from any book or MSS. in this catalogue, or in Dove Cottage, may be taken—whether to be reproduced or merely retained—without the special permission of the trustees of the cottage personally granted.

Room F., we notice, is filled with portraits of the guests who have slept in Dove Cottage. The list is interesting, and includes De Quincey, Scott, Landor, Lamb, Southey, Coleridge, Dr. Arnold, and Matthew Arnold.

Academy 1902

GOOD FRIDAY AND THE FACTORY ACT.—J. H. Bigland, baker, was fined 13s. 6d., including costs, at Southampton Police Court, for having employed a boy in his bakery before 6 o'clock in the morning. The lad was packing buns on Good Friday morning up to 5.30. The boy said he was there on pleasure, and received no wages.——At the same court, Oliver Simmonds, 62, Orchard Lane, was charged with employing a boy at 5.10 on Good Friday morning. A fine, including costs, of 11s. 6d. was inflicted.

"Nature has written a letter of credit on some men's faces which is honoured almost wherever presented." This is what we might term face value, and is a valuable asset to any man. Another good thing is "Book-keeping for Small Traders," 2s. 8d. post free. Can be had from the publishers of this journal.

British Baker 1903

AUGUST BANK HOLIDAY TRAFFIC.

THOUSANDS of excursionists availed themselves of the admirable facilities offered by the Great Central Railway Company from Marylebone to Stratford-on-Avon, Leicester, Nottingham, Sheffield, Leeds, Huddersfield, Halifax, Bradford, Manchester, Liverpool, Southport, Isle-of-Man, York, Cleethorpes, Scarborough, Bridlington, and other renowned holiday resorts on the north-east and north-west coasts accessible by this Company's picturesque and comfortable route. Numerous special express trains were run to accommodate this holiday traffic, in addition to many of the ordinary trains being duplicated. Large numbers travelled by this Company's route from the Midlands and the North to London, and the bookings from their provincial stations to the many popular watering places and holiday haunts North, East, South, and West, reached by the Great Central line also compare most favourably with previous returns for the same period.

Chic 1904

CERTAINLY the comfort of the English hotel is not a lost possession. It has found a prophet in an American journalist, Mr. H. Gilson Gardner, who, writing in a Chicago newspaper, expresses the astonishment with which he discovered how delusive was his previous belief that the Englishwoman is never taken into account in our hotel life. He writes :—

> While seeking in the evening for the bar—which I never found—I came on a most delightful, large room, with fireplace, sofas, easy chairs, writing desks, tables, and tobourets, and filled with women in evening toilet and men in dress suits, all lounging and chatting and sipping at various cheering drinks. Behind a screen of palms, an orchestra discoursed sweet strains. Further on was another room frequented by men alone and similarly furnished. . . . But a place for the women to lounge with the men, and have coffee or lemonade or champagne as their taste and purse might suggest, was a notion quite foreign to our theories of hotel-keeping.

It has been more than hinted in American papers that the treatment their hotels afford to women is by no means too cordial, but we do not pay much attention to such suggestions. Still it is evident from the above that Cousin Jonathan may learn something from John Bull even at his own game of hotel-keeping.

Caterer 1901

EQUINE PENSIONERS.

New Year's Day Dinner at a Horses' Home of Rest.

In public state at the Acton Home of Rest yesterday, fifty-seven horses—some thoroughbreds, others of less exalted lineage—partook of their special New Year's Day repast.

Punctually at half-past two the chestnut Max, an aristocratic veteran, put his head out of his loose-box and rang the dinner-bell—a feat accomplished by seizing a rope in his teeth.

This was the signal for stablemen and boys to commence serving out boxes of carrots and apples; bread, white and brown, lump sugar, and biscuits; all chopped into appetising slices which could not try the tenderest teeth.

The aged guests of the lady who has given this feast for twelve successive years, like human beings well past their allotted span, look old and world-weary, for these old pensioners think nothing of thirty years, and one Methuselah has attained the great age of thirty-eight.

But blood tells, and many of the retired steeple-chasers look thoroughly game, though coat and mane are silvered. A Colonel's charger, who led the Coldstreams for fifteen years, is a supremely gentlemanly old fellow. To see him gently whinny and caress his master in response to a kiss on his white-starred forehead is a lesson in the art of deportment.

Quite at the other end of the social scale is the little rough coster's moke, who was rescued from ill-treatment and pensioned by a tender-hearted lady. One of his eyes is blinded by a flick of the whip, but the other looks out on life cheerily.

Some explanation seemed necessary for the presence of four mettled steeds, for it was evident that neither old age nor weakness was responsible for their relegation to the retired list.

"Motoring," said the head groom, laconically, indicating two handsome carriage horses.

"The lady has taken up with automobiles and altered her stables."

Daily Mirror 1904

Suffolk and Norfolk.

"Nosey."—(1) Chelmsford, Witham, Colchester, Clacton. (2) Walton, Dovercourt, Harwich, and steamer up Orwell to Ipswich, or ferry to Felixstowe. (3) Woodbridge, Orford (castle) by beach and ferry to Aldeburgh (if rough work objected to then cut Orford), Saxmundham, Walberswick or Southwold. (4) Lowestoft, Yarmouth, Caister, Stalham. (5) North Walsham, Cromer, Sherringham and back. (6) Norwich, Scole, Diss, Earl Stonham. (7) Ipswich, Colchester, Braintree, Dunmow. (8) Harlow, Epping Forest, home.

Wales, etc.

F.F.S.—The boats run from Weston to Cardiff daily in three-quarters of an hour, but I doubt if there is a Sunday boat (write P. and A. Campbell, Cumberland Basin, Bristol). You will, however, do well to wait until the Monday as you have ample time. Do not ferry at Bath, nor use the bridge at Barmouth; and do not miss Dolgelly; better have the bag sent to Barmouth; Harlech is a tiny place. From Beddgelert by Carnarvon. There are no tolls worth naming. Mr. Throup's Sixpenny Guide (post free 8d.) T. Throup, 27, Fairbank Road, Bradford.

Cycling 1903

The main rendezvous, however, was the Shaftesbury Holiday House at Loughton, on the border of Epping Forest. Here an acre of ground encloses the Superintendent's house, with a dozen beds for guests, and large kitchen accommodation; and three large halls or sheds with tables and seats for 800 children. Five days a week, from July to September, 500, 600, or 700 children arrive from various districts of the metropolis in special trains. Sunday schools, as such, are excluded, the aim being to lay hold

AN old custom is still practised in the pretty old village of Bainbridge. Every winter's night a horn is blown at nine o'clock from the village green, and is meant to guide travellers to the town who may have wandered on the surrounding fells. The fine horn now in use was recently presented to the village, and at one time adorned the head of an African bull. The ancient horn in previous use is a good deal worse for wear, and is kept as an interesting relic.

Tourist 1905

MR. TAGGS'S WATER PARTY TO CRIPPLE CHILDREN

British Monthly 1902

of the roughest and most neglected class of children. Sometimes it is the entire attendance of a Board or Voluntary School in the poorest neighbourhood which reaches the Forest ; or some Mission School whose teachers have walked the streets on Sunday morning at eight or nine o'clock as the surest way of finding parents and children at home to recruit their party.

The railway company does not provide Pulmans for these clients, whose delight is boundless, though often less noisily expressed than might be imagined. At Loughton station they form into line and march to Shaftesbury House. Here each receives a large meat pie and some needful instructions.

"THIS comes of allowing chickens to run about in the road," grumbled a motorist as he pulled up in a country village to pay an old lady for one of her pullets which he had run over and killed.

"I can't allus keep 'em in the fowl-house, sir," she explained, as she eagerly pocketed the halfcrown tendered as compensation.

"No, an' she don't want to," interposed a jealous neighbour. "Whenever she wants a chicken for dinner she drives 'em into the road, and the moting cars do the rest, and as they 'as to pay for it, she gits the money and the pullet into the bargain!"

An angry retort from the owner of the chickens did not allay the motorist's suspicion that there was probably a basis of truth in the accusation.

Tourist 1905

London Welshman
1906

END OF THE WOLF.

KILLED AT CUMWHINTON.

A VICTIM OF THE SCOTCH EXPRESS.

The wolf hunt which has lately been exciting the farmers on the borders of Cumberland and Northumberland has finished, not with a "Tally-ho" on the part of the pursuers but by an agency as surprising as it was unforeseen. It is curious that the marauder whose escapades have carried us back to the "good old times" should have fallen a victim to that comparatively modern invention— the railway train. Yet such is the fact. The wolf who for weeks has been eluding hounds and hunters has fallen a victim to the Scotch express at Cumwhinton.

The wolf was one of a pair purchased at Newcastle some months ago by a gentleman who resided at Shotley Bridge, North Durham. The pair were confined in his grounds, but a few weeks ago one of the two escaped. Then it commenced a series of wanderings in Southern Northumberland which have everywhere been marked by disaster to farmers. Its tracks were first observed in Hexhamshire. From there it proceeded to Allendale, numbers of slaughtered sheep showing its trail. So great was the damage wrought that a hunt was arranged, a committee being organised for the purpose. The Braes of Derwent Hounds were brought into requisition, and it is estimated that at times as many as 200 people have been taking part in these searches. But the wily wolf managed to elude all their efforts, and although at times he was observed in different neighbourhoods, it seemed impossible to run him to earth.

Among the last places where the wolf was seen were Lanes, Dipton and Eltealey woods, the last-named covering 70 acres. From there he must have travelled along the east fells by way of Croglin. Passing by Armathwaite he would reach Cumwhinton. Here it was that he was seen by Mr Stewart, coal-agent, about eight o'clock on Wednesday night, proceeding from the Cotehill direction; and Mr Stewart subsequently observed him jump over the wall into Mr Pugney's field. About midnight an elderly lady living in a farmhouse near the village was awakened by four loud, dismal howls. A horse had been killed and bled on the farm during the day, and the scent of the animal's blood had evidently attracted the marauder's notice.

How the wolf, whose career has been arousing so much attention throughout the country actually met its death cannot be precisely described, but can be easily surmised. It is evident that at about four o'clock in the morning the beast found itself near the railway line between Cumwhinton and Scotby, less than half a mile from the former station. Probably its object in crossing the line was to reach some sheep which were to be found in a field adjoining the opposite bank. However, at this point there is a sharp curve in the line and the wolf, taken unawares, was knocked down by the Midland express proceeding from London to Scotland, and cut clean in two.

Carlisle Patriot 1904

Lifeboat Saturday
Parade, Southsea,
1902.

DISTURBED CONGREGATION.

In accordance with a resolution adopted by the elders and office-holders of the Rehoboth Calvinistic Chapel, Llangollen, Mr. W. P. Williams last night forwarded a strongly worded communication to Mr. J. Herbert Roberts, M.P., protesting, on behalf of the denomination, against the band of the Volunteer Battalion of the Royal Welsh Fusiliers playing in Victoria Square, Llangollen, on Sunday last, and interfering with public worship in the chapel, and asking the hon. member to bring the matter under the notice of the authorities with a view to preventing a recurrence of the incident. On Sunday morning the members (of the H (Llangollen) Company were ordered to assemble at the armoury, which is contiguous to Rehoboth Chapel at 10.15 for church parade. They were to proceed to the Parish Church, where service begins at 11 o'clock. The service begins at the Calvinistic Methodist Chapel an hour earlier. At 10 o'clock a special motor tram, conveying the battalion band, thirty-five strong, from Wrexham, arrived, and playing military airs marched along Castle Street to Victoria Square. The band continued to play after it had reached the Square. Within the Chapel a congregation of some six or seven hundred was endeavouring in vain to follow the sermon which the Rev. W. Foulkes was delivering, with extreme difficulty, until at length he completely failed to make his voice heard and had to stop speaking. In a lull of the music he exclaimed: "Truly it has come to something if we are not to conduct our services without molestation? who will go out and protest against this disturbance?" Mr. W. P. Williams (conductor of the choir) volunteered to do so, the congregation in the meantime joining in the singing of a hymn. Mr. Williams' protest was treated with indifference, and as the band continued to play the chapel service had to be curtailed.

The Furness Railway Company have arranged a fine set of circular tours between Blackpool and the Lakes, and these form a combination of sea, lake, rail and coach.

Leaving Blackpool by train at 10 a.m. passengers arrive at Fleetwood in time to catch the Furness Railway Company's steamer, "Lady Margaret," to Barrow. Ramsden Dock is reached in about an hour's sail across Morecambe Bay, and passengers for the circular tour soon leave that station by a special fast train for Windermere Lake Side Station. During the journey the tourist catches a passing glimpse of the famous ruins of Furness Abbey, described in our illustrated article in this number.

NORTH EASTERN RAILWAY COMPANY'S MOTOR CHAR-A-BANC

At Lake Side lunch is provided at the Pavilion Restaurant, after which visitors embark on one of the Furness Railway Co.'s steam yachts for Ambleside. Here the visitors find char-a-bancs waiting to take them to Coniston, where, after a brief stay for refreshments and a visit to the Ruskin Memorial Cross, the homeward journey is commenced.

Tourist 1905

"COOK'S TOURISTS' HANDBOOK FOR PALESTINE AND SYRIA." London : Ludgate Circus (pp. 376).—This 7s. 6d. volume is the best, completest, and most reliable and up-to-date guide book to the Holy Land. It is easily consulted upon points of detail, and is always luminous and interesting. No tourist in Palestine, nor those who are looking forward to that pleasure, ought to attempt to do without this "guide, philosopher, and friend." It is truly a friend in need, and it can never be consulted without getting precisely the information we desire. But the volume will prove of priceless worth to pastors, local preachers, Sunday School teachers, and divinity students It is a treasury of important and much-needed information to them. Its section maps—and especially the full map in the pocket of the book—are very fine and very full. They add much to the permanent value of the guide. It is an ideally got up guide book, by a firm which knows better than any other from practical and prolonged experience just what intelligent travellers require. This handbook, therefore, ought to be in ever-widening demand.

Gentleman's Journal 1901

❧ OLD TIME VILLAGES. ❧
IN RURAL BUCKINGHAM.

Health Resort 1907

THE Italian railways are incorrigible. The robberies from passengers' luggage are much on the increase, and whereas they were formerly limited to cash and jewels, the thieves are now taking wearing apparel. One passenger travelling between Rome and the Riviera actually had his boots abstracted from his portmanteau on the way. The heating of carriages during the recent very severe weather has been absolutely neglected, rendering travelling a dangerous ordeal for persons in delicate health.

A WRITER in the *Times*, speaking of the unpunctuality of the trains in Italy, says: "Only yesterday an Italian friend of mine travelled from Leghorn to Florence; his train managed to lose an hour and a half on the two hours' journey—though that is nothing unusual; but, though the day was an intensely cold one, the carriages were not heated in any way. The engine, which for some time had shewed signs of exhaustion, at last completely broke down about 400 yards outside the Florence station; there the passengers had to alight, and, in the teeth of a piercing *tramontana* wind, had to carry their own hand-luggage to the station, for, as usually happens now, there were only a few porters visible."

THE terrible state of the Italian railways has again and again been the subject of remark in these columns. When the State took over the lines in the summer of 1905 we were told things would improve. They have not; they have simply retrograded. Italy has scenery which tourists delight in, and visit again and again; but there is a limit to endurance. Other countries possess scenery and antiquities as well as Italy, notably Spain. The stream of tourists, and the ensuing flow of gold, will be diverted from Italy, unless a speedy and a radical reform is effected in the railways.

A host of attractions is centred in the delightful valley of the Misbourne, and perhaps the ancient villages of Chalfont St. Giles and Chalfont St. Peter and the interesting properties which surround them are among the principal. Chalfont St. Giles, famous with the English-speaking races as the place where Milton sought refuge from the terrors of the Great Plague of 1665, and where he wrote "Paradise Lost," has frequently been selected for paintings by some of our best artists, which have from time to time appeared on the walls of the Academy. The cottage in which Milton lived still stands, and of all the abodes of the poet this quaint house has the exceptional interest of being the only residence remaining which he is known to have occupied. In the Jubilee Year of the late Queen Victoria an effort of our American cousins to purchase this cottage and remove it bodily across the Atlantic was happily prevented by the timely intervention of a local landowner, who succeeded in raising by voluntary subscription sufficient funds to secure the premises, which are now used for the purposes of a local museum.

World Travel Gazette **1906**

OUR HAPPY LAND!

A millionaire, who left Queenstown on board the Mauretania on her latest voyage to New York, paid no less than £600 for his suite of rooms for the trip, which lasted under six days.

Three men, who stole a haddock because they were hungry, were sentenced at a provincial police court to terms of hard labour varying from two to one months' hard labour each.

Reynolds Newspaper **1907**

THE jealousy that exists between the two main islands of the Canarian Archipelago is deep-seated and hoary with age. Tenerife and Gran Canaria are, to use a familiar phrase, at it again. Last month some sort of undefined sickness made its appearance in the port of Santa Cruz at Tenerife, and fears were expressed that it might possibly be plague. A bacteriologist was sent from Madrid to pronounce an expert opinion, and he pronounced that there was no evidence of bubonic fever, but that there were a few cases of typhus fever, and that the port authorities were issuing clean bills of health which were endorsed by the various Consuls. Gran Canaria has been spreading abroad the tale that Tenerife has the plague—at least, the Tenerifians assert that the persistency of the rumour is due to that quarter. The consequence is that the port of Santa Cruz de Tenerife has lost its coaling and other business, and Las Palmas has proportionately benefitted.

Health Resort 1907

KING AND XMAS.

OLD ENGLISH FARE.

HIS MAJESTY'S GIFTS.

King Edward and Queen Alexandra will spend Christmas at Sandringham, as they have done for some years past. The festivities will be on an extensive scale. On Christmas morning the Royal Family will attend church, and, returning about one o'clock, a dinner, consisting of Yuletide fare, will be served. A special feature will be roast cygnets, which have been born and bred on the River Thames. There are also sucking pigs, roast turkey, roast goose, and large barons of beef. These will be followed by a tremendous plum pudding, which will be carried all ablaze into the dining hall by two gorgeously-liveried footmen. Mince pies will also be served, and are made from a special Sandringham recipe which is kept an inviolable secret. After the repast the King's and Queen's Christmas gifts will be inspected. In addition to the King and Queen, the Prince and Princess of Wales, Princess Victoria, Prince Edward and Albert, and Princess Mary will be present. King Edward will arrive at Sandringham to-morrow.

Reynolds Newspaper 1907

OLYMPIC REGATTA.

SOCIAL PROGRAMME.

The social side of the Henley Olympic Regatta, for which a very full programme of entertainments has been arranged, opened last night with a municipal reception at the Town Hall, at which the mayors of the three counties—Berks, Bucks, and Oxon—welcomed the competitors and visitors.

To-day there is to be a garden party at Park Place by invitation of Mrs. Noble, followed by a pastoral concert at Phyllis Court. To-morrow (Sunday) special church services will be held at the Roman Catholic Church and the Congregational Church, and the competitors will lunch at Taplow Court as the guests of Lord Desborough.

On Monday the competitors will be entertained at luncheon by the Phyllis Court Club. Afternoon excursions have been arranged by launch to Holme Park, Sonning (by invitation of Mr. Martin John Sutton), and by motor to Crowsley Park Wild Gardens (by invitation of Colonel Baskerville), and on to a garden party at Greys Court (by invitation of Mrs. Stapleton). In the evening an al-fresco river concert off the Mayor's Lawn, Bird-place, is announced.

On Tuesday, the first regatta day, competitors will lunch with Sir Frank Crisp, at his boathouse. An al-fresco concert follows in the evening in the regatta enclosure.

On Wednesday the competitors and their friends will lunch at Greenlands, as the guests of the Hon. W. F. D. Smith, M.P., and a dinner is to be given to distinguished visitors. Massed bands of the 7th Hussars and Royal Irish Fusiliers will play in the regatta enclosure, and there are to be fireworks at 9.15 p.m. On Thursday the competitors will lunch at Greenlands, as guests of the Hon. W. F. D. Smith, M.P., and in the evening a river concert will be given off Mr. W. L. T. Foy's Lawn, Manor Garden, with another display of fireworks at 9.15 p.m.

Daily Telegraph 1908

BEDFORD & DISTRICT MASTER BAKERS' ASSOCIATION.

MR. & MRS. ROFF WELCOMED HOME.

On Thursday evening the Bedford Association of Master Bakers held a social gathering at the Central Restaurant to welcome home Mr. and Mrs. William Roff after their tour round the world. Mr. and Mrs. Roff, who are looking extremely well, have been 2½ years away from home. They first visited Australia, and went into every State in the Commonwealth. At Sidney Mr. Roff represented the National Association at the conference of the Commonwealth Association of Bakers. From Sidney they went to Hong Kong by way of the east and north coasts of Australia, visiting the island of Timor, passing through the Celebees Sea to the Phillipines, and stayed at Manilla, where, we gather that Mr. Roff acquired the art of smoking cigarettes. After a few days at Hong Kong, Mr. and Mrs. Roff went to Shanghai, and there met a number of Bedford people, among them Mr. Dudeney's eldest son. He also witnessed a Rugby football match in which seven Bedford boys were players, three of whom scored tries and one a goal. They next went to Japan, and Mr. Roff paid a flying visit to Yokohama, but unfortunately Mrs. Roff took a severe chill, and they were unable to remain, but went on to Victoria, the capital of British Columbia, where, at Alberni, they had been staying with their daughter some 18 months. Travelling homeward by the Canadian Pacific Railway they broke the journey at Winnipeg, Toronto, Montreal, and Quebec, where they saw their grandson off to the Bedford Modern School. After a visit to their daughter at New York, they caught the "Car-mania" (which is Mr. Roff's little joke for motor car enthusiasm) and arrived in Bedford a week ago.

Ampthill and District News 1908

THE CHRISTMAS POST.

The Post Office announces that on Christmas Day there will be no collection of parcels in London and its suburbs, but that the first morning delivery will be made. Only the first morning delivery of letters will be made throughout London and the suburbs, and no express letters and parcels will be accepted for delivery by special messenger. On Boxing Day only the first morning delivery of letters and parcels will be made, and collections from the offices open will be made about noon.

Reynolds Newspaper 1907

Rapallo.

Prelude to the Winter Season.

THE autumn season at Rapallo is always full of movement and bustle, serving as a kind of prelude to that of winter which commences after the Christmas festivities.

The season on the Riviera de Levante is even longer than that of the Riviera proper. The English and American colonies at Rapallo are always very large, from Portofino right down to Santa Margherita.

The English swarm to the town in November and December, and leave—when the weather gets too hot—about the end of April to make room for the Italians.

The Mole, Rapallo.—Showing bathers.

Continental Express 1908

AUGUST HOLIDAY FREE.

A MONTH BY THE SEA FOR YOURSELF AND FAMILY.

This week five fortunate winners in our Limerick Competition have received £22 8s. 0d. each. What a splendid holiday they can have! They can go to Blackpool, Brighton, or even to Granville or Ostend, with plenty of money in their pockets. At the end of this week comes the August Bank Holiday. Can you afford a glorious jaunt for yourself and family? Would you like to be able to say good-bye to work for a couple of months?

Look at our "MONEY FOR BRAINS" column, and pit your wit and skill against those of our other readers. You may receive one of the five glorious first prizes. Don't forget that your attempt must reach us by Tuesday morning.

Reynolds Newspaper 1907

Fairlop Sunday.

Fairlop Friday has now given place to "Fairlop Sunday." If anyone is curious let him take his stand next Sunday evening in the road which runs through Chigwell—made famous by Dickens in "Barnaby Rudge"—and he will be astonished at the hundreds of vehicles that will pass him laden with East-Enders on their way home. They have been keeping up Fairlop Sunday in the remnants of Hainault Forest already referred to.

The scene is typical of an East London holiday, and affords much amusement to the uninitiated who watch the merry-makers driving uproariously home. In former days, when Fairlop Fair was in full swing, the roads in the district were practically impassable, and the police were fully occupied in endeavouring to keep order.

It is said that Queen Anne once visited Fairlop Oak, and the event is commemorated in the following lines :—

To Hainault Forest Queen Anne she did ride,
And beheld the beautiful Oak by her side ;
And, after viewing it from the bottom to the top,
She said to her Court, "It is a Fair-lop."

It is interesting to note that the pulpit in St. Pancras Church is made of wood from Fairlop Oak.

Evening News 1904

THE RIVIERA PALACE
AT MONTE CARLO.

Traveller de Luxe 1909

VIEW OF RIVIERA PALACE HOTEL, MONTE CARLO, FROM GARDENS.

Notes from South Wales.

(From our Special Correspondent.)

The Whitsuntide Holidays.

Glorious weather prevailed at Whitsuntide, and the population of South Wales, needless to state, enjoyed it to the full. Thousands patronised the cheap excursions by rail and pleasure steamer, and the railway stations and embarkation piers presented a most animated appearance. Thousands also patronised the Eisteddfodau at Caerphilly and Llanharran, and amply demonstrated the fact that the Cymric love for the ancient institution of Wales is as strong as ever. It was an inspiring sight to see the orderly and well-dressed crowds in the Eisteddfod pavilion, at the seashore, and in the country. Pleasant also to see were the bands of merry boys and girls accompanying their various Sunday Schools on the occasion of the annual treats. In years to come, these boys and girls may enjoy great riches, but the latter will never give them the same amount of delight and real pleasure as the Sunday School treat!

London Welshman 1906

It was a plan for a new hotel, in a situation unsurpassed on this lovely coast. "Here," thought the pioneer, "here at last is the ideal site. There is no finer view in the Riviera. The air is superb; the access is easy. Ha! First of all I will secure the ground, so that unsuspecting gossips hereabouts may think I want to live like a landed proprietor upon a charming estate."

But provision is made, too, for indoor exercise, by the immense Hall and Winter Garden, with about two thousand square yards under cover. This Garden shelters the back of the Hotel, already protected from the north wind by the mountains. Rain—it sometimes, though not often, rains in the Riviera with a needless profusion which suggests malice is baulked of its prey by this forethought. When the visitor is cramped within doors and deluged without, he may have a touch of melancholia; but, with such a Winter Garden to ramble in, he can wait cheerfully for the return of the sunshine which is the true mantle of these beautiful hills.

The approaches to the Riviera Palace from Monte Carlo have no lack of facility. Advantage has been taken, in the first place, of the Turbie Railway, which passes the end of the garden. It was clear from the outset that the railway interest and the interests of the International Sleeping Car Company must be identical. They are so closely related now that the Company has a station (Monte Carlo Supérieur) which is distant only three minutes from the Casino, and stands in the very garden of the Hotel. Moreover, there has now been completed a more direct method of communication between the Hotel and the Town, by means of a Private lift or Funicular Railway running from the Casino gardens right into the basement of the Hotel, a continual service being maintained up till the closing of the rooms.

Restaurant Cars.

These are attached to all Trains-de-Luxe of the International Sleeping Car Company, and to almost every express train of importance on the Continent running during the day time, as may be gleaned from the tables given in another part of our impression. Some of the more important trains have also Saloon Cars, smoking and non-smoking

Traveller de Luxe 1909

1910–1919

SOME CHRISTMAS VARIETY STARS.

TIVOLI.—Marie Lloyd, Little Tich, Amélie de L'Encles, Vampire Dance, and Lionel Rignold and Co.

OXFORD.—Joe Elvin and Co., Chirgwin, Victoria Monks, T. E. Dunville, George Formby, and Charles Austin and Co.

LONDON PAVILION.—Vesta Victoria, Harry First and Co., Fred Russell, The Gothams, Jock Whiteford, and Ernest Shand.

HOLBORN.—Arthur Roberts and Co., May Moore Duprez, Bromley and Fontein, Arthur Lennard, and George Gilbey.

KILBURN.—Fred Karno's Co., Lindon's Entertainers, Lelia Roze, Franco's Midgets, and Syd Cotterill and Co.

EMPIRE, LEICESTER SQUARE.—"Round the World," Velanche's Dogs, Olga Tcharna, and Evelyn D'Alroy and Co.

ALHAMBRA.—"Our Flag," Gobert Belling, Gardner and Stoddart, and " On the Heath."

METROPOLITAN.—Marie Lloyd, Ernest Shand, George Formby, and Ruby Celeste and May Hallett.

LONDON HIPPODROME.—"The Arctic," Cinquevalli, Henry Ainley and Suzanne Sheldon, and Vampire Dance.

COLISEUM.—Seymour Hicks and Co. ; Olga, Elgar, and Eli Hudson ; Chanti, and Old English Country Dancers.

PALACE.—Mr. and Mrs. Arthur Bourchier, Margaret Cooper, Jack Lorimer, and Vesta Tilley.

STANDARD, PIMLICO.—Dutch Daly, Arthur Aldridge, Frank Seeley, and Dan Lipton's Co.

EMPRESS.—T. E. Dunville, Jordan and Harvey, Herbert Rule, and Charles Austin and Co.

MIDDLESEX.—Charles Benson and Co., Flying Orenins, and Brull and Hemsley.

CANTERBURY.—Joe Elvin and Co., King and Benson, The Romps and Horace Hunter and Co.

PARAGON.—Lionel Rignold and Co., The Gothams, Tom Leamore, and Charles Coborn.

CHELSEA.—Fred Karno's Co., Fred Russell, Phil and Nettie Peters, and Jock Whiteford.

EUSTON.—Leo Stormont and Co., Chris Richards, Charles Whittle, and Harry First and Co.

SOUTH LONDON.—Kate Carney and Co., Beattie and Babs, H. A. Moore, and Phoebe Mercer and Co.

TOTTENHAM.—Whit Cunliffe, Ella Shields, John Donald, and Chirgwin.

WALTHAMSTOW.—"Puss in Boots" pantomime.

EAST HAM.—"Babes in the Wood" pantomime.

HOLLOWAY EMPIRE.—Chung Ling Soo, Takio, and George Leyton.

NEW CROSS EMPIRE.—Fred Karno's Co., Tom Davies Trio, and The Courtiers.

STRATFORD EMPIRE.—Alice Esty, D'Arco's Marionettes, and Herbert Shelley.

HACKNEY EMPIRE.—Raymond, Marie Kendall, and Mr. and Mrs. Leslie Faber.

SHEPHERD'S BUSH EMPIRE.—La Sylphe, Paul Barnes, and Baron's Menagerie.

BEDFORD.—W. T. Ellwanger and Co., Leo Dryden, and "Fight in the Lighthouse."

Referee
1910

WHAT MAKES A HOLIDAY

It is not change of air nor change of scene that makes a holiday, but change of sound.

The silence of the country is a tonic to the nerves after the rush and roar of the city, but the country dweller is invigorated by escape from that very silence to the tumult of the town.

Hence it is argued that town people should vary their noises with as much silence as they can get, while country people should recreate themselves with noisy games and brass bands.

Let a woman who has been working all the morning over the countless details of housekeeping by herself indoors go out for a brisk walk.

If it is only for fifteen minutes it will do her untold good. The noise and bustle of outside life will then refresh her. Her head will be clearer and her heart lighter.

Time thus taken is not wasted, but the best kind of an investment, as she will find she can do much more in the long run.

The World and
His Wife 1910

The Children's Corner.

UNCLE NED'S CHAT.

MY DEAR CHILDREN,

Uncle Ned has not sent a letter this week, and I expect he is too busy on his holiday. It will not be long before his holiday will be completed, and then you will hear all about how he spent his time. THE EDITOR.

◆

Dear Uncle Ned,—I am sorry that the weather is so dull for your holiday. I shall not have mine until we break up from school, and my holiday will commence from Bank Holiday Monday, when I shall go to the seaside for a week with my sisters and brothers. I have two sisters and three brothers, and as we are all going together I expect we shall have a nice time. I hope the weather is nicer then, although I would have liked it to be nice now for you. I have been in for an examination and have passed the first section, and if I pass the second which will be held in a few weeks, my father says he will buy me a bicycle, and I shall be able to attend the higher grade school free of all cost. I am pleased I passed the first, and thought you would like to know. I am looking forward to my holiday, and I intend to work hard at school until that time, when I am going to make the best of it.—With love,

AGNES RUSSELL.

◆

Dear Uncle Ned,—I shall be pleased to hear how you have spent your holiday when you return. It is a pity the weather is not brighter, although I think it will be a bit better for a short time. I have not been out much lately, so have been spending most of my time painting, and I am sending you some flowers which I painted. We often have a painting contest, and I got the most marks twice out of six. The one who does the best painting is allowed to help the others to paint, and also gets threepence from the teacher, so you see I have won sixpence up to the present. I did not read of your great painting competition until it was too late to compete, but if you have another one I should like to try and win a prize, as I am greatly interested in painting. I do not know yet where I shall go for my holiday in August, as my father is at present away from home, but I shall know when he returns at the end of the week, and I will write you later and tell you all about it. I think this is all for this time, so will now close. With love and best wishes,—I am, your loving niece,

BESSIE CLEMENTS.

Dunstable Borough Gazette 1910

KING'S GUEST SHOT.

An unfortunate accident occurred to a member of the King's shooting party on Deeside on Wednesday, Lord Kilmarnock being injured.

The accident happened about two o'clock in the afternoon, when Captain Hood and Lord Kilmarnock were in adjoining butts. The captain got on to the line of a bird just crossing between his butt and that of Lord Kilmarnock, who, unknown to Captain Hood, was facing him forty yards away, when the trigger was pulled. Lord Kilmarnock at once shouted to Captain Hood, who ceased firing immediately.

Several pellets struck his lordship. One pierced his right ear, another his nose, two lodged in his right arm, and the lenses of his eyeglasses were broken.

At the close of the drive the mishap was reported to the King, who expressed sympathy with both Lord Kilmarnock and Captain Hood.

In an interview, Lord Kilmarnock said he was very sorry for Captain Hood, who was feeling the matter more keenly than he was, and regretted it extremely. The force of the pellets was well spent before they struck him, and the result was that the injuries were comparatively slight. When the lenses of his eyeglasses were smashed he thought he had received some damage to his eye, but fortunately that was not the case. He had now no pain from the wounds, and was really feeling none the worse.

A ghillie, who was in attendance on the party, was also slightly injured.

Dunstable Borough Gazette 1910

THE BANK HOLIDAYS.

Lord Knollys has sent the following reply, dated April 3, to a correspondent who wrote urging that the two days proclaimed as holidays during the Coronation festivities would inflict considerable hardship on poor people, as, generally speaking, holidays were not paid for, and, further, that, as many workshops would also close on the following Saturday, a large number of families would only receive half the usual wages during Coronation week :—

Owing to the inquiries I had to make, the reply to which I have only just received, I have been unable to send you an earlier answer. From what I am told I do not think poor people have much reason to complain of the inordinate holidays at the Coronation, as there will only be one day for the whole country and two for London, and as regards the London holiday (June 23), employers can conduct their businesses if they wish to do so, the holiday only being proclaimed because owing to the Procession it will be impossible to open the banks in the City.

The Times 1911

LONDON'S CROWDS.

EXCELLENT BEHAVIOUR DURING CORONATION.

Scotland Yard is on very good terms with itself. And not without reason. For London never behaved better during a national festival. Indeed, as was evidenced at the police courts yesterday, crime was below the normal. Drunkenness was less prevalent than on an ordinary bank holiday, and, more remarkable still, there were no fatalities and very few serious accidents. Scotland Yard does not attribute this happy state of things to chance. It was achieved as the result of many months of administrative activity, and much vigilant labour on the part of the Criminal Investigation Department. Every well-known "crook" and "sharper," home and foreign, was kept under observation, his residence and movements noted, and the man himself in many cases warned that it was hopeless for him to attempt operations. Mr. Froest, of the Criminal Investigation Department, informed a Press representative yesterday that crime was below the normal within London's inner area, while from the suburbs

No Cases of Burglary

were reported. Even "Bill Sykes" seemed to have been on holiday. But the suburbs were not left to take care of themselves. Reserve men patrolled deserted streets and terraces, while superintending officers on cycles sped over the various divisions with an eye vigilant for wrong-doing. Of the Coronation crowds a highly-placed official at the "Yard" spoke in terms of the highest praise. For orderliness, good conduct, good humour, and marvellous patience, he said, the crowds were unique. They made the onerous and trying duties of the police more or less of a waiting sinecure. There was good-humoured chaffing—it is impossible to suppress the Londoner on holiday—and the wise latitude given by the police all played a part in securing the absence of untoward happenings. The elaborate arrangements made for provisioning and relieving the police worked with perfection, and the great body of the force has come out of the ordeal of about three days and nights' continuous and exacting duties without appreciably affecting the sick list.

King's Thanks to Police.

His Majesty has sent an expression of his thanks and appreciation of the services of the City and Metropolitan Police on the days of the Coronation and of the Royal progress through London. The letter contains this striking tribute to the members of the force:—

His Majesty realises, and greatly appreciates, the patience and tact displayed by the police in the performance of their especially arduous and trying duties, and their conduct has earned the general admiration of his Majesty's foreign guests.

People 1911

THROUGH FRANCE IN A MOTOR—II.

By FRANK HARRIS

I THOUGHT Grenoble one of the most beautiful and most interesting towns I had ever seen. Placed in a valley just above the meeting of the two rivers—the Isère and the Drac—with mountains from 5,000ft. to 10,000ft. in height walling it in on both hands, it would be difficult to find a finer position. The museum is wonderful, as I have said, and the town itself is a sort of epitome of the past. The old part of the Law Courts dates from 1480; the church of St. Laurent was built about 1050, and there is a crypt below with columns of Parian marble from the sixth century; the very name of the town, a corruption of Gratianopolis, carries one back to the time of the Emperor Gratian, who ruled towards the end of the fourth century; one can trace the growth of civilisation in Grenoble for fifteen hundred years.

But we had heard so much of Annecy and its joyous, bright lake that we resolved to visit it. At first our way led along the Durance by the great bastion of Mont Eynard, some 5,000ft. in height, which we had already admired on account of its bold, rocky outline. As we went on, this mountain became still more picturesque: first came vineyards and orchards and crofts; then a long pine-clad slope for a couple of thousand yards, and far above the pines a thousand feet of porphyric cliff like a wall. I do not know that the rock was porphyry, but the colour of it was that peculiar reddish brown. On the other side across the stream were mountains of all shapes—breasts, and pyramids— while behind them showed a higher range of snow-clad peaks.

A little later and the scene on our left hand became entrancing. Mountains of various shapes sprang up in front, and between them one caught sight of the vast porphyric bastion frowning down above them, the top veiled in clouds. Here and there waterfalls streamed down between the cliffs; now the water was blown into foam, now it was whirled about like veils of lawn tossed in the wind. As we drew towards Annecy the mountains fell away on either hand, losing their majesty. Nor did Annecy, charmingly situated as it is, nearly 1,500ft. above the sea-level, make up in beauty for what we had left behind. It is a delightful little town, the old part intersected by broad canals, a sort of quaint Venice among the mountains looking out over the gayest, brightest lake imaginable.

Academy and Literature **1911**

UNDRESSING ON BEACH.

SUGGESTED TIME ALLOWANCE FOR LADY BATHERS.

How long should lady bathers, who disrobe on the beach, be allowed to remain undressed? The question was raised at a meeting of the Whitley and Monkseaton District Council, when complaints were made of the non-observance of the by-laws regulating the costumes to be worn. It was also said that the notices which had been set up marking off the beach so as to provide for the separation of the sexes during the undressing and dressing by bathers in the open air had been ignored. The clerk pointed out that unfortunately they could not specify in a by-law what was a reasonable time which ought to elapse between the doffing of the last garment and the donning of the next. He could not credit, for instance, that lady bathers who prepared in the open air for their dip in the sea would take more time than necessary in dressing or undressing. If it could be shown that anyone wilfully acted indecently, proceedings could be taken. The chairman said the surveyor was aware that from time to time there were occurring breaches of the by-laws such as had been mentioned regarding costumes, and the differentiation of the sexes, but at the same time there was no doubt that a great improvement had taken place since the new regulations came into force. The Council did not wish to act too harshly, seeing that the by-laws were quite new, but they would be quietly and firmly brought to notice.

News of the World **1912**

Cannes's memorial to King Edward VII. will be unveiled in March, and takes the form of a statue of our late King in yachting costume with a telescope under his arm. At the foot of the statue is seated a female figure, and the sides of the memorial are decorated by two bas-reliefs, the one representing the Cannes regatta and the other a battle of flowers. The sculptor is M. Denys Puech. Everything is ready for the commencement of the polo season, the prospects for which are very bright, and Capt. Miller has already arrived, and will once more be in charge. At the Hôtel des Anglais there have been many arrivals recently, among whom are the Hon. Mrs George Chetwynd, Col. Kennedy and party, Mrs Dickson, Miss D. Shaw, Miss M. Shaw, Mr Algernon Mandlesley (whose yacht is to take part in the local regatta), Mr and Mrs Cochrane, Mrs Capel Holden, Lady Jackson, and Mrs Philip MacGregor (who is making this hotel her headquarters while she is touring in the neighbouring country in her car). Bridge and dinner parties are numerous at the hotel, which is once more living up to its name. At the Carlton Sir Edward Sassoon and Sir John and Lady Aliston are expected to arrive shortly. Mr Davison Dalziel's yacht, the Capercailzie, has arrived from Marseilles, where she has been undergoing repairs, and her owner is to join her this week.

Queen **1912**

AT A FRENCH WATERING-PLACE.

Mother. "TOMMY, WHY DON'T YOU TRY TO TALK TO THOSE OTHER CHILDREN IN THEIR OWN LANGUAGE?"

Youthful Briton. "WHAT'S THE GOOD? IT ONLY ENCOURAGES THEM!"

Thomas Cook archive, c. 1912

EIGHTY IN THE SHADE

We have had an old-fashioned summer. How often during the last few sun-starved years has the lament gone up that the seasons are not as they used to be when we were young. That assertion and its sequel remind one of Leech's reply to a complainant that *Punch* was not as good as it used to be: "It never has been." The summers of the two years of Victorian Jubilee and that of the marriage year of the King were very similar to this present summer of the Coronation. The sun has lately given us a rare taste of his quality. We have had spells of tropical heat that have well-nigh broken the record. Already in the early days of August the dry leaves come pattering down in clouds; the horse-chestnut is turning rusty; and even the bracken begins to look played out. The blossom of that glorious weed the great convolvulus begins to assert itself like the modern Teuton. It reminds us that we are drawing on toward the fringe of autumn.

He who has not seen tropical forest trees half-smothered in the embrace of their attendant creepers can have little conception of the meaning of the phrase "the struggle for existence." The great convolvulus, clutching and seeking to strangle any living tissue which blocks its way, is perhaps our nearest approach to those villainous weeds which the tropical tree nurtures in their youth, protects from the fierce heat of a point-blank sun, and which later in the season reward their protector by a hug more deadly than that of an anaconda or a grizzly. The struggle of most living things as we see them in the Tropics is for light and air. When streams of heat quiver across our line of vision, the dog will coil up in the hottest corner he can find and absorb as much of the actinic force as he may. A healthy child will do the same. He will bask and bathe in the sunlight, and rejoice in its abounding sense of growth. "Dogs and Englishmen," say the Mexicans, "walk in the sun."

Academy and Literature 1911

HIS MAJESTY'S RED ROSE.

KING RETURNS FROM SHOOTING VISIT.

Yesterday morning the King concluded his shooting visit to the Hon. John Ward at Chilton, near Hungerford, and, travelling by special train to Paddington, proceeded to Buckingham Palace. At Hungerford Station school children, wearing favours and carrying Union Jacks, sang the National Anthem. On arrival at Paddington His Majesty, who wore a heavy serge overcoat with a red rose in the buttonhole, appeared in excellent health, and, alighting from the train, chatted with Viscount Churchill, chairman of the Great Western Railway. The King took leave of several of the house party from Chilton who had travelled on the train, and then, entering a closed carriage, drove direct to Buckingham Palace. Large crowds assembled outside the station cheered the King as he drove off. It is expected that his Majesty will go to Newmarket on Tuesday morning.

TAKING A REST CURE.

HAPPY SOLUTION OF YOUNG LADY'S DISAPPEARANCE.

In consequence of the wide publicity given to the case in the Press, Miss Mabel Davey, a young lady from Exeter, who disappeared suddenly in London a fortnight ago, has been found. It appears that Miss Davey, after leaving a house where she was staying in Marylebone-road, felt somewhat out of sorts, and on reaching the City took train for Southend instead of Walthamstow, fearing that the round of visits she had planned to make in London would result in a complete breakdown. In Southend she stayed at a quiet boarding house in Burnaby-road, enjoying a rest cure. The publication of her description and the account of the anxiety caused by her disappearance led to her being identified by a resident. Miss Davey, who is now much better, has returned to Exeter.

COCKROACHES IN BED.

REMARKABLE STORY OF MEDITERRANEAN TRIP.

LADY'S STORY OF CAPTAIN AND PASSENGER.

Voyaging from Manchester to the Mediterranean on board the steamship Carib Prince last year, Mrs. Frances Vivian Campbell of Ongar, Essex, had, according to her story, some very unpleasant experiences. She now sued the Prince Line, Ltd., of Newcastle, for damages for alleged breach of contract and warranty and alleged negligence.—Mr. Raymond Asquith, for plaintiff, said Mrs. Campbell was the widow of a relative of the Duke of Argyll, and upon her husband's death the duke advised her to take up journalism. Some time ago she became engaged on business of a somewhat confidential character, in which she was associated with the late Mr. W. T. Stead. Her complaint was that she and her daughter and cousin, who accompanied her, suffered hardships and inconveniences on the voyage. She alleged that the food was inferior, badly served, and badly cooked, and gave her ptomaine poisoning, which resulted in serious injury to her health, and the loss of the sight of

MRS. FRANCES VIVIAN CAMPBELL.

one eye. After her return Mrs. Campbell wrote a letter to defendants' London agents in which she stated :—

Our beds were alive with cockroaches and the bed linen dirty and evil-smelling. We had only the cheapest, coarsest, and roughest food possible to imagine. The mutton and beef were often in a state of decomposition. . . . Actual starvation drove us to eat what were called mutton chops after leaving Malta, and we each and all were poisoned and are still suffering from the effects of ptomaine. . . . We had also to submit to every kind of annoyance from the captain, who tried to force on us a lady who came on board at Alexandria. I refused to know her, principally because she passed most of her time in the captain's cabin, going up on the bridge, where, during rough weather, she would even have her meals. I also objected to the manner in which he walked about the deck with her and in which she entered her cabin—walking in and out as if it were occupied by his wife, without the formality of even calling her or knocking.

—Mrs. Campbell, giving evidence, said that owing to the cockroaches she

SLEPT ON THE TOP OF THE BED,

with an overcoat round her. Once she went to have a bath, but found a dirty pail and brush in it. She asked the stewardess to do what was necessary, and received the reply that the stewardess was a lady and not accustomed to such work. Consequently she had to clean the bath herself and wash in sea water. Plaintiff said that when the boat was off Alexandria she asked for an egg, but was told there were none on board. Plaintiff stated that 100,000 quails were brought on board at Alexandria, and many of them died. Those that could be reached were thrown out by Arabs, but others dead at the back of the coops could not be got at. Mrs. Campbell said the chief steward selected some of the dead quails and put them in the storehouse. Quail on toast was served at dinner, but she had none. The dead quails smelt something like the odour she noticed after the great flood in Queensland, when thousands of dead cattle were lying on the plains. At one meal some of the veal served was green and shiny. After this witness was taken ill, and while showing symptoms of ptomaine poisoning felt a sudden sharp pain over the eye of which she had lost the sight. —Mr. F. E. Smith (cross-examining): I suggest that this story about cockroaches is a ludicrous and grotesque exaggeration?—It sounds like it. (Laughter.) Witness said she had to sleep outside the sheets because she did not like the cockroaches walking over her feet.—Mr. F. E. Smith: Did they do it all the time?—Yes.—Almost a constant procession?—Yes.—Did you find the captain an untruthful man?—The captain has taken proceedings against me for libel, said to be contained in a letter I wrote to the Prince Line.—You accused him of undue familiarity with a lady passenger?—I accused him of trying to force her upon us and of refusing to come to us unless we allowed him to bring her to tea.—The hearing was adjourned until Tuesday.

News of the World 1912

CHARLES DONALD ROBERTSON TRAVEL FUND.

This fund, in memory of the late C. D. Robertson, Fellow of Trinity College, has been founded for the purpose of enabling junior members of the University, who would otherwise be unable to do so, to take an open-air holiday, preferably abroad and among mountains. It is hoped that enough money will be available to provide such a holiday for at least two persons. Anyone who would care to have his name considered in connection with the fund for the present summer is requested to communicate either directly or through his college Tutor, before May 11th, with one of the undersigned, who have agreed to act as Trustees, and by whom the Fund will be administered as informally as possible.

Signed H. O. JONES
(Clare College).

A. C. PIGOU
(King's College).

A. V. VALENTINE-RICHARDS
(Christ's College).

G. WINTHROP YOUNG
(Trinity College).

Granta 1912

JEANNIE'S JOY JAUNT.

Servant Girl Who Had a Royal Time for a Week

ON MISTRESS'S STOLEN MONEY.

Refused to Work, & Dismissed for "Cheek."

How a servant girl spent money at the rate of about £1 a day, which belonged to a former mistress, was told in the Manchester Police Court.

The prisoner was Jeannie Harrison, a neatly-dressed young woman, who appeared in the dock wearing a heavy coat and large picture hat.

The girl had been discharged from her employment as general servant in a Cheetham-hill house about eight days ago. Since then she had stayed at Ashton House, and throughout the whole of the time it was stated she had lived luxuriously, and had treated her friends with great liberality.

She took one for a day trip to the seaside, and on other occasions she had given them music-hall tickets. One night she and a friend took a box at a Manchester theatre. In this way over £10 was disposed of in a little over a week.

The suspicions of the police were at length aroused, the young woman was watched, and her appearance in the Police Court was the sequel.

Come to the Police Station.

Detective-sergeant Allan, when called, said that in consequence of her mode of living recently the prisoner had been under close observation for some days.

Yesterday, when in company with Detective-Inspector Mather, he saw her in Market-street. She was spending money freely, and the officers approached her.

The witness said to her, "You have been spending a lot of money lately. You have had new dresses and other things, and I believe you are in possession of a considerable quantity of cash now. You must come to Albert-street Police Station and give an account of yourself."

While passing through the Parsonage, Harrison handed over £5 2s 6d, with two purses, saying, "This is what is left."

At the station she said she had been in service at 29, George-street, Cheetham Hill, and on inquiries at that house the occupant, Mrs Wilkins, made a statement. Later prisoner was charged with having stolen from a purse at the address named, on January 28th, the sum of £18 15s, the property of her late employer.

In reply to the charge by the police, Harrison said, "Not £18; £15." She added, "I bought a clock for 13s, a skirt 4s 6d, boots 8s 6d, gloves 3s, electric hair pad 10s, and combs 2s. I took a girl to New Brighton and back, which cost 10s or 12s. The other money I have spent at music-halls, and we had a box at the theatre, and there were other things."

The statement was made in reply to the inquiries by the officers as to where the money had gone.

The Mistress's Evidence.

Mrs Wilkins said she had engaged the girl shortly before Christmas, and had discharged her without notice on January 28th. She did not miss any money until the police officers called yesterday. Then she found that a purse in her room which had contained £25 in gold, 25s in silver, and 14d in copper, now contained only £8 10s in gold, £1 in silver, and 1d in copper.

Prisoner: She did not give me enough to eat.

Witness denied there was any truth in the statement, and the Stipendiary pointed out that the remark was not material to the charge.

Prisoner (to witness): Did you not mark the butter and the bread?

Mrs Wilkins said the suggestion was ridiculous, as there was not a drawer or cupboard that was locked in the house.

The Stipendiary: Why did you dismiss her? For being cheeky.

The prisoner pleaded guilty, but added, "I only took £15 out of the purse."

The Stipendiary: It is not a sufficient reason for stealing, to say you were not comfortable in your place. You should have given notice to leave. There is no great difficulty, I understand, in getting situations as domestic servants. I do not for one moment say it is true what you suggest about your place, but it is no excuse even if it were true.

Inquiry at a former house in which she had worked showed that she had been discharged for refusing to work. There was, however, no suspicion of stealing against her then.

TRAVEL IN PLEASANT PLACES

WHERE TO STAY

"HEARTH AND HOME" can be found at all the undermentioned Hotels

CONTINENTAL HOTELS

FRANCE
Evian-les-Bains

Fashionable watering-place; finest thermal establishment in Europe; every form of bath and massage; celebrated Cachet springs; casino; fishing; boating; motoring; sporting golf course; tennis; Venetian fêtes.

Splendide, 1st class; park 20 acres; same management as Royal.

ITALY
Milan

Lanza d'Intelvi (prov. di Como). Hôtel-Pension Villa, Annunciata, April, October. Health resort. 2,800 ft.; facing Lugano. Modern comforts. Moderate terms, Splendid woods.

SWITZERLAND
Geneva

Well-known city on the Lake of Geneva. University; fine schools. Delightful to visit in spring, summer, and autumn; large English and American colonies; centre for excursions.

Beau-Séjour Champel, built 1907; country, city combined; open all year.

Hotel National, superbly situated in gardens on Lake Geneva.

Richemond, on the Lake; 1st cl.; moderate prices; pension terms.

Victoria, comf., fam. hotel, near lake and English gardens.

Champel Les-Bains (5 min. from Geneva).

Hydro, select; diet, rest treatments; fine site; immense park; 3 Drs.

Vevey

Favourite four-season resort on the Lake of Geneva; mild climate, high-class schools for boys and girls; 9 hours from Paris.

Grand Hotel and Palace, fine site on Lake; gardens, tennis.

Park Hotel Mooser, fine, healthiest site. Prop., C. Schwenter.

Lausanne

Well-known University town; English colony, churches, and clubs, noted doctors; excellent schools; centre for excursions.

Hotel Gibbon, 1st cl., modern comforts; historic garden.

Carlton, 1st cl., near English Church and Club; tennis gardens.

Cecil, 1st class., modern family hotel; recently built; unrivalled view.

Le Grand Hotel, Hotel Beau-Site, Hotel Richemont reunis.

Mirabeau (opened 1911), 1st cl. hotel, handy to station.

Victoria, 1st cl. mod. family residential hotel; near station. Prop., F. Imseng.

Ouchy

Picturesque lake-port of Lausanne; town quickly reached by tram or funicular.

Savoy (opened 1911); 8 acres gardens; 3 tennis courts; garage.

Signal (above Lausanne, 5 min. by funicular)

Majestic, new, 1st cl.; open all year; tennis; grand views.

Montreux

Grand Hotel Suisse up-to-date, best position in the town.

Gstaad (Bernese Oberland)

Noted winter sport centre, rising summer resort; excellent walks and views.

English Pension. Best position, open all the year, except April; moderate terms.—Miss Quihampton.

Hearth and Home 1913

A VETERAN TO HIS SON.

The sky she is blue as the sea, with a lather
Of billowy cloud: from a neighbouring thicket
The blackbird she heralds the summer, or rather
She heralds the season of cricket.
So come in the garden and bowl to your father
At sixpenny bits on the wicket.

My bat she is old, and as red as a fiddle,
And heavy, and mottled with liberal pegging,
But many a ball has she hit in the middle
And never a one has gone begging.
So send up that ball with a bit of a twiddle
(And mind you, I haven't a legging).

Well bowled, you young sinner! You bowl quite a
fast one,
But keep that right arm up as high as you're able.
(Its wonderful how these full tosses get past one)
Why, here are your mother and Mabel!
So bowl me another full toss like the last one
And watch it go over the stable.

J. N.

Granta 1914

HUNTING ON FOOT.

By LADY SYBIL GRANT.

THIS IS A PASTIME recommended to those who, vagrants by nature, snatch at an excuse for a day in the open air. Of course, no one really needs an excuse for a day in the open air, but in England, during the winter, it is as well to be prepared with one when your hostess, apologising for its being a hunting day, urges you to accompany her to the meet, and then to return to the library fire and a good book. If you have once lived in a hunting country, and have hunted yourself, there are few more odious experiences than that of "just motoring to the meet and back." Upon the other hand, if you come back for a day or two into that country with neither horse nor habit, and yet are anxious to elude the library and a good book, you can share not a little of the excitement and plenty of the humour of the chase if you take to your feet. In fact, those who hunt on horseback often miss some of the quiet fun that is enjoyed by those who hunt on foot, although I am not otherwise comparing the two ways of hunting; who could?

Queen 1914

THE KING APPLAUDS SOME BALL GAME.

Keen Royal Interest In White Sox Win.

MARVELLOUS FIELDING.

Play Described From All Points Of View.

Chicago White Sox 5
New York Giants 4

Many Englishmen saw their first baseball match yesterday at Stamford Bridge, a game which was watched by the King and many other distinguished persons.

His Majesty, it was noticed, was keenly interested in the play, frequently laughing and applauding.

What appealed most particularly to the novice amongst the onlookers—especially one who is used to cricket—was the really marvellous fielding, lightning-like balls being casually and nonchalantly held with one hand.

To the uninitiated the safeguards are rather alarming. The catcher padded and helmeted; even the spectators hidden behind a sort of House of Commons ladies' grille.

ROUNDERS — ELECTRIFIED.

The Game As Seen By An Englishman For The First Time.

The general impression in this country is that baseball is "something like rounders."

It is, but in that something there is all the difference that there is between a tiger and a kitten, or a rifle and a popgun.

Baseball is rounders geared up, galvanised and electrified into what is probably the fastest ball game played in any country.

It is fast from the moment the striker takes his place in his box, or base, until the game is over.

The players run on and off the field, the catcher puts on and takes off his mask with the quickness of a conjuror, the warnings of the coach sound across the field like a phonograph geared up to a maxim gun.

When a side is out the fielders rush off at top speed throwing their catching gloves on the turf, and before they have got to their bench the other side have taken up their positions on the field.

A baseball player gets on and off the field in about half the time a cricketer takes to get his centre.

Daily Sketch 1914

No Gloves.

Have you noticed since the warm weather has come how many women are going about without gloves? I believe it was the Duchess of Manchester who started this summer fashion a few years ago. The Duchess comes from Cincinnati and is daring. Women say her notion is delightfully comfortable.

THE PRINCE CHATS WITH MARKET FOLK.

Spends Easter at Darmstadt with Grand Duke of Hesse.

CHOCOLATE SOUVENIR.

(From Our Special Correspondent.)

DARMSTADT, March 23.—The Prince of Wales motored here yesterday from Wiesbaden to spend Easter with the Grand Duke of Hesse and to meet Prince Henry of Prussia, the Kaiser's brother, who is also a guest at the Grand Ducal Court.

The Prince to-day attended both the eight o'clock early Communion service and Matins at eleven in the Royal Chapel in the old palace, lent by the Grand Duke for these special English services. The Rev. Hope Jones, a retired Army chaplain invalided home from South Africa, officiated and preached at Matins.

The Prince declined a seat in the royal gallery, preferring to sit below in a pew. The congregation numbered seventy.

The chaplain says the Prince is the most unaffected and agreeable young man he has ever met.

Before leaving Wiesbaden yesterday the Prince spent half an hour shopping, buying postcards and trinkets, accompanied only by Professor Fiedler.

Fully 200 people saw the departure of his Royal Highness in an open motor-car at ten o'clock. Taking a circuitous route by Homburg, the Prince reached Frankfort about two o'clock, and spent an hour strolling through the picturesque mediæval portions of the city. He wore a bowler hat and a lounge suit, without overcoat, and not three people in Frankfort recognised him

AT THE EASTER TOY STALLS.

With Professor Fiedler and Major Cadogan, the Prince visited the cathedral. He showed special interest in the garish Easter toy stalls of Romerberg, the spacious historic market-place, where little children played around him and stallkeepers answered his fluent questions, utterly ignorant of his identity.

In the evening the Prince dined with the Grand Ducal Family.

To-morrow, which is not a German holiday, the Prince will probably inspect some of the chemical and drug factories, which are Darmstadt's special pride. He did not ascend the cathedral tower yesterday in Frankfort, but he bought a chocolate hare, of which millions are sold in Germany at Easter.

The Prince, according to the *Cologne Gazette*, wanted to be the first to leave the steamer on returning to Bingen, but was waved back by the man in charge of the gangway, to whom he attempted to hand his ticket, and motioned to take his place in the line and give his ticket to a sailor. "Duly intimidated," says the journal, "the Prince withdrew, and for a minute or two the young man found himself sandwiched between a motley crowd of market women, tradespeople, priests and navvies."

Daily Mirror 1913

Sunday Pictorial 1916

JAPAN CHINA
THE PHILIPPINES

THOS. COOK & SON

1917

New Note in Holidays.
English Gala Week at Le Touquet.

A new idea in holidays will be carried out at Le Touquet, near Boulogne, from September 12th to 19th. A health and pleasure carnival has been organised by the Le Touquet Gala Committee, Sardinia House, Kingsway, and the beautiful seaside resort in a forest will be at its merriest. For an inclusive fee of ten guineas visitors will travel first-class and by private motor cars, will stay at the most luxurious hotels, and, without cost, will be guests at the casinos, the opera house, balls, concerts, golf, tennis, dancing, and auction bridge tournaments. Even tips will be provided by the Committee, in fact, no one taking part in the round of gaieties need spend any money. English ladies will act as hostesses, and Miss Floyd Ariston, the well-known society singer and song writer, will supervise the entertainments. A feature of the week will be a tango dancing competition controlled by Miss Harding, well known in society dancing circles. For this competition Miss Ariston has composed a new time, a dance tempo which is expected to replace rag-time melodies. For the tango, tennis, golf, and auction bridge tournaments prizes will be given, and these will be presented at the Grand Bal de Casino on the last evening of the visit. Visitors will be conveyed by the South Eastern and Chatham Railway Co.'s trains and boats by the most popular route to the continent via Folkestone and Boulogne.

Gentleman's Magazine 1915

WELCOMING TOMMY.

Christmas Tears and Kisses at Waterloo.

Tommy on Christmas "leaf" is a great sight, especially in bulk. Waterloo, the naval and military clearing-house of England, was packed with him to-day, full of loud-lunged, boisterous youth; and every fresh train that came in added to the crush and din.

"Don't Be Late in the Morning."

Frank, merry souls all, they frolicked like schoolboys, tumbling, jostling, laughing; greeting old friends and making new ones, and telling each other on no account to be late in the morning.

"Not half, chummie," shouted one; "I'm going to sleep in a real bed to-night, with all my clothes off, and I don't care if I never get up."

By companies and battalions they raised the national slogan that all London might hear—protesting that they were NOT downhearted.

A Mixed Assembly.

At noon Waterloo was more like a barracks than a railway station. Train after train, packed with odds and ends of regiments, drew in from Aldershot and other prohibited areas; big men of the Highland Light Infantry, the Royal Scots, the A.S.C., the shorter and thicker men of the new Army, giants of the Borderers, fresh-cheeked Canadians of the Western Cavalry, men of the British Columbia contingent, Field and Garrison Artillerymen, and men of the Buffs.

There was that keen, quick look in their eyes that spoke of life in the healthy open, and the bloom of wind and rain on their faces.

"Cheero!" was the countersign. Everybody said it. Men who had never seen each other before and likely would not again cried "Cheero!" as they passed.

The girls were beautiful too. Mothers and wives and sweethearts crowded seats and disengaged trucks all over the station, and as each train came in they flocked to the barriers. Then what a kissing and a cuddling! They ran at their men with wet eyes, and the big soldiers, nothing abashed, lifted those who could not reach.

Under the Mistletoe.

There was mistletoe too. The Highlanders had each a twig tucked in their bonnets, and probably the festive plant was never so overworked. You could hardly hear the trains come in.

Here and there stood a young mother, a baby in her arms, and another at heel, waiting patiently for daddy. These by a natural sympathy collected into groups and compared babies.

A Homely Scene.

Said one, crooning over a bundle of snowy lace, "My boy hasn't seen this one yet. Three months old next week. He'll be all over it."

There was nothing at all warlike in the proceedings, no patriotic fervour. The interest was domestic only, wives and husbands, mothers and sons, young men and maidens, meeting once more after a dreary absence.

Star 1914

Men from Flanders

One of the greatest joys this Christmas has held for us has been the sight of men on leave from the Front mixing with the crowd in London. Great laughing children, many of them, with all the delight in their leave shown in every look and action. Without these boys Christmas would have been a dull, thoughtful festival. It is so essentially a family festival—the annual re-union—and, alas! what family now has not some sad gap in its ranks? "Absent Friends" was the toast everywhere. The dear ones who will never come home again and the brave ones in the trenches were the invisible guests everywhere. There must have been many burning ears in Flanders this Christmastide. But who could be melancholy with the returned warriors, gay and careless, enjoying every minute to the full—and, of course, children "of a lesser growth," without whom Christmas would not be worth having?

British Supremacy 1916

PUTNEY: ENTERTAINMENT FOR WOUNDED SOLDIERS.—An entertainment, consisting of concert, tea, and Christmas tree, was given by Mrs. Arthur Baker, of Magdala, St. Symons Avenue, Putney Hill, to wounded soldiers from Gifford House, on January 6, and from Rochampton House on January 13. The pretty little hall known as St. Simon's Hall was hired for each occasion, and was artistically decorated. The men were all given cigars, cigarettes, ties, handkerchiefs, and soap from the Christmas tree. A baby doll, a "thumbs up," and a handsome box of chocolates were drawn for, not forgetting a jovial gollywog, all causing much merriment. The arrangement of the entertainment, which included songs, recitations, dances, &c., was in the hands of Miss Freda White. Before dispersing, the Rev. J. Livesey on the first occasion, and Mr. Crossley on the second, proposed a vote of thanks to the generous donor of the entertainment, and called for three cheers for Mrs. Arthur Baker, which were unanimously accorded.

The Tablet 1917

The outbreak of the war caused something like consternation in the Christmas card trade. It emphasised the fact that a large proportion of the cards sold in this country, though they might have been designed in England, were actually printed in Germany. An ultra-patriotic agitation for buying none but British-made goods threatened the business with heavy loss. By the end of July, 1914, stocks of German-printed cards of a value amounting to many hundred thousand pounds were either in the retailers' hands or in process of delivery by the wholesale houses. The practical common sense of Queen Mary and Queen Alexandra gave considerable help in this predicament. Their Majesties placed specially large orders with the trade, and the announcement of what they had done helped to retrieve the situation. How Germany had secured so much of the very best class of this business was explained by Sir Adolph Tuck in a communication to the *Stationery Trades' Journal*. The finest small stipple work could only be secured by very delicate lithography, for which it was necessary to go outside this country. His own firm had tried to do this work in England, and had imported for the purpose some of the most skilful men in this branch, but in the first year they lost £4,000 over it and could see no likelihood of ever making it a successful commercial proposition.

Common Sense 1916

Spectator 1915

OH, THAT ATLANTIC ICE!

WILL THE SUMMER BE LIKE LAST YEAR'S?

Are we going to have a summer as bad as last year's?

Professor Bassett, of University College, Reading, who believes that the weather can be foretold by the character of the water in the Irish Sea, hints that we shall.

"I draw my conclusions," he said to an "Express" representative, "entirely from the nature of the water we find in the Irish Sea—the amount of salt in it and so on, and I find there are fairly striking variations in that from year to year.

The observations have only been continued for six years, but so far as they have gone we can divide them into four different types, and it looks as if those different types correspond to four different types of summer.

"The changes we get in the Irish Sea, I consider, give an indication of the changes going on in the open Atlantic, and the weather we get appears to be very largely dependent on what is happening out there.

"This year I find the sort of water obtained is similar to what we had last year, and it looks to me as if we are in for a summer similar to that of last year."

The professor added that his theory was supported by the appearance of numbers of the small floating animals known as Portuguese men-o'-war, as was the case last year, and by the fact that Atlantic ice was again coming down much further south than usual.

The Tablet 1917

ST. WINEFRIDE'S WELL.
RUN DRY.

The stream and ancient Well of St. Winefride, which has been flowing for fourteen hundred years, and which has been celebrated for the miraculous cures obtained, on January 5 ran dry. In the evening a press representative was able to walk on the floor of the outer bath. It appears that for some time tunnelling has been in progress in the neighbourhood, with the object of draining old lead mines in the district, and the flow of the water in the Well has been steadily decreasing. At last on the afternoon of January 5, when the men of the Holywell Halkyn mines and Tunnelling Co. were engaged in exploding a blasting charge there was a great rush of water from which the workmen had to flee for their lives, and shortly after this it was noticed that the flow of the Well had ceased. The flow is normally over 2,000 gallons per minute, and has been so from time immemorial. The stream served many mills along its banks, and the spring has been celebrated for the miraculous cures that for hundreds of years are alleged to have been obtained by bathing in the waters.

The deaf, dumb, blind, and the paralysed for centuries have sought its healing virtues, and cures have been effected even within recent years, as attested by the crutches, chairs, and other votive gifts hung over the Well by pilgrims who have been able to discard them. A hospice for the reception of the poorer class of Catholic pilgrims was opened in 1870, and since then interest in the shrine has greatly revived. Naturally the stoppage of the flow has caused consternation in Holywell, and will be received with regret by Catholics all over the country.

North Eastern Daily Gazette 1918

How the City received the News.

"Just before eleven o'clock on Monday," writes a City correspondent, "we learnt that the armistice was signed. A few people were lingering about the front of St. Paul's Cathedral, as usual, two American nurses sightseeing, and children feeding the pigeons. For a brief moment, as the cannon, guns and maroons boomed out on the stroke of eleven, they looked startled, and the pigeons wheeled and wheeled again. Inside the Cathedral some score of people knelt in silent thanksgiving. In less than ten minutes the City was delirious with excitement. Suddenly the streets were gay with flags and bunting, as at the bidding of some super-conjurer. Every vehicle, from taxi and 'bus to coal lorry, was commandeered and invaded by shouting, whistling, flag-waving crowds. Parties of munition workers, curiously garbed in Union Jacks and paper hats, waltzed and danced westward. Standing at the top of Northumberland-avenue, one had a never-to-be-forgotten view of a seething mass of people of every class and age filling Trafalgar-square, tightly wedged in the Mall, the Strand, and St. Martin's-lane, noisily abandoning themselves to feelings pent up for over four years. Contrasts there were also. Two well-dressed elderly men stood watching a group of jolly young officers, while unheeded tears ran down their cheeks. A little post-woman turned to the wall and wept bitterly. 'What is the matter, mother?' said a young soldier to an old flowerwoman who was weeping copiously; 'bad bad news?' 'No, lad, no,' said the old lady, smiling through her tears, 'it's the good news that makes me cry so!'"

British Weekly 1918

— The Food Controller has revoked Clause 36 of the Rationing Order, 1918, which limits to an ounce and a half the amount of bread, cake, bun, scone, or biscuit which may be served at public eating-places between 3 and 5.30 p.m.

British Weekly 1918

Armistice Day in Galway.

In this far-away town in the West of Ireland, writes a correspondent, the news came in this morning of the signing of the armistice. It is a lovely sunny day, so calm and so appropriate for such news. Very soon flags appear on various private houses, on some of the banks and hotels, also on the County Club, and the air seems full of holiday-making. Most of the passers are wearing the red, white and blue. The docks are gay with all sorts of flags and bunting, trawlers and patrol boats have put out every pennon and ensign aboard, and as I write the fine band of the Connaught Rangers is pouring out first "Rule, Britannia" and then the "Marseillaise."

British Weekly 1918

END OF THE WAR.

The glorious news of the end of the great world-war was made known on Monday forenoon, and throughout the kingdom was received with manifestions of popular rejoicing. There are few homes in the land upon which the war has not laid some share of its sorrow and suffering, some cause for abiding grief, but in the thrilling hour of victory our first thoughts and feelings were those of heartfelt thanksgiving that the long agony of blood and tears is over.

On receipt of the glad tidings we had a copy of the wire immediately displayed in the window of the "Herald" Office, and simultaneously had the flags hoisted. Crowds soon collected, and speedily spread the news. At the same time we must candidly admit that we were disappointed at the reception given to the most momentous announcement. Flags appeared very slowly, and not in great numbers; no mill Horns were blown, and some time elapsed before the church bells were rung. A few of the factories ceased work, but larger concerns "carried on." It was altogether unlike Lisburn, and unworthy of the occasion. What a contrast to other towns in Ulster! On Tuesday, the mill operatives were given a half-holiday, and in the evening there was an unorganised demonstration, with a bon-fire in Market Square. The Silver Band marched through the leading streets as did also a drumming party, but the whole affair lacked enthusiasm, and occasioned a good deal of comment, as well it might. Our City Fathers, too, didn't evidently consider it their duty to send a loyal message of congratulation to his Majesty. Other municipalities did, and have received the King's gracious acknowledgment. What's gone wrong with "Loyal Lisnagarvey?"

At Plantation, on Monday night, there were big celebration bonfires at Mr. T. M'Connell's and Messrs. Todd. Bros'. farms, but Lisburn was asleep and didn't see them.

Lisburn Herald 1918

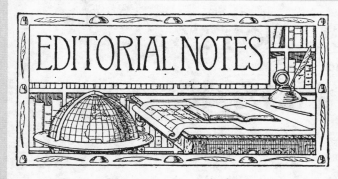

AERIAL TRAVEL FOR BUSINESS OR PLEASURE.

IMPORTANT NOTICE.

THE story of the development of transport from the days of the pack-horse to the present time is as interesting as any in the annals of Progress. Nothing has been so wonderfully revolutionized as locomotion. Science itself has made no greater strides than is seen in the methods of travelling obtaining now and, say, a hundred years ago; and for more than three-quarters of that period Thos. Cook & Son have been engaged in popularizing and in devising facilities for utilizing each new development as it appeared.

The latest development and most wonderful revolution of all is the Aeroplane, which is about to take its place as a recognized method of transit for travellers. Although for the moment, and probably for some little time to come, civilian flying for long journeys will be more or less limited, we have the pleasure to announce that we have been appointed to act as the official

PASSENGER AGENTS FOR
THE PRINCIPAL COMPANIES
OPERATING AERIAL LINES

in the same way as we act in that capacity for the chief Railway and Steamship Lines of the world.

Aerial travel is, of course, in its infancy, but most people already recognize that for transit purposes its possibilities are boundless. In the words of Mr. J. A. Whitehead, "Space will be annihilated, and the cities of the world brought within the reach of all. If we feel in need of a change we shall be able to start out for Venice to feed the pigeons of St. Mark's, to fly off to Norway to witness the spectacle of the Midnight Sun, or to spend the week-end in Cairo."

This was not mere rhetoric, as the world will shortly realize. People marvel less to-day at the flight of the Atlantic than they did when Bleriot flew the Channel with his monoplane, yet to-day the Channel is a mere ditch over which the aviator flies in the ordinary course of his work. In March last, one Handley-Page machine alone carried over 700 passengers between England and France.

Particulars of the services to Continental and other cities will be announced later on, also of more extended tours by aeroplane as soon as the necessary arrangements with the connecting aerial lines abroad have been completed.

Pending the completion of these arrangements we have issued "The New Highway in the Air," an illustrated booklet showing the comfort of aerial travel in machines expressly adapted for passenger traffic. It may be had at any of our Offices.

Traveller's Gazette **1919**

As quickly as possible the guests were then driven to the Battersea Town Hall, an ample number of carriages, supplied by Messrs. Tilling, Ltd., being in attendance for the purpose. Here the reception was held, the guests, about one hundred, being received on arriving by Alderman and Mrs. Rees, the genial host and hostess. The distinguished company included the Mayor of Battersea, three ex-Mayors, and several Councillors and their wives.

The hall was beautifully furnished, and the tables tastefully arrayed with flowers, etc. Several large tables on one side of the hall proved a great attraction, they were covered with presents, many of which were costly and handsome, comprising articles of ornament and usefulness. The catering was entrusted to Messrs. I. Stanley, and was quite up to the usual standard of this well-known firm in so far as the present conditions permit. The genial Mr. Barrow, who was present as a guest, superintended.

The company soon settled down to the tempting refreshments, and after a while, the glasses being filled, the Mayor, in a pleasant and affectionate speech, proposed the health of the bride and bridegroom, in which the company heartily joined. The bridegroom calmly replied and thanked all present for the way they had responded to the toast, and further assured the generous donors of the beautiful presents that he should always remember them. "I am not going to let your gifts be put out of sight but see that my wife uses them every day," he said, "you have all just heard her promise to 'obey,' and I intend to insist!" (Much laughter).

The bride then cut the cake and Lieutenant Dormer proposed the toast of the bridesmaids. Short *a propos* speeches in connection with the customary toasts were also made by Alderman Rees, Councillors Haythornthwaite, R. H. Johnson and H. C. Bigden, and also one by Mrs. Haythornthwaite. Their remarks were mostly complimentary, humorous and witty, quite in keeping with the festive occasion. It was all very pleasing to hear and must have been enjoyed by the speakers themselves who, by-the-way, owing to their public positions, are frequently making speeches of a very different and less pleasant character.

The speeches were interspersed by songs very ably rendered by Miss Daisy Rees, Miss Ruby Kipping and Miss Irene Rangecroft, each being much appreciated and very deservedly encored.

During the reception the newly-wedded couple left to spend the honeymoon in Scotland. The bride being tastefully dressed in a Serbian blue gabardine costume and white georgette hat. Their departing became the signal for a hearty cheer, sincere greetings and another storm of confetti.

*Clapham Junction
Review* **1918**

Traveller's Gazette 1919

Travel Notes and News.

STEAMERS ON THE THAMES.

THE steamers are now running for the season between Kingston and Oxford, and on page 13 we show how this delightful holiday may be made. It is a ninety-one miles voyage from Kingston to Oxford, through typical English scenery of a soft, quiet, pastoral character, and a broad shining waterway placidly winding through a panorama of woods and meadows and sunny hills and dales, with here and there gushing sluices and foaming cascades and

IN THE HAYFIELD.

quiet backwaters, with lovely homesteads nestling amid the trees and flowers of fairyland gardens.

INTO THE DEPTHS.

BREAKING ROPE PRECIPITATES MOUNTAINEERING PARTY.

News is to hand of an exciting accident which occurred to a mountaineering party in the Haute Savoie.

A party of tourists, whilst attempting to reach the summit of the Avaudruz, near Samoens, were all precipitated into the abyss below, through the breaking of the connecting rope.

M. Lutzud, a former Governor of Algeria, who was one of the party, was afterwards discovered suffering from serious injuries to the shoulder.

Tavistock Gazette 1919

BOY'S ORGY AT SEASIDE.

A boy of 15, who stole £150 in notes from a chest of drawers in his father's bedroom, was remanded at Old-street Children's Court in order to be sent to a reformatory. The boy, George Wilhemly, of Waley-street, Stepney, pleaded guilty.

It was stated that when the theft was discovered the father went to Southend, where he found the lad at work. With the exception of 6s. 8d., all the money had been spent in less than a fortnight.

Tavistock Gazette 1919

1920–1929

CENOTAPH DAY PLANS.

Seats by Lottery in Whitehall: 14,000 Applications.

The King has been pleased to approve the recommenda-tion of the Cabinet Committee that on Armistice Day, November 11, there shall be complete suspension of all normal business, work, and locomotion, through-out the British Empire, during the two minutes' silence commencing at 11 a.m.

FINAL details are now announced of the programme for the celebration of Armistice Day, for the burial of the unknown warrior in Westminster Abbey, with the King as chief mourner, and for the unveil-ing of the Cenotaph in Whitehall.

The destroyer which has been se-lected to bring the body of the un-known warrior from France is H.M.S. Verdun, specially chosen for its name as a compliment to our Allies. She will arrive at Dover with the body on Wednesday afternoon. At Dover there is to be a fitting military cere-monial.

The high officers who have accepted the invitation to act as bearers with the gun-carriage in the funeral pro-cession from Victoria Station on Thurs-day morning include Admirals of the Fleet Sir H. Meux, Earl Beatty, Sir H. Jackson, Admirals Sturdee and Madden, Field-Marshals Sir Henry Wilson, Lord Methuen, Sir W. Robert-son, and Earl Haig, General Lord Horne, and Air-Marshal Sir H. Trenchard.

Maroons Once Again.

The dropping of the veil from the Cenotaph by the King will be an-nounced throughout the suburbs of London by maroons. Overlooking the simple yet impressive ceremony in Whitehall from one of the Home Office windows will be the Queen, Queen Alexandra, Princess Mary, Princess Victoria, and other Royal Princesses.

Probably for the first time in history a lottery with the consent and approval of the Cabinet has been held in a Government office. The event took place yesterday in the Conference Room of the Office of Works, when Sir Lionel Earle, Permanent Secre-tary to the Office of Works, and Chair-man of the Cabinet Sub-Committee for the Armistice Day Memorial Service, assisted by a number of officials, acted as "drawer."

For the limited accommodation available in Westminster Abbey, where the "unknown warrior" will be buried, in Government office windows and on the pavements of White-hall over fourteen thousand ap-plications, many of them extremely pathetic, had been received from widows and relatives of those killed in the war, and it was found impossible to allocate seats for all. It was decided, therefore, to divide the applicants into three classes: (a) Women who had lost their husbands or only sons, (b) mothers or fathers who had lost all sons, or an only son, and (c) widows.

Result of the Draw.

Bereaved mothers and wives, totalling 103, were allotted seats in the Abbey, including the widows or mothers of three dead V.C.s, 599 mothers or fathers who had lost all sons or an only son, and 359 widows.

The accommodation provided in the windows of the Government offices overlooking the Cenotaph, and the north door of Westminster Abbey has been given up exclusively to the bereaved, and in these cases only women are to be accommodated. The drawings resulted in the following:— Class (b), 840; Class (c), 555.

In addition, space is being reserved for 105 women, selected by the over-seas High Commissioners from amongst the applications they have received.

The last class to be drawn was for the accommodation on the pavement in Whitehall, and this resulted as follows:— Class (b) 2,000; Class (c) 1,200.

Wreaths for Ypres.

In addition to a wreath on the Ceno-taph, the Ypres League is depositing another before the Cloth Hall ruins at Ypres on Armistice Day. Both will bear the following inscription:—

"In honoured memory of those who died in the defence of Ypres. On the 11th November, 1914, the Prussian Guard were finally stopped and the way to Calais barred."

The Ypres wreath is to be carried to Ypres by an ex-sergeant of the Guards, who took part in all the Battles of the Salient. Those de-sirous of sending wreaths to Ypres and vicinity for Armistice Day should communicate at once with the Honorary Secretary, Ypres League, 20, Berkeley Street, W.1.

HOLIDAY HINTS

The day before you set off for the seaside or country—

Grease all bright steelwork—such as fenders, fire-irons, and ordinary steel knives—to prevent rusting.

Turn off the gas, electric current, and water before leaving the house.

Thoroughly clean all sinks and lavatory basins and remember to pour a little disinfectant down each drain.

Dispose of all perishable foodstuffs. Cereals and non-perishable foods should be stored in air-tight tins so that mice and other pests will not be encouraged.

If the house is to be left entirely unattended all house plants should be placed in a shady part of the garden.

Cancel delivery of the daily papers and give notice to tradesmen that supplies will not be required.

Cover delicate upholstered furniture and carpets with dust-sheets in preference to drawing the blinds and curtains.

Good Housekeeping c.1920

£5 FOR A HOLIDAY IDEA.

HAVE you any really bright ideas for a holiday this summer, something that gets right away from the humdrum seaside fortnight? If so, don't keep it to yourself, let us know about it. It doesn't matter how wild it is, so long as it is within the purse-reach of the ordinary individual. If you have a good scheme or can think of one, write and tell me about it, and I will reward the sender of what I consider the best, most novel and most useful idea, with a £5 note. Address your letters to the Holiday Editor. PEARSON'S MAGAZINE, and post to arrive not later than Wednesday, June 22nd. Keep them short!

Pearson's Magazine 1921

DUKE OF YORK'S CAMP.

Jolly Good Time for the Boys.

The Duke of York has arranged a camp for some 400 boys from Eton, Harrow, and other public schools throughout the country, and a number of representatives of working-class organisations.

As a preliminary to their going away to the camp, which is situated at Littlestone Aerodrome, New Romney, the 400 were entertained yesterday to luncheon in the Royal Riding School at Buckingham Palace Mews, and were afterwards shown round the mews before going to Charing Cross to entrain for New Romney.

The Duke of York sent them the following message:—

"Tell them to enjoy themselves, and have a jolly good time. Say that I am going down to see them on Tuesday next, and to spend a couple of days with them, and if they are not having a good time I shall jolly well want to know the reason why."

Illustrated Sunday Herald 1921

KING OF MIRTH LOST & FOUND

Elusive Charlie's Wonderful Day in London : Kissed by Girls and Mobbed by Children.

RAN INTO THE "ARMS OF THE LAW."

Charlie Chaplin, described by the Mayor of Southampton as the King of Mirth, took London by storm yesterday, and in a wonderful day had the following experiences :—

- Mobbed at Waterloo.
- Kissed by London girls.
- Speech at the Ritz.
- Threw carnations to crowd.
- Walked down Regent-street.
- Eluded his friends.
- Taxi ride to Kennington.
- Strolled in old haunts.
- Children mobbed him.
- Escaped in taxi.
- Alighted once again.
- Distributed chocolates.
- Ran into the arms of police in escaping crowd.
- Vanished into the Ritz.
- Made dumb show from balcony.
- Dined at West End restaurant.
- Visited New Oxford Theatre.

When he arrived at Waterloo thousands nearly tore him off his feet in a wild rush. Within four minutes he had been hurried through the cheering multitude to his hotel.

Before he had been in London two hours Charlie had vanished. He went to his old haunts in Kennington for a quiet stroll, but the children recognised him with shouts of " Here's Charlie." He had to beat a retreat from the boisterous welcome that followed.

To-day he is expected at Clapham and Tagg's Island.

Illustrated Sunday Herald 1921

A MOTOR TOUR IN THE HIGHLANDS

Appeals for a " lift " were not uncommon. Our first passenger was a little, tired stonemason, with anxious face, who had walked from Dundee (over a hundred miles), and was going to Inverness, where he heard there was a job. He was terribly poor; the night before he had sold his shirt for a night's lodging. But he was not uncheerful, for the cottage women were kind, and would often give him a bowl of broth or cup of tea and a scone newly off the girdle.

And so we went on and on, now hugging the coast, now running inland, until we reached Inverness, with its unusual stir and its fashionables on the way to moor and loch for shooting and fishing. Thence, still heading north, to Dingwall; and after that 169 miles straight run to John o' Groats. Here, indeed, we seemed to be on top of the world. The little octagon-shaped house marks the Land's End of North Britain, and London and Piccadilly and Fleet-street seem very far away.

We return by the West Coast this time, and now we revel in the gorgeous beauty of the Highlands— towering mountains, purple clad and snow capped, brown streams where trout lie; roaring cataracts and rushing rivers, where the salmon beguile the angler; pine forests, rowan trees in full berry, moor and crag and torrent; and over all the infinite tender charm of " the fall o' the year," golds and browns, reds and russets. Through the soft September twilight on the way home.

Holiday Maker 1921

Everywoman's

Seaside Flirtations

IT is the flirtation that makes the holiday. There's no denying that, however one may pretend to be superior to and independent of such side lines. Neither girl nor man is really intended to take his or her amusements separately; that is proved beyond a doubt by the extra amount of enjoyment that can be crammed in when they take them jointly.

And, after all, why not? For one blessed fortnight in the year he can put his hand on a more or less unlimited supply of cash, the result of months of saving, and she can wear her daintiest dresses without wondering if there will be enough left over from her weekly pay to meet the laundry bill. Relief from petty considerations of that sort, plus immaculate flannels and a background of sparkling sea, turns a very ordinary young man into an Adonis of sorts. It gives her, too, a sparkle unknown to the office. Therefore, given the time and the place, what more natural than the loved one should be sought.

Everywoman's Weekly 1922

Chit Chat

One of our national bad habits is specially connected with the holiday season, and with all holiday excursions. It is the thoughtless and untidy practice of throwing down paper bags, pieces of newspaper, empty bottles, banana skins, etc., after the *al fresco* meal, and thus disfiguring the natural beauty of the seashore, the field, and the forest. It is not a punishable offence, but every individual who recognises that it is none the less reprehensible, may help to spread the right sense of responsibility. We blame the children who wantonly destroy flowering plants and trees, and, after all, this is only another mode of destroying beauty.

Schoolmistress 1923

HOLYHEAD DISTRICT.—It was unfortunate that the good weather should break just as the season was beginning for us. This being a holiday district the season is a short one, from the middle of July till the middle of September.

There was a two days' regatta at Holyhead at the beginning of August, in connection with the Menai Straits regattas. It was an attempt to revive the old annual regatta. The Royal Dee yacht club had charge of the racing one day and the Town Regatta committee the other. The bad weather kept all the yachts but one away, and the racing was provided by small boats from Holyhead and Trearddur bay. A feature of the regatta was the race for "hobblers" or pilot boats, big open boats rigged with a dipping lug and leg of mutton mizzen. This race was keenly contested and the boats were very smartly handled in the fresh breeze. The regatta will be repeated next year on a larger scale.

Merrimaid, ketch, 107, which used to belong to Mrs Workman, was here several times during the season. Hoshi, sch. 40, came round from Bangor for the regatta, bringing Mr Charles Livingston, Mr John Jellico and Sir Charles MacIver, three well-known north of England yachtsmen. Several other yachts came into the harbour during the season. The C.A. boatman is a smart man and has given every satisfaction. At Trearddur bay the sailing club held races for its three classes as usual during August, but the weather was not altogether favourable. The first day's racing had to be abandoned owing to a fresh S.W. breeze which had kicked up a heavy sea.

That's the worst of Trearddur bay. There is no shelter from a S.W. wind. On each of the last two days there was more wind than was required, and a boat capsized each day. The races held for novices were a feature of this year's programme. These were a great success, being attended with perfect weather and did much to encourage the young people to take an interest in sailing.

Cruising Association Bulletin 1921

Punch 1922

Beneath a picture :—

"Racing, the sport of Kings, is resuming its pre-war standard in England. The picture shows Tetrameter, the winner of the Goodwood Stewards Cup, approaching the winning post on which were seated the King and Queen."
Canadian Paper.

Our home papers somehow missed this picturesque detail.

MERAN.

SITUATED in the gracious valley of the Adige in the Southern Tyrol, Meran has of recent years attained a world-wide reputation as a health resort and justly earned her title as the "Jewel of the South Tyrol."

Little known at the latter end of last century, the climatic perfection and lovely situation of Meran began to be spoken of at the beginning of this century. The years 1910-11 saw the size of her population ten times what it had been forty years previously, and now her attractions and the accommodation she offers are firmly established.

Possessing the advantages of an Alpine climate (exceptionally clear sky, an unusual amount of sunshine, freedom from wind and few rainy days) without many of its drawbacks, Meran and her suburbs Obermais, Untermais and Gratsch are a little over 1,000 feet above sea-level. North, east and west mighty mountains shelter her. To the south stretches a broad valley. Thus even at mid-day in winter the temperature scarcely ever falls below freezing point, while fogs are almost unknown. Summer is not unendurably hot, and in autumn the atmosphere has the pure and bracing quality one associates with the perfect Alpine resort. As a health resort Meran has indeed much to recommend her.

FOR THE INVALID.

Invalids may rest assured that in Meran their every want will be satisfied and that everything possible has been provided to alleviate or heal their ills. Firstly, perhaps, the water, brought from high-level springs and giving a pure supply; milk is there in abundance, grapes unrivalled. In 1907 there was added to the attractions in this category the Health Establishment, or "Kurmittelhaus," containing perfectly appointed baths of every description—electric, mud, salt-water, pine and a magnificent swimming bath. Again for the invalid, of doctors there are plenty. During the "season" (which may be estimated at from September to June) these generally number over fifty and include many leading authorities and specialists in most branches of their professions.

World Travel Gazette **1923**

IN THE DESERT.
By F. K. Hosali.

AT BISKRA we hired three mules from one of the best hotels to ride to Sidi-okba (an oasis) for a day's excursion. One mule had strings for stirrup-leathers; one was very old and stiff in the legs, and really only fit for slaughter. The guide got it along by incessant beating, somehow. When we started to return in the afternoon it had stiffened up, and could barely walk; the second had gone lame—only the third was fit. We could only ride in misery at a walking pace, and sunset saw us with some six kilometres before us. At that time that part of the desert was not safe after sunset, and I don't know how we should have got on but for the lucky chance of a European dog-cart with an Italian and a Frenchman coming along the track, which was very unusual so late in the evening.

We asked them to help us, and they crammed us in. We put the guide and mules into an Arab camp for the night, and they drove us back to Biskra, revolver in hand. An Arab, afraid of being robbed, ran beside us for some distance.

We refused to pay, on principle, more than the fee to the guide. Our pleasure was spoiled by the condition of the mules, and it might have been rather unpleasant if the dog-cart had not come along. Afterwards we were always careful to say before-hand that we should look at the animals before we started, and Arabs always brought good animals, and seemed to take a pride in showing them off.

World Travel Gazette **1923**

Schoolmistress 1923

Traveller's Gazette 1924

Times Educational Supplement 1924

ENGLISH CATHEDRALS.

A double purpose is served by the artistic addition, entitled "Cathedrals," which has just been made to the publications of the Great Western Railway Company. It not only directs attention to the very large number of important centres of Church life within the area served by the "G.W.R."—the book deals specifically with Westminster and Bath Abbeys and 20 cathedrals as far apart as Truro and Manchester—but also provides an illustrated guide of unusual interest and beauty for the use of visitors.

At a time when many of those responsible for the care of the cathedrals are showing an increasing desire to interest the public in them, the publication of the book is opportune, and if arrangements could be made to reprint for local use the several chapters dealing with the individual cathedrals, many of the Church authorities concerned would doubtless welcome the opportunity.

When the King and Queen visited Swindon recently a presentation copy of the book was handed to them in the Royal train, and the Queen at once asked for further copies.

The book, which consists of nearly 120 large pages, is freely illustrated by means of 74 photographs, beautifully reproduced, and an equal number of black-and-white drawings, and contains a useful section, entitled "Cathedrals and How to Understand Their Architecture." The chapters are conveniently arranged, on the assumption that the reader is making London the starting-point of a tour of the principal cathedral cities. The book can be obtained from the Superintendent of the Line, G.W.R., Paddington, and the price is half a crown.

Traveller's Gazette 1924

COMRADES LOOKING ON THE WEST.

MR. SPARROW.   MR. MARSHALL.   MR. BUTLER.
We apologise for this photo.   It was reproduced from an American Newspaper.

Granta 1924

The Idol of America.

Disquieting rumours are reaching Cambridge from across the Atlantic. It is said that Mr. J. W. G. Sparrow, of Trinity Hall, the Secretary of the Union, is fast becoming the idol of the United States. It is not merely his forensic skill, nor the brilliance of his brain or scalp, that has placed him in this position. It is also that he is "so English." Meanwhile Cambridge is beginning to wonder whether it will ever see its Union Officers again. The pathetic cry, "Will ye no come back again?" is being heard on all sides. In this connection I may draw the notice of our readers to the cartoon of the Cambridge debaters that we reproduce this week from an American newspaper.

GASSED IN THEIR SLEEP

Holiday Couple Saved by Police Sergeant

Owing to an accidental escape of gas in their bedroom at Southend, Mr. and Mrs. Mahoney, of Oxton, who were on holiday, had a narrow escape from death.

When their landlady knocked at their door she received no answer, and when a police sergeant was brought he found the couple unconscious. Artificial respiration was successfully applied.

It appears that the gas had been turned off the previous evening at the main by the landlady, and that when she turned it on again to cook the breakfast next morning there was an escape in the room where Mr. and Mrs. Mahoney were asleep.

Daily Sketch 1924

PILGRIMS' RETURN.

GREAT ENTHUSIASM AT PRESTON.

PARALYSED MAN'S CURE.

Scenes of great enthusiasm greeted the return to Preston last evening, of the local contingent of the pilgrimage to Lourdes, which included James Salisbury, of St. Mary's-street North. The train was an hour and a half late, but the crowd waited patiently and raised cheers as Salisbury was piloted by police, ambulance men, priests, and others to a taxicab and hurried to his home.

Round the streets where his home is situated hundreds of people had congregated, and again loud cheers were raised. Salisbury went straight to the bedside of his sick wife. It appears that his wife, who suffers from heart trouble, had been overcome by the excitement of the occasion, which was increased by the enthusiastic crowd.

Paralysis Cure.

Salisbury has been a familiar figure for the past two years, shuffling a few steps at a time with the help of two sticks. From the waist downwards he has been apparently hopelessly paralysed, and has tried many doctors and specialists, electric baths, and all kinds of massage treatment, but nothing has ever done him good.

Now he has come back from Lourdes, and, judging by the way he stepped in and out of the taxi, something in the nature of a complete cure has been effected.

He is about 32 years of age. He served in the war and prior to his accident was an amateur boxer.

Scenes at Southport.

Shortly before midnight the 20 odd pilgrims from Southport to Lourdes returned home amidst enthusiastic scenes. The pilgrims, who were brought by special train, save for half a dozen, one a cripple, who went on to Southport—detrained at Birkdale, where a crowd, estimated at several thousands, filled the station and the roadway.

This was in readiness to greet the two boys who went as cripples and returned cured, carrying their leg irons, and in one case a boot with an enlarged iron heel, which they had previously used as aids to walking. The boys were Joe Macarthy, aged 12, of 51, Canning-road, Southport, and Edward Maccumsky, aged 15, of 76, Banastre-road, Southport. Maccumsky, who was at the end of the train, was carried shoulder high, but Macarthy, who slipped from the front portion of the train almost unobserved, was lost for a time in the crowd.

The boys, quite free in their action, were subsequently driven amidst the cheering crowd to their homes in a cab.

Northern Daily Telegraph 1925

AN ANIMAL HUNTER ON THE AMAZON.

An interesting creature is the manatee, or cowfish, which attains a length of eight feet and weighs about four hundred pounds. It has a face not unlike that of a cow, hence the name cowfish. It suckles its young at the breast. Its flesh, which resembles pork or veal in flavour, is considered by the natives as a delicacy. It is found on the Rio Negro, Tapajos, and Uassa rivers; and I decided to catch a pair and bring them over to the London Gardens. I accordingly built some special steel traps, and went off down the Tapajos looking for manatees. It was many weary weeks before our luck was in. But one night a pair, male and female, got into the net. Now a four-hundred pound fish is not an easy creature to hold. In their efforts to get loose they are likely to break the mesh of the net and get free. But we quickly hauled them up on to the shore, when they were helpless. We placed them in two crude tanks and set off home for Para. Unfortunately a rebellion had broken out, and the revolutionary authorities sent us to Obidos, where our prized treasures were commandeered for food. It was disappointing, but when things had quieted down I set off manatee hunting once more, and eventually succeeded in getting another pair to my depot in Para. Here I taught them to feed on green food which could easily be procured in England. I procured two wooden oval tanks, 8 feet long, 3 feet wide and 11 feet deep, placed the fish in them, and got them on board a liner bound for Liverpool. When we reached Lisbon all the green food had been consumed, and though I hunted all over the city I only procured fifty-six bunches of carrots, of which only the green tops were of use. Despite every care, one of the manatees succumbed while passing through the Bay of Biscay, and the other five hours after we had dropped anchor at Liverpool. It was a bitter disappointment; but I am off again shortly, and mean to have another try, and hope this time to be successful in bringing to Europe a living specimen of this strange fresh-water mammal.

Windsor Magazine **1925-1926**

BOY CAMPERS' TRIBUTE AT SOUTHPORT.

The boys at the Birkdale Summer Camp, headed by the Windsor Institute prize band, marched in procession yesterday afternoon to the war memorial, and the youngest boy, aged 7, and the drum-major there placed a wreath.

Subsequently, the residence of Mr Hoyle, father of Mr H. A. Hoyle, the hon. secretary of the camp, was visited, yesterday being Mr Hoyle's 80th birthday.

The celery crop in North Nottinghamshire is much earlier than usual, and is of excellent quality.

Northern Daily Telegraph **1925**

Granta **1924**

CARAVANNING
I VENTURE FORTH.

I am probably one of the first "holiday" caravanners who has ventured forth this year with his caravan behind his car, his lockers well stocked with provisions, bound for a favourite beauty spot. As I write these notes, just a week before Easter, my caravan is pitched behind me in the shelter of a large and very ancient holly bush, from which is suspended the aerial for our wireless set. It is one of many good pitches in the New Forest. In front of me is a delightful pond with sandy banks, and to my right, looking north, is the most glorious view over the tops of the trees, in the valley in which is hidden Rufus Stone. As far as the eye can see over the counties of Hampshire and Wiltshire are trees, with occasional stretches of green fields or hills covered with gorse and bracken.

SOME DETAILS.

We are only here for three days, just a break from ordinary routine, but we are already planning our next week-end trip, and then, later, our summer holiday.

Our holiday home, when pitched ready for habitation, is much more than a mere caravan. We have a

The "Lean-to" Provides an Excellent Dining Room.

canvas "lean-to" on each side, forming with the caravan, three rooms. This arrangement not only gives us all the accommodation we want for a party of six, but it helps to keep the caravan warm, an advantage when taking a holiday so early as March.

The "lean-to" is a very roomy affair, and as it takes only about ten minutes to erect, our holiday home is ready to use about twenty minutes after we have selected our site. Of course, the caravan is ready to use as a house as soon as we have stopped and let down the legs.

Holidays, Tours and Travel **1926**

IN THE WILDS :—Travellers who find it needful to use mules, donkeys (or burros), and horses should be careful. The horses or mules should be inspected. Choice is not always possible, but experienced travellers find that by insistence they are often able to obtain "bestias" of more endurance than others from the same owner. The staying power of the animals is important in the mountains, where an accident may cause serious delay.

Wayside sleeping accommodation is indifferent in the less frequented parts of the country. A traveller expecting to stop at a tambo should carry his own hammock, bed linen, and mosquito netting. Tinned food may advisably be carried as an emergency ration.

In mountaineering, it is incumbent upon the traveller to take his own saddle and blankets. A good and comfortable saddle is particularly necessary, and care should be exercised in adjusting the straps, which are often subject to severe strains.

South American Handbook 1925

ARGENTINA'S CLEARING HOUSE

A Pleasurable Experience.

Another result of British influence is the growing popularity of all classes of British sports. Football, cricket, tennis, golf, polo, boxing—most of these have a wide circle of adherents and are given considerable space in the daily press. Racing is exceedingly popular.

The manufacturer, or representative, who pays a business visit to Argentina, will find that his journey is accompanied by considerable pleasure. The people are hospitable, the English community will make him welcome, and he need not be deterred by ignorance of the language. There are English hotels (*e.g.*, The Phœnix Hotel, in Calle San Martin), where the majority of the staff speak English. The example mentioned is noted for a bill of fare that is irreproachable, a convenient situation and a moderate tariff—judged by Argentine standards.

The climate of Buenos Aires is equable and exceedingly pleasant, the winter being less severe than is the case in England and the summer considerably longer and warmer. Snow has fallen but twice in three hundred years.

No description of Buenos Aires would be complete without a reference to Calle Florida— the Bond Street of Buenos Aires. It is the fashionable shopping street, and is thronged daily with a concourse of fashion such as cannot be excelled in London, Paris or New York. Between the hours of five p.m. and seven p.m. traffic is suspended in this particular thoroughfare and it is given over to a nightly promenade —a spectacle on no account to be missed.

Empire Mail 1927

A TRIP TO FRANCE.

All Seats Booked.

Whitsun railway bookings are brisk, and given a fine week-end they should be heavy on Monday. An interesting trip to France will take place on Sunday. No seats are now available; the number of tickets being restricted to the boat accommodation. The train starts from Bedminster at 6.20 a.m., Temple Mead 6.27, and Bath 6.45. Stops will also be made at Trowbridge, Frome, Yeovil, Dorchester and Weymouth. The steamer will leave Weymouth quay for Cherbourg at 9 a.m., and there will be several hours ashore before the return. The trip has proved most popular, and there are many disappointments in Bath, and presumably at other places along the line.

This revival of Continental trips, after a lapse of several years, has proved a signal success, and will probably lead to a revival of the entente cordiale.

Bath and Wilts Chronicle 1927

Visit to Prince of Wales's Hospital.

In response to an invitation from the Prince of Wales's Hospital, Tottenham, N.15, a profitable afternoon was spent there on Saturday, February 5th, by a mixed party from the H.S.A. Group F.176, and representatives from several other Groups formed in the Northern Area.

A tour of inspection was made under the guidance of Mr. Drewett, the director, and Miss Bickerton, the Matron, who gave most interesting information relative to the practical working of each department, which included the domestic quarters, the sterilising plant, disinfecting chambers, store rooms, nurses' quarters, dispensary, operating theatres, testing rooms, etc., etc.

Most interesting was the explanation as to the use of an electric diathary: a practical demonstration was also given in the Rontgen-ray department. In the wards, almost everyone was "listening-in" and thoroughly enjoying the programme which was being broadcast from the local football match. The children's ward attracted great attention; comfort and relaxation was in evidence everywhere. Later on we were taken to the Lecture Room, where the Matron and her staff served a most enjoyable tea. The Group Secretary, on behalf of the guests expressed appreciation of the privileges and courtesy which had been accorded to them and he handed to Mr. Drewett the sum of £1 9s. subscribed by the guests in aid of the funds of the hospital. Such visits to our hospitals cannot but help to bring more Contributors to the Hospital Saving Association so as to help the Voluntary Hospitals in their splen did work.

Contributor
1928

WHY NOT A MOUNTAIN HOLIDAY?

—

By A. Woman Traveller.

□ □ □

Foreigners are astonished by the number of English women who spend holidays abroad alone. One tiny hotel in the Italian Alps is never without at least one rambling woman artist.

Wealthy tourists never reach these mountain villages. Tariffs are fixed, and one may secure a delightful bedroom with meals for less than £3 a week. Tourist agencies are able to advise such places, or the Italian State Railways, Spanish Travel Bureau, and similar organisations will do everything for you—including getting your passport.

Take English £1 notes with you. These are accepted everywhere abroad, even by motor car drivers. Motoring is expensive abroad, but a day's drive along roads high up among mountains is a thrilling experience if your nerves are strong. Hotels usually have a car for hire attached to them. You should always arrange the price before starting. The chauffeur expects 10 per cent. of the bill. Don't tip too much — a reputation as a wealthy person is sure to prove expensive.

Traveller and Clubman 1928

The Lady
1928

NEW SPORTS FASHIONS

Trousers for tennis are a striking innovation in sports clothes seen at the British
Artificial Silk Exhibition at Holland Park Hall

Around Europe with a Car—(*Continued*).

Belper News 1927

Dresden, the Florence of Germany

GENERALLY speaking, the part of Germany making the strongest appeal to the motorist and lovers of mountains and quaint towns is the south-west, whilst Saxony, with its beautiful city of Dresden, the Florence of Germany, is a dream of delight. We leave out Berlin since it is so well-known, and pass thence to the sunny south. The motorist will not regret devoting several days to Dresden and its lovely hinterland ; there are gorges and woods, pinnacled rocks and craggy cliffs, and always the picturesque reaches of the winding Elbe.

South of Dresden lies Czecho-Slovakia, reached through forests of pine. It is a great district for the " Wandervogel "—not wild animals or rare flowers, but the foot-slogging German youth of either sex or both sexes. We came upon them in small parties each with a rucksack and usually one with a guitar tramping along these fine roads, happy and hatless. The " Wandervogel " is a symptom of the new Germany, a sign of virility, a gigantic movement with pre-war roots and post-war developments.

✳   ✳   ✳

—A Country—Not a Cocktail !

OUR entry into Czecho-Slovakia was by a pass in the Erz Gebirge, and on the edge of this dividing line we came to the frontier post. It is ninety-four kilometres to Prague, the capital, through the sugar-loaf hills of Bohemia. We were in a new country, comparatively speaking.

" When our State was newly-established I had to go up and down Europe and America explaining that ' Czecho-Slovakia ' was a country and not a new cocktail," Jan Masaryk, the son of the President, told us.

There are all sorts of things to be seen in the capital of old Bohemia, but we do not advise anyone to learn Czech. Having travelled far and seen much, we had acquired a certain knowledge of tongues, but Czech is in a class by itself. What, for instance, can one say when asked to pronounce this, " Strc prst skrz krk "; or, if you want an ice-cream, you must ask for " Zlmzlina."

WANTED A HOLIDAY.

CLOWNE SCHOOLBOYS' ADVENTURE.

The precocity of four Clowne schoolboys who wanted a holiday, and, to satisfy their ambition disappeared from home, caused no little amount of amusement in the village, though at first their absence from home led to considerable anxiety on the part of their parents and friends.

It appears that the boys left home the other morning ostensibly to go to school, but their failure to return for dinner aroused the suspicions of the parents, who instituted inquiries and ascertained that the youngsters had not presented themselves at school at all that morning. Expectations that they would return in the evening were not realised, and the suspense of the parents was not broken until the following day when a wire was received from a relative of one of the boys at Huddersfield announcing their safe arrival in that town.

It transpired later that the lads had set out to walk there, but succeeded in getting a lift on passing vehicles during a portion of the journey. Having no money in their pockets they were hungry and tired and were glad of the rest and food which awaited them at their destination. They arrived home during the week-end and were at school on Monday looking little the worse for their adventure.

MISS LAURA THICKETT AND TALK OF "SECRETS."

Describes as "All Piffle" the Stories about the Butler Straw.

FAREWELL LETTER TO HER.

A Clue to the Butler: Two Postcards from Paignton, Devonshire.

MISS THICKETT, the secretary of the missing rector.

Evening Standard
1928

THE deepest mystery still surrounded to-day the disappearance from his parish of the Rector of Doddinghurst (Essex), the Rev. Franklin Isaac Hutchinson, from whom nothing has been heard since July 25, when apparently he left to go on holiday in Ireland.

The whereabouts of Herbert Straw, his butler and handyman, who left the rectory a few days before Mr. Hutchinson, are also unknown. He is supposed to have gone away to Torquay for a holiday.

This evening, however, the "Evening Standard" learned that two post-cards with the mark of Paignton, Devon, dated July 25, have been received in Swinton from Straw.

The postcards are addressed to John Aireys, aged 16, and Basil Aireys, aged 10, who live in Church-street, Swinton, near where Straw formerly lived with his mother.

On the postcard to the elder boy was written: "Dear Jack, How are you going on, old lad? Lovely weather in Devon.—H.S."

On the other card is written: "Dear Basil, Lovely weather in Devon.—H.S." The Aireys recognise the handwriting as unmistakably that of Straw.

This afternoon a police superintendent and other officers arrived at the rectory from Brentwood and were conducted into the grounds by the Rector's churchwarden. (See Page Ten.)

THE "YARD" ASSISTS.

The local police were accompanied by two inspectors and one sergeant from Scotland Yard.

Some of the officers entered the premises and inspected the interior; the others searched the grounds.

Shortly after their entrance men were posted on the gates.

LETTER TO MISS THICKETT.

Mr. A. G. Weymouth, joint principal with Mr. Hutchinson of St. Peter's College, Lewisham, said to-day that on August 2 he received a letter from Mr. Hutchinson, addressed "My dear Weymouth," and stating:
This is to say good-bye. I wish you every happiness with your loved one—happiness which a rotter robbed me of. I am broken in heart through overwork. I feel I am of no further use to the Church, this college, or the world, so I am leaving it.

Miss Laura Thickett, the rector's secretary, now at Swinton, Yorkshire, told the "Evening Standard" to-day that she also had received a letter there from Mr. Hutchinson.

In this letter Mr. Hutchinson said he was not continuing his work at Doddinghurst, and bade her good-bye.

Miss Thickett said she destroyed the letter.

MISS THICKETT'S STORY.

From Our Special Correspondent.

SWINTON, Thursday.

TO-DAY Miss Thickett gave me further information about the movements of the man Straw and about his relations with Mr. Hutchinson, the rector of Doddinghurst.

She said Straw left the rectory at 9 a.m. on July 21 for a two weeks holiday, but she did not know where he was going.

"The vicar took him in his car to Brentwood Station, which is about five miles away. I have not had much to do with Straw.

"He first went as outdoor and odd-job man at the College at Lewisham, but when the old butler and his wife left the Doddinghurst Rectory, Straw went there to do housework for Mr. Hutchinson.

"There were to have been more servants at the rectory at the beginning of next term.

"Dr. Hutchinson was very good to Straw, and on the friendliest terms with him."

THE ONLY GUEST IN THE INN.

□ □ □

Have you ever been the solitary traveller at the lonely inn on a stormy night — that familiar figure in fiction which has stood so many novelists of the old shool in good stead in opening their three-decker romances?

Business took me late one day to a remote village on the edge of Dartmoor. It was more inaccessible even than the farcical Ippleton; it was not even on a branch line.

From a junction a small train with a panting engine took me as far into that bare moorland region as the iron road penetrates, and the journey had to be completed by motor-omnibus.

It was blowing hard and the rain was pelting down as the omnibus headed for the moorland, crawling along the narrow roads between time-worn and moss-grown stone fences.

Once or twice we stopped at cross-roads to set down a few passengers, mostly women with baskets and parcels, who had been shopping in town. It was a single-decker omnibus, with the entrance platform at the front, and every time a woman alighted the driver would flash a ray of light on to the vehicle's steps with an electric torch so that she should not plunge headlong into the darkness. At the same time he would be handing out her parcels.

The conductor seemed to know his passengers as a shepherd his sheep. I alone was the stranger.

"Where might you want to be set down?" he inquired, as we rumbled into the village.

I named an hotel — the only one I had come across in a hurried consultation with the faithful "Kelly".

"We pass there," he confided, "and I'll put you down."

* * *

It was after nine o'clock when I pushed open the door of the little inn. A dim light was burning; no one was about. The prospect was about as cheerless as it could well be.

Then a trim maid appeared from a kitchen. "A room? Certainly."

She grabbed a chair and scampered upstairs. On the landing she mounted the chair and lit the gas. They were lighting up for my benefit.

I came downstairs five minutes later, after unpacking my bag, to find her on her knees at the hearth lighting a fire. Soon there was a roaring blaze, and a steaming supper on the table.

I was the only guest that night, and if the visitors' register was correct, there had not been a visitor staying there for a week, but I could not have been made more welcome if I had been a member of the family.

Last touch of thoughtfulness, a hot-water bottle was put in the bed to help to lull me to sleep while the storm raged outside.

It is not an epic story, but it is a grateful tribute to one British innkeeper who will greet a late and lonely guest with a smile and do his best to make him comfortable.   X.

Traveller and Clubman 1928

Tourist Topics
1928

Motoring Adventures in the Balkans

E ACH country has its peculiarities and curious ways of doing business, which may be irksome to the traveller. For instance, difficulties about money increase as a grand European tour proceeds. Already we had paid out in Dutch guilder, German reichmarks, Czech kroner, Polish zloty, Rumanian lei, and Yankee dollars.

Owing to the parlous condition of national finance, it is not easy to secure fresh currencies. You cannot walk into a Balkan bank, present a cheque, or a letter of credit, and depart with the cash all in a minute. They don't deal with real money in the Balkans in that easy-going way.

"You want to draw money," says a swarthy-looking official, frowning in darkest disapproval. "Why do you want to draw money?" When you come to think of it, that is a disconcerting question. Why does one want to draw money? It is no use telling him you want to spend it. You might say that you are making a collection of the world's paper money for a scrap-book, or that the money, if paid, will save you from the workhouse or the police; but there is no sense of humour in a Balkan bank. You say you want the money because you have none, and that makes him suspicious.

Then you warm to the task. "Look here," you say, "it's my money you've got and I mean to have it." He stares, pales, and vanishes behind a screen, to reappear after a long interval with more forms and a large colleague, who comes to look at the stranger wanting to draw money.

Motor Touring Abroad

Motoring in Norway and Sweden

The Automobile Association announces reduced charges for the conveyance of motor-cars and motor-cycles accompanied by passenger, on the Ellerman's Wilson Line steamers from Hull to Norwegian and Swedish ports. A flat rate has been secured of £4 3s. 4d. for any size, or make of car, and £1 1s. for motor-cycles.

Concessions to British Motorists

The Automobile Association states that British tourists visiting Sweden are now exempt from payment of the motor-car taxes for a period of four months. Owing to the initiative of the A.A. and the various national clubs, the principle of allowing four months' exemption to British motorists has now been adopted by the Governments of Spain, Holland, Belgium, Norway, Sweden and Denmark. In several of these countries the concession is already in force, in others the necessary arrangements are being made for its introduction.

In all the above countries the concession is of a reciprocal nature, so that British motorists are allowed the benefit of it because the British Government has for many years granted exemption from the motor vehicle tax to all visiting motorists whose stay in Great Britain does not exceed four months. Italy has for several years granted exemption for three months. In Great Britain and Italy the exemption is not based on reciprocity.

Tourist Topics
1928

Summer Holidays in Canada.

The success of the conducted tours last year by the Canadian Pacific Railway have led to the repetition of the tours in 1929. They will embrace periods ranging from three or four weeks (which would enable the tourist to take in Quebec, Montreal, Ottawa, Toronto, Niagara Falls) to a more extensive trip of eight or ten weeks, to cover the Atlantic journey on a Canadian Pacific steamer and a visit from one end of the Dominion to the other, embracing stays at the beauty spots in the Canadian Rockies, such an Banff, Lake Louise, etc., terminating with a visit to Vancouver and Victoria on Vancouver Island.

Empire Mail 1929

THE TRAVELLER IN ST. MALO

A Popular British Rendez-Vous at the Scotch Tea Rooms

Eight years ago two enterprising Scotch girls came to St. Malo to seek their fortune. They found an old pork and sausage shop to let; rented it and set to work. And it needed hard work and grit and all the energy that Scotch girls possess to transform the ancient and none too clean premises into an up-to-date and charming Tea Room. At the end of four years the original founders retired and the business passed into the hands of a South of Ireland woman. The new owner had spent many years during the War, cooking in various Red Cross Hostels in France, and had afterwards gained much experience while working with the War Graves Commission and so was well able to keep up the high standard of efficiency already possessed by the Scotch Tea Room. Indeed its sphere of usefulness has been considerably extended. As it opens at 7 a.m. travellers arriving by the Southampton Boat can have breakfast at once on landing.

Town and Country Life 1929

Afrikaans for the Traveller.

The *Travellers' Practical Manual*, No. 4, gives a wide range of sentences in English and Afrikaans. It will enable the English-speaking tourist in South Africa and Rhodesia to travel confident in the knowledge that he has sufficient command of Afrikaans to get any want attended to in places where English is not much used. The conversations and sentences have been compiled by Mr. Leonard W. Van Os in a facile manner. Messrs. E. Marlborough & Co., Ltd., 51 and 52, Old Bailey, London, E.C.4, publish the handbook at 1/6 (in wrapper) and 2/- (in cloth).

Empire Mail 1929

1930–1939

WHITE ROCK PAVILION, HASTINGS.

Miss Dora Labbette is singing at to-night's concert, and also at those to-morrow (Sunday).

Mr. Cameron conducts to-night the "William Tell" overture, German's "Nell Gwyn Dances" and Grainger's "Shepherd's Hey"; on Sunday afternoon, Svendsen's "Norwegian Rhapsody," the Siegfried "Idyll," and Saint-Saen's "Samson and Delilah" selection; on Sunday night, Tchaikovsky's "Casse Noisette," Litolf's "Robespierre" overture, when also Messrs. Hopkins, Whitehouse and Attwell will play trios for harp, violin and 'cello. Many of their orchestral works will be included at the three concerts.

This (Saturday) afternoon's orchestral programme, to be conducted by Mr. Basil Cameron, will be rendered the more interesting by the performances of a Bach Concerto for two pianos, to be played by two pupils of Miss Hilda Garland. A collection will be made for the "Frank Shaw" Ward now being erected at the Buchanan Hospital.

Mr. Basil Cameron will conduct a special symphony concert with an augmented orchestra of 50 performers next Saturday afternoon. This will be the last day but one of his season here, and it will also be marked by the appearance of England's greatest violinist, Albert Sammons, who will play a violin concerto with Mr. Cameron. Seats for this concert, and those on the final Sunday, may now be booked at the box office.

Bexhill-on-Sea Observer 1930

SPOILING THE WEST PARADE.

To the Editor of the " Bexhill Observer."

SIR,—I feel I must express the great abhorrence and dismay at the Council's action in placing a lavatory in the centre of the Parade Front, at the bottom of Richmond-road. Richmond-road is one of our finest approaches to the sea, terminating as it did at the bastion by the flagstaff. The bastion, offering a more extensive view of sea and beach, was one of the most frequented and most enjoyable spots on the Front.

It will be a very different thing with this lavatory in the middle of it. The public will give it a wide berth, and we shall not see the cars drawn up there as before. However, the building is going up, and I suppose nothing can be done now; it will be a lasting eyesore and source of regret to the public, and not redound to the Council's credit.

Of course, everyone knows that lavatories are necessary, but let them be sunk under ground or otherwise hidden, as in other seaside towns, and not dumped down on a most frequented, enjoyable spot.

I hear that there is a proposal also to provide a lavatory in the little garden in Town Hall Square; I know nothing of any plans, but that little open space of garden is much frequented in summer, and there seems no room for a lavatory without spoiling it entirely. Surely it should be preserved as a bright show spot in the centre of the town.

Perhaps some other plan may be thought of.

Yours truly,
G. E. BELCHER, M.A. Oxon.
43, Collington-avenue, Bexhill.
13th March, 1930.

Bexhill-on-Sea Observer 1930

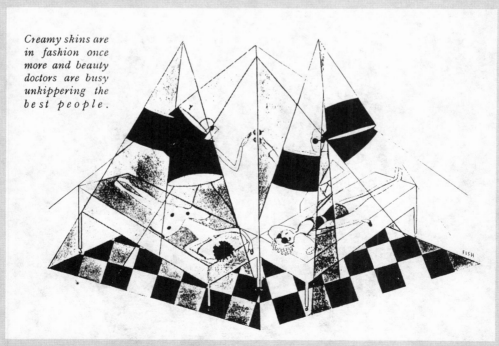

Creamy skins are in fashion once more and beauty doctors are busy unkippering the best people.

Harper's Bazaar 1930

When Oshkosh opens its arms

At the end of a long journey your Oshkosh opens its arms to you and straightway you feel at home with your surroundings.

Unpack? Why, no! Your Oshkosh is a wardrobe in itself with everything instantly ready to your hand. You are unpacked already! And when you rejoin your friends downstairs they say "How spick and span you look—how do you do it after such a long journey?" And you reply carelessly, "I dunno," but to yourself you are thinking, "Oh, my dear blessed old Oshkosh!"

OSHKOSH
TRUNKS

Sold at Harrods, Selfridges, Army & Navy Stores, John Pound, The Revelation Suit Case Company, Whiteley's, Shoolbred's, Aquasol and other well-known West End shops. Also Forsyth's in Glasgow. If you have any difficulty in obtaining Oshkosh Trunks, write to Oshkosh, Kingsway House, Kingsway, London. Telephone Holborn 7082 (interesting booklet sent on request)

Stuarts

Harper's Bazaar
1930

Harper's Bazaar 1931

Oh! to be in St. Moritz when the snow is there, and take one's ease in cosy splints on arms and knees at the end of a perfect day. Excelsior!

Overhead Cables in Bronte Country.

A Protest and an Appeal.

To the Editor: "Halifax Courier and Guardian."

Holly Bank, Oxenhope,
Nr. Keighley, April 17, 1931.

Sir,—Saddening as the fact is, it cannot be overlooked that even more serious and frequent are the reports that reach us from localities far and near of menaces of one kind or another to the scenic beauties of the countryside. One such, perhaps as recent a one as any, relates to that region on the border of Yorkshire and Lancashire, famed throughout Britain, and indeed far beyond, as the Bronte country. This is to the effect that the Yorkshire Electric Power Company—in a scheme covering most of the West Riding—has decided that it would be advantageous for the transmission of current to link up two important stations of supply—one at Hebden Bridge in Caldervale with one at Silsden in Airedale.

To do this, it is decreed that overhead cables—those monstrosities whose presence in so many parts has disturbed us quite enough already—shall be erected right across country—a line of a dozen miles or so—between the two places. A landscape, itself of no mean attraction, apart from its classical associations, is thus to be disfigured by these unsightly poles, standing 50ft. or 60ft. high.

To start with, the cables will encroach on Crimsworth Dean, as charming a valley as any in the district, and one as yet unspoilt. They will then cross the Cockhill Moors—quite close, for some distance, to the familiar highway that sweeps from Oxenhope to Hebden Bridge—i.e., the road of "stoups" vividly depicted in Emily Bronte's "Wuthering Heights," Halliwell Sutcliffe's "Man of the Moors," "By Moor and Fell," etc. Across a tract of valley and upland—rather barren, but of distinct beauty—they will reach the edge of Haworth Moor itself; and thence pass downwards into the flowered and sorgful valley that to Halliwell Sutcliffe is "Hazeldene." Over hill and dale again, they will traverse the environs of Oakworth—the heights above Sutton—and at last, the fields of Airedale.

Independent of this, under the grid scheme, it is proposed to lay a section of cable up the Ponden Valley (verging on the "Lonely Valley"), and over the moors to Lancashire.

One would at once suggest that, in preference, the cables be laid underground, as is done in certain parts where the scenic features are spectacular, and where encroachment upon them would be obviously ruinous; but I am told that in these particular instances it is hardly practicable to do so. The one fact remains, however, that in the process of these erections the Bronte country is sure to be despoiled; and no matter how urgent, commercially, such schemes may be, the preservation of the country as it has been from early time, is, I submit, supreme.

Owners may have sanctioned the erection of the cables on their land, but so far as I can judge none of them is wishful that the scheme should materialise, and incidentally, none of the farmers will derive any supply of electricity from the system.

The Haworth Ramblers have deputed me to oppose the scheme on their behalf; and Mr. Jonas Bradley (Stanbury), who is president of the Society, and who is also one of the oldest members of the Council of the Bronte Society, unreservedly associates himself with this appeal. I am, I know, expressing here the feelings of many more, and to the desired end I need hardly, I feel, invoke the sympathies of nature-lovers, moor-wanderers, literary pilgrims, and all who have at heart that treasured bit of country.—Yours, etc.,
MARSHALL HOLMES.

Halifax Courier and Guardian 1931

Miss Violette Cordery is going to drive an Invicta car from London to Edinburgh on first gear, to Monte Carlo and back on third, to John o' Groats on second, and to finish to run 25 miles on Brooklands in reverse. The gear-box should be run in by the finish anyhow.

Motor World 1930

Northern Echo 1931

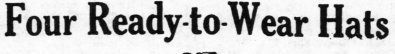

Four Ready-to-Wear Hats

FOR
EASTER HOLIDAYS.

Small knitted Angora Cap. This is delightful for sports and can be had in all the new shades; also will fit any head.

Price 10/6

Charming sports hats are made of Angora, fitting snugly to the head, and an example of which is shown here.

Then there is the medium-sized brim, also sketched, much welcomed after a long retirement.

These and a varied selection of models are to be seen daily in our showrooms.

Smart Flecked Hat, giving a Tweed effect, with the new drooping brim; in Brown and White, also Green and White.

Price 12/11

Fine quality Rough Fur Felt Hat, with a stitched crown and brim; most useful for golf or a tailored suit; in Green, Saxe, and Beige.

Price 25/9

Close-fitting stitched Taffeta Tam, soft and easy to pack; in Black and White, Navy and White, also Saxe.

Price 18/11

Everyone is at liberty to walk through our Departments and Showrooms without the least obligation to buy.

PARKINSON & CLARK
PARADE HOUSE, BRADFORD

Halifax Courier and Guardian 1931

YORK RUGBY LEAGUE CUP FINAL
At Wembley, Saturday, 2nd May.

SPECIAL NORTHERN ECHO
ORGANISED EXCURSION.

The Northern Echo, in conjunction with the L.N.E.R. and Messrs. Dean & Dawson, has arranged a Special Excursion YORK to LONDON in connection with the above match.

1. On arrival at King's Cross the parties will be met by **Luxury Type Motor Coaches** and taken for a Sight-seeing Drive; after which,

2. Substantial Lunch at Restaurant.

3. After Lunch, Drive to Wembley, where Motor Coaches will be parked in Special Enclosure and where they will be easily accessible after the match.

   (For those who do not desire to visit the match at Wembley, an Afternoon Drive to Hampton Court may be substituted.)

4. Return to London for substantial Meat Tea at Restaurant.

5. Evening at Leisure.

ALTERNATIVE METHODS OF BOOKING.

(a) The above "all in" arrangements, including Railway Fare **26/-**

(b) Railway Fare only **15/6**

In the case of (b) passengers will make their own arrangements on arrival at King's Cross for the remainder of the day.

NOTE:—The above charges do not include admission to Wembley for the match, but Tickets are available at all prices of admission.

Train times will be announced later.

A deposit of 10/- on the "All-In" Arrangements or 5/- Railway Fare only may be made, the balance to be completed by 8.0 p.m., 25 April, at the address below.

Book Now at Northern Echo Office, 1, Castlegate, York.

Northern Echo 1931

Northern Echo 1931

Spring-time at SOUTHSEA

Sunshine in abundance, Spring flowers in super-abundance, the sea and the great ships that only Southsea possesses.

Fill in this coupon and send to the Manager, Enquiry Bureau, Southsea, and the Guide, Hotel List, and a magnificent panorama of Southsea, 40 x 8 ins., by the late Mr. W. L. Wyllie, R.A., will be sent post free.
Name and Address to be written in Block Letters.

NAME .... N.E.4.

ADDRESS ....

....

Northern Echo 1931

WEARY CYCLISTS WHO TOOK A CAR.

THEFT AFTER " PERFECT DAY " AT SCARBOROUGH.

The story of how three weary Cleck-heaton youths stole a motor car from a private garage on their way home from Scarborough after a " perfect day " at the seaside was told at the North Riding Court at Scarborough yesterday.

The defendants, Norman Baxter, aged 26, Maurice Spencer, aged 16, and Clem Shaw, aged 25, came to Scarborough on pedal cycles on Easter Monday. They spent the day in the town and went to a dance hall in the evening.

ADVENTURE AT DAYBREAK.

At daybreak they set off to ride home when the wheel of one of the cycles collapsed near Stoney Haggs. The garage attracted their attention, and they took the car, worth £80, which was the property of Mrs. Millicent Leach.

At 9 a.m. on the Tuesday, Mrs. Leach went to the garage and found that her car was missing. Information was given to the police and a description of the car was issued. In the meantime a constable of the West Riding Motor Patrol near Tadcaster saw the car and had his suspicions aroused by seeing two bicycles tied to the back.

CONSTABLE CONGRATULATED.

He went to the car, found the three defendants inside, and they tried to borrow money off him to buy some petrol. Instead, however, the constable arrested the trio on suspicion.

All three were given good characters and had no previous convictions against them. In view of this the Bench took a lenient view and they were each fined £1 and had to pay 11s 2d each costs. P.C. Eric Gordon, who arrested them, was complimented by the Bench for his smart work.

FLYING by the ROYAL MAIL

A WEEK ago to-day the first of the regular services to the Cape left Croydon Airport, and should have arrived in Kenya, Capetown being reached on Sunday afternoon. Paying passengers will be carried in a month's time, just as soon as the personnel have settled down to routine work, the air fare to be £130, freight and excess baggage at 13s. a kilo., and letters at 1s. per half-ounce. For the first time an air liner had the insignia of the Royal Mail painted on its side, and all the speakers at the lunch given by Imperial Airways after the event referred to this day as an historic occasion. Sir Samuel Wilson reminded the guests of the part played by the late Capt. "Tony" Gladstone and by Sir Alan Cobham in preparing the way for the regular service. It was at the Governor's Conference, held in Nairobi during the winter of 1927-28, and attended by these two pioneers, that the East African Colonies and the Sudan agreed to bear their share of the subsidy. This was augmented at a later date by contributions from Southern Rhodesia and South Africa, the latter promising no less than £80,000 a year so that the Home Government might be relieved of a large part of the financial burden.

Sir Vyell Vyvyan, seen on the left, and Lady Vyvyan at Croydon before departure for Cape Town on the first of the regular mail services. Major E. S. Grogan, who is standing between them, walked most of the way from the Cape to Cairo some thirty years ago, taking two years for a journey which is now to be accomplished regularly in 8 days

Londoner 1932

Northern Echo 1931

VISIT LONDON

with a Cinema Display on the Journey

The Northern Echo, in conjunction with the L.N.E.R. Company and Messrs. Dean and Dawson, is organising an outing to London

on Wednesday, 2nd December,

This excursion is arranged for during the run of the CYCLE AND MOTOR-CYCLE SHOW at OLYMPIA, and those taking part will have the opportunity of

SEEING LONDON'S SHOPPING CENTRES IN THEIR CHRISTMAS SEASON'S DISPLAYS.

IN CONJUNCTION WITH THE L.N.E.R. CO. AND THE PATHESCOPE COMPANY AN INTERESTING DISPLAY OF CINEMA FILMS WILL BE SHOWN ON THE TRAIN EN ROUTE. Each display will last about forty minutes.

Special Dining Car Train leaves Newcastle at 6 a.m., Chester-le-Street 6.15 a.m., Durham 6.25 a.m., Ferryhill 6.45 a.m., Darlington 7.5 a.m., Northallerton 7.25 a.m., Thirsk 7.35 a.m., York 8.10 a.m.

From Sunderland 5.10 a.m. and East Boldon 5.17 a.m. to Newcastle to join main line train.

Bookings from Hartlepool 5.23 a.m., West Hartlepool, travelling by 5.32 a.m. ordinary train, calling at Greatham at 5.40 a.m., Billingham 5.47 a.m., Stockton 5.55 a.m., Eaglescliffe 6.5 a.m.

Bookings from Saltburn, travelling by 5.4 a.m. ordinary train, picking up at Redcar East Halt 5.17, Redcar 5.22, Grangetown 5.32, South Bank 5.36, Cargo Fleet 5.39, Middlesbrough 5.45 Thornaby 5.54, Eaglescliffe 6.3 a.m. Dinsdale 6.15 a.m., arriving at Darlington at 6.23 to join main line train.

Breakfast served on outward train journey and Supper on return. Lunch and Tea at Lyon's Corner House, Piccadilly, motor coaches meeting party at King's Cross to convey them to lunch. Return train leaves London about midnight.

Afternoon Motor Coach Drive through London's principal streets and passing all the points of interest, with visit to the Tower of London and admission to the White Tower and Westminster Abbey is being arranged. The Bank of England, Mansion House, Royal Exchange, London Bridge, St. Paul's Cathedral, Law Courts and Buckingham Palace will be seen. This interesting and educational motor coach drive of three and a half hours is strongly recommended.

Mablethorpe Convalescent Home.

*Town and Country
Life* 1932

The management of this Home is carried out by an executive committee, and everything possible is done to ensure the comfort of the patients. The Committee is fortunate in having the services of the present Matron, Miss S. Brown, S.R.., whose unremitting care for the health of the patients is remarkable for its great efficiency.

A unique feature of the Home is the Hot Sea-Water Baths, which have contributed so much to the restoration to health of patients suffering from rheumatism and kindred complaints. These Baths are also open to visitors at a moderate charge. The Bath House has in recent years been restored at great expense and brought thoroughly up-to-date.

The Home's equipment and appointments, in fact, leave nothing to be desired, and the Committee does everything in its power to ensure the happiness and comfort of patients. The bracing air of Mablethorpe has much to do with the benefit to health which invariably results from the patient's stay of three weeks. Admission of patients is per Recommendation Forms, issued to subscribers.

THE BLIGHT OF SABBATARIANISM IN RHYL.

By NOMAD.

A fortnight ago I issued a challenge to the good people who are running a Sabbatarian crusade in Rhyl to justify their actions on religious grounds. I asked them to produce one iota or tittle of Biblical evidence in support of their attitude. I considered this of importance because it had been assumed that the movement in favour of Sunday games and a brighter Sunday in general was instigated and supported by secularists and unbelievers. So far there has been no response to my challenge. Therefore I am at liberty to assume that our friends are unable to produce such evidence.

Now this time I am going to look at the Sunday question from another angle— from an economic standpoint. All the readers of the Journal will agree with me that Rhyl's main industry is catering for visitors. I believe also that we are agreed that in order to attract visitors we should make the town as bright as possible. There is a movement on foot the object of which is to induce Britishers to spend their holidays at home and also to attract holiday-making foreigners to British resorts. Concurrent with this is an endeavour on the part of organisations whose function it is to benefit British holiday resorts to promote a Brighter Sunday movement. This movement aims at the abolition of irksome Sunday restrictions which make the seventh day of the week a day of gloom in so many British seaside places, particularly in Wales. Now visitors will no doubt choose the brighter places. They have plenty of gloom and glumness at home and they seek a change. They will select a resort where they may enjoy reasonable liberty. And inasmuch as many of them are week-end visitors it is important that they should have a cheery Sunday. The average visitor will not book rooms in Prude's Paradise.

THREE FAIRS TO BE HELD ON MIDSUMMER COMMON

It is probable that there will be three fairs on Midsummer Common this year.

The Commons Committee of the Borough Council have granted permission to Mr. Bertram Mills to bring his circus to Cambridge for one week in the early part of April, while Messrs. William Thurston and Sons have hired a portion of Midsummer Common for an amusement gala on Whit-Monday and Tuesday.

According to the *Cambridge Chronicle*, the Committee have also decided to raise no objections to the annual Midsummer Fair being held this year.

CORRESPONDENCE.

RHYL'S BRIGHTER SUNDAY.

Sir,—May I make a few remarks regarding the suggestions made by a deputation to a recent meeting of the Rhyl Council on the Brighter Sunday question? This deputation, to my mind, represents a small, sedate minority possessed of prejudiced ideas and selfish instincts. Unless they are strongly opposed, they might easily ring the death-knell of Rhyl as a pleasure resort. Rhyl differs from other resorts in having such a short season, and little or no winter attractions. Landladies therefore have to work intensively during the restricted holiday period in order to meet the demands of the rate collector. A portion of our visitors belong to the working class, some of whom are able to spend only week-ends away from home. Tradesmen also find it difficult to leave their businesses longer than from Saturday to Monday. If Sunday recreation and amusements are banned in Rhyl, is it likely that these people will come to us, in preference to other resorts where no such restrictions obtain? What is the motive of this interference with public rights? If the deputation and those for whom they speak are not disposed to indulge in Sunday recreation, that is no reason why they should try to prevent other people doing so. I don't attend either church or chapel, but subscribe to these institutions and try to live a clean and moral life. Are there not good and bad both inside and outside the church? In the good (or should it be bad?) old days, when there were fewer pettifogging laws and restrictions, such as D.O.R.A., this was a tolerably free country. Less vice and immorality existed, and still less would exist to-day if rational sports and recreation were more unrestricted. I have long passed my youth, and have replaced the active sports of my younger days by less strenuous pastimes and amusements. What I don't feel inclined to patronise I avoid, but I don't try to interfere with those who do indulge. I appreciate anything in reason, especially if it creates revenue and benefits the community at large. These are times of abnormal assessments, overburdened ratepayers, and worried business men, and anything which tends to the restriction of the free flow of money is contrary to the best interests of all.—Yours, &c.

Rhyl.

J.A.M.

Rhyl Journal 1932

NOMAD AND THE SABBATH.

Sir,—I don't wish to enter into any controversy with "Nomad" regarding the way in which Sunday should be spent, but one or two questions occur to me which I should like to put to him, namely:—Is it his wish that all distinctions between Sunday and other days should be eliminated? Does he believe that it would be in the real interest of Rhyl if it should happen? Would he personally prefer it to, say, the Sunday of twenty years ago?—Yours,

T. ELIAS JONES.

Bryngwyn, Rhyl.

Rhyl Journal 1932

SUNDAY AMUSEMENTS.

Sir,—May I state the following reasons why I oppose Sunday trading and amusements :—

Because during the last two seasons which I spent at Rhyl, with the exception of one fortnight in my native county, I talked with scores of visitors, chiefly of the middle class family type, coming from all parts of the country. Quite ninety per cent. of these people openly expressed their utter disgust at the open shops and places of entertainment and general trading on the Sunday. Many of them, who had young children with them, told me definitely it was the last time they should bring their family to Rhyl for a holiday.

Because these visitors forced on me the conclusion that the seaside resort which advertised a full six days programme of pleasure and amusements, but kept Sunday as a day of rest, would reap a rich reward, not from religious people but from a host of decent living citizens who have a strong inborn respect for Sunday as Sunday.

Because while some eight millions of workers can only get about three days work a week, and three millions cannot get any work at all, why should places of entertainment and other pleasure haunts demand a seven days week? —Where is the equality of sacrifice?

Because the pre-war sixty hour working week is now reduced to forty-eight hours only, and the Summer Time Act gives still another extra hour every day for play. When we add to this the great amount of short time worked and the cruel unemployment that exists, the cry for more time for amusements is nothing less than sheer hypocrisy.

Because at the present time millions of people are crying out for more work and less pleasure.

Because during the last three years our greatest economists and thinkers, statesmen and business men have stated over and over again that we are spending far and away too much time and money on an orgy of pleasure at a time of appalling trade depression and unemployment.

Because every working man and woman who supports the so-called Brighter Sunday movement is beyond all doubt helping to bring about what will eventually mean seven days work for six days' pay. This is inevitable.

Because a million brave sons of British mothers—our only son (our all in life) amongst them—gave their lives on the battlefield in order that we might live in peace in a land made nobler and better by their supreme sacrifice, and not for a Sunday joy ride or game, while thousands of those who stayed behind safe and snug at home and sponged on the blood and sorrow of other people's homes, cannot even pay respect on one day of the week to the memory of the heroic dead. That, sir, is why, by pen, vote and voice, I will fight to the bitter end against this outrage to those silent heroes of the battlefield.—Yours, etc.,

A MERE MAN OF THE WORLD.

West Parade, Rhyl.

Rhyl Journal 1932

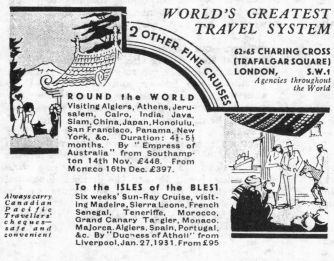
Harper's Bazaar 1930

Bournemouth Evening Echo 1932

"HOLIDAY FARM" CRITICISED.

Lymington Council Discussions.

BUNGALOWS AT CHEWTON GLEN.

Naish Farm, near Chewton Glen, where bungalows have been erected for the accommodation of holiday-makers, formed the subject of a discussion at the meeting of the Lymington Town Council yesterday.

It was stated that for some time past there have been complaints from residents in the vicinity regarding the character of the buildings and the lack of a proper drainage system. The matter has previously occupied the attention of both the new Lymington Town Council and the old Milton Urban District Council.

The General Purposes and the Public Health Committee yesterday reported that the Town Clerk had submitted the report of the special meeting appointed to inspect the farm, and also a report of Dr. Wood. The committee also reported that the Town Clerk submitted lengthy correspondence on the matter with the Ministry of Health, Major Blades, and Mr. Maggs, of Barton-on-Sea.

The report went on to say that the refuse dump on the farm had not been closed by the owner, as instructed, and it was recommended that statutory notice for the closing of the dump be served, and that in the event of the owner failing to close it, the dump be closed by the Borough Engineer, the cost to be charged to the owner.

South London Press 1933

The Family Bus from Dulwich

ITS CLIENTS NEVER VARY

Every morning for several years now a party of East Dulwich people have travelled up to Town from the Grove Hotel on the same bus, a "St. George," the only one in the service.

Every evening they come back by the same means.

That bus has nothing of the grim impersonality of the ordinary public vehicle. It is **their** bus.

Its passengers hail each other every morning, and greet the drivers and conductors by their christian names.

One of the passengers is a Mr. Gill, of 210, Dunstan's-rd., and Mr. Gill, with one of the conductors, has made a happy family of all the passengers.

On Saturday they held a party at the Moore Park Hotel, Forest Hill, when over 70 of the "regulars" attended.

Drivers, conductors and passengers took turns at thumping the piano and giving "turns."

When the party was over the bus came and fetched the revellers and took them home.

In the summer an outing is held and all the passengers have a day at the sea. How do they get there? In the bus, of course.

SEASIDE GAMES
Heavy Fines For "Pure Chance" Amusements

Fines totalling £60, or £30 each with 30s. costs were imposed by the Bournemouth magistrates yesterday on Eustace Russell Parsons, of King's-road, Swanage, and Harold Anley Percy, of Lowther-road, Bournemouth, in respect of six summonses against each under the Gaming Houses Act, 1845, and the Betting Act, 1852, relating to "games" in the Bournemouth Amusement Park, Exeter-road.

Both pleaded guilty.

Inspector McCallum said when he visited the Amusement Gardens two stalls were being used for "the racer." People paid twopence and stood round.

Certain jockeys' names and horses were then revolved, and lights went up and down opposite jockeys' names on an indicator. The game was pure chance. When the lights stopped at a certain jockey's name the persons standing at the stall in front of the corresponding name received a prize worth half-a-crown for his twopence outlay.

At another stall people paid sixpence to endeavour to knock half-crowns, placed on a ball in the centre of a chalk circle, out of the circle, and received the half-crowns which fell outside the circles. There was another similar game for coppers, and a third for knocking down packets of cigarettes.

The chairman (Mr. M. Williams) said the magistrates felt that these games of chance were such an evil for children who had not the ballast of older people. Children lost their heads and got into trouble, and probably it led to worse things as they grew older.

Gloucestershire Echo 1932

"SKY-LINER" EXCURSIONS
CHEAP FARES TO COAST

DAY-TRIPS IN 'PLANES TO HOLD FORTY PASSENGERS

BUSINESS BOON

BY A SPECIAL CORRESPONDENT

BRITAIN'S air supremacy is going to make the whole of Britain air-minded. New records—such as the splendid R.A.F. non-stop flight to South Africa, and Mollison's crossing from Europe to South America, in the past week—help to stimulate interest in flying and to give the general public still greater confidence in the air as a means of travel.

> More than 1,000 miles of inland air-lines are to be opened up in this country during the coming spring and summer.
>
> Big air-liners are to make daily pleasure tours.
>
> A network of business men's air-lines is to connect the Midlands and the North with the London air-port.
>
> * "Seaside air expresses" are to be a feature of the holiday season.
>
> "Air-ferry" services are to be extended widely.
>
> Final plans are in hand for the erection of great aerial landing-stages above railway stations and groups of large buildings in the centres of population.

Sunday Dispatch 1933

SUNDAY CINEMAS REJECTED

Manchester and Salford Councils Decide Not to Apply for Orders

MANCHESTER'S BIG MAJORITY

The Manchester City Council yesterday after a lengthy debate approved a motion proposed by Councillor Ackroyd and seconded by Alderman West that the application of the local branch of the Cinematograph Exhibitors' Association for a draft order from Parliament sanctioning the opening of cinemas in the city on Sunday be not agreed to. This decision of the Council, which was approved of by an unexpectedly large majority, 73 votes against 17, settles the vexed question of Sunday opening for six months. At the end of that time the exhibitors may, if they have mind to, reopen the question with a similar application.

The arguments of Councillor Ackroyd and his supporters were based on an unwillingness further to secularise the English Sunday and upon the opinion that the large majority of films shown were unsuitable, in any case, for exhibition on Sunday. Alderman Titt and others who opposed the motion argued that the citizens should have a right to decide the matter for themselves by the procedure of a town's meeting and a poll. The course of the debate showed that there were powerful arguments on both sides, and after the even balance of speakers the voting came as a surprise. Both the Conservative and Labour parties left the question an open one for the individual decision of their members, but the Liberal party followed the agreement arrived at in the caucus meeting the previous day—to support the motion and not, as previously stated, to leave the question open.

It will be seen from the report in an adjoining column that Salford Council also voted against Sunday cinemas by 28 to 22.

Manchester Guardian 1933

TORQUAY.

Queen city of the English Riviera, set like a jewel, seeming in its fragrant beauty to stand half-way between the deep blue sea and the infinite variety of green sub-tropical foliage and flowers.

For the first time, visitors to this beautiful resort, especially those of artistic temperament, must feel a strange stirring of the soul as they gaze upon the everchanging, wonderful panorama presented.

Surely, one must find here in such a romantic setting everything to satisfy the desire to roam which lies in the hearts of all.

Most seaside resorts fail to stir the imagination, and consist mainly of a long street or curved promenade, and you can stand in the centre looking left and right and absorb all that is to be seen in one casual glance. But in Torquay, with its great variety of coves, hills, and inland scenery, with the majestic heights of Dartmoor, the heads of the tors crowned with yellow gorse, in the Summer the hills ablaze with purple heather, the dread spirit of monotony cannot exist.

One moment you are looking over the wonderful harbour portrayed, the next you are sitting in a deck chair enjoying the wonderful sunshine at Abbey Sands. In the afternoon you rest in perfect peace and contentment amid the quietude of Anstey's Cove, Babbacombe, or Oddicombe Beach, and looking down from Babbacombe Downs into Babbacombe Bay. Surely no artist, however clever he or she may be, can truly portray the wonderful scene which will lie before your eyes.

The tired business man, the weary housewife, those who cannot find rest or refreshing sleep, surely in this lovely atmosphere surrounded by so much fragrant beauty, coupled with the strong air from the sea they will at night at last find the peace both of mind and body which they have previously sought in vain.

To those who merely desire a seaside resort, to those who expect to find a whirl of gaiety, side shows, round-abouts, etc., Torquay has no appeal.

It reserves all its glories for that vast majority of men and women who seek the real beauties of life, which are reflected in the glorious scenery with which they desire to surround themselves.

By day the glorious sun shines with full intensity, and ultra-violet rays confer maximum health upon those who are lucky enough to be resting or living in the " English Riviera."

By night, when the sun has set in a blaze of golden or red glory behind the distant hills, there is very little difference of temperature, perhaps a soft cooling breeze blowing in from the sea ; and standing on some nearby hill looking down upon Torquay with its thousands of coloured and reflecting lights, over the hills one must get the impression that the beauty portrayed is not of this earth but something more nearly approaching what we all imagine Heaven to be.

Throughout the ages the hospitality of the West of England people has been renowned, and to the visitor it is best reflected not in a blaring welcome of trumpets but in the quiet, old-world courtesy which they receive from all.

This publication, the " English Riviera," will be issued each month. Its policy will be to tell the people of England that there is no necessity to travel abroad for beauty, no necessity to undertake long steamship and railway journeys to find rest. Here, in this beautiful county, 3¼ hours from London, you step from the train into a land which will fill all your requirements, and when, by force of circumstance, you must leave, it will be with regret and a real longing for an opportunity to return quickly.

English Riviera 1932

THE Isle of Wight was without electric light for over half an hour last night, owing to a breakdown at the generating station at East Cowes. Nearly all the streets were thrown into darkness, and one cinema audience spent the period during which the programme was interrupted by indulging in community singing.

The Scotsman 1934

South London Press 1933

GOLDEN RULES
. . for
HOLIDAY BATHERS

AUGUST is the holiday month, the month of all the year to which thousands who work hard during the other eleven months look forward with eagerness.

Maybe you will be going with your family to the seaside or the river, and if the summer continues as it has begun the young people will certainly want to bathe. Whether they are swimmers or not, it is still important that they should remember certain rules for safety.

* * *

In these days, only the children who are physically unfit are non-swimmers, but many a swimmer who fancies his chances in a swimming bath or in the place where he generally does his bathing may find a very different state of affairs where the holiday bathing is being done. The river bather, for instance, knows nothing of rough waves and cross currents, little whirlpools round the rocks, etc., whilst the bath swimmer is as unacquainted with these as with the deep pits the river bather has learned to beware of. So, when you do your holiday bathing, take care.

* * *

A good general rule for all bathers is not to use those quiet little coves so beloved by many. You may like seclusion, but seclusion means danger if help should be wanted. Make a rule then, of bathing only at the recognised places where the attendant will give advice as to pitfalls and where a boat is available in case of trouble.

* * *

Do not bathe when overheated, and never bathe shortly after a heavy meal. At least an hour should elapse between a meal and a bathe. It may seem unnecessary to emphasise this oft-repeated point, but every year brings evidence that the rule has been disregarded, either through ignorance or carelessness, with unpleasant, if not worse, results.

* * *

Always leave the water immediately you begin to feel the slightest cold; a cold feeling often precedes cramp, and while cramp, in itself, is seldom more than unpleasant, it is the primary cause of a good many bathing fatalities, as the swimmer who is attacked by it gets unduly nervous and drowning often results.

* * *

If attacked by cramp, keep cool. Shout for help by all means, but keep the arms under water and then it is unlikely that you will sink. As soon as the arms are thrown out of water the submerged body has to support additional weight, which causes the head to sink, and even an expert swimmer could not prevent this happening.

* * *

If a bather finds himself being carried away by a strong current, the best plan is not to attempt to fight against it. Shout for help, and, in the meantime, swim or float with the current, gradually working towards the end of it, if possible. In this way strength is conserved, instead of being wasted in a vain attempt to beat the current, which will certainly be stronger than the swimmer.

* * *

The most valuable advice which can be given for use in emergency is to keep cool and keep the hands under water.

Western Times 1933

HOLIDAY HAUNTS

REDESIGNED FOR 1933
8,000 ADDRESSES
700 RESORTS
TO CHOOSE FROM.

The New "Holiday Haunts" Guide is a fascinating production of more than 1,000 pages that intending holiday seekers cannot afford to be without. The 300 photogravure illustrations, executed in an entirely new style, are in themselves a sheer delight.

ON SALE EVERYWHERE
6d.

TRAVEL **GWR**

Sheffield Daily Telegraph 1933

(Right) Princess Marie Louise (centre) photographed with Princess Helena Victoria and Captain E. Clarke on the bridge of the "Alcantara" before leaving for a cruise to Madeira and the West Coast of Africa

The Lady 1933

TREGYNON SHOW AND SPORTS.

To THE EDITOR OF THE County Times.

Sir,—I beg to ask your kind favour for a little space for this letter. I attended the Tregynon show and sports and appreciated the quality of stock that the show has produced, but I should like to ask the committee to provide more sports which attract visitors, such as pillow fights, apple and bucket races or musical chairs—something with some go in it. With regards to the poultry section of the show, I do not think it fair that the committee should provide in the schedule for a pair of hens, and then allow an exhibitor to show a pair of pullets which have not laid an egg. In fairness to the judge, who has a very difficult duty to perform, and to the exhibitors, there ought to be separate classes for pullets, such as 2 pullets and a cockerel for a pen of 1933 hatched produce. It would enable the exhibitors to understand the position. I was informed that the judge could not get a saucer to break one egg of each exhibit, which should have been done as sizes of eggs vary much to their qualities. Wishing the show every success.—Yours etc.,

DONOR AND EXHIBITOR.

POWYSLAND MUSEUM.

To THE EDITOR OF THE County Times.

Sir,— During August the Powysland Museum was open to the public for the first time, the honorary curator and Mr. A. Stanley Davies, taking it in turn to be on duty, during the holiday of the regular staff. You referred to the matter in last week's issue, but by an unfortunate typographical error stated that the number of visitors was twenty. Actually the number of visitors was 231, although it was only possible to open the Museum in the afternoons. This is the largest number of visitors in a month for many years. The renovation of the building, and rearrangement of the exhibits have been appreciated by the public, as there have been five times more visitors this year than formerly.—Yours etc.,

T. SIMPSON JONES.

Montgomery County Times 1933

LIFEBUOY TOWN.

YOU CAN BUY A 'FREEDOM FROM COLLECTORS.

Every one who goes to Southend this week will be expected to wear a tiny model lifebuoy, dangling from a blue life line.

It is carnival week, and the streets will be thronged with 1,000 collectors.

For a shilling one can buy one of the lifebuoys, and so gain immunity from the attentions of the collectors for the rest of the week.

The carnival, which opens to-morrow, is in aid of the New General Hospital.

A small village will be erected in Chalkwell Park, where a non-stop day and night fete will be held.

PAYMENT FOR HOLIDAYS.

SHOULD MANUAL WORKERS BE INCLUDED?

Should manual workers not "on the staff" be paid for holidays? This point was raised in a recent letter to the "Mail," and has evoked correspondence from other readers. A selection of letters is appended:—

NO OVERTIME PAY.

Sir,—Surely your correspondent, "Young England Anew," is hardly fair to office staffs in general. Those who receive Christmas-boxes, double week's pay and a bonus cheque are in the minority and, most probably, confined to City offices.

Of course, members of the staff are paid for their holidays, and rightly so, for they are forced to work until any hour their employers deem necessary, and without overtime pay. Also, the majority of office workers receive a smaller remuneration than the average manual worker.

Further, is it not possible for manual workers to put aside each full working week just a small amount to tide them over the holiday periods and the inevitable short weeks which follow?

E. T. L.

MANAGEMENT'S RIGHT.

Sir,—Replying to "Young England Anew," surely the management can do just as they like with their own money. When a man takes on a job he usually knows what the wage agreement is, and whether he is likely to get paid for holidays or not. In other words, he contracts his services for a stipulated sum, and gets it. Then why grumble?

Generally speaking, the majority of people continue to pay their way quite well irrespective of holidays. My experience is that the people who fail to meet demands after holidays are usually those who miss on the slightest provocation. EXPERIENCED.

ARTISAN'S CLAIM.

Sir,—I consider the letter signed "Young England Anew" is sensibly put and logical. If we grant that something is due to those on the staff who have to stay over to see things through without any benefit in extra pay, then surely the same claim can be put forward by the workers who are hard pressed to get the work done, besides being penalised for their quickness by lower rates of pay.

Moreover it is not extravagant to claim that it is the skill of the factory worker that creates the business, and satisfies the customer, not the one who packs it up, and books it.

The sooner we get things squared up by just recognition and impartiality the sooner we shall see the ills removed that now beset industry, which will eventually place the artisan first as an unquestioned right. A. C. CASHMORE.

THREE QUESTIONS.

Sir,—Your correspondent shows in the first place a very practical mind when he refers to the short week of the piece or time worker, but appears to forget the other side of the question, i.e., overtime. I would reply to him by asking three questions.

(1) The address of any employers who pay for that which they do not receive.

(2) The name of any company giving the staff a cheque for their holidays.

(3) Who is the factory hand willing to work 12 or more hours (including Sundays) per day without extra pay during rush periods?

STAFF.

Birmingham Mail 1934

Sunday Express 1933

Blackpool Expects More Visitors Than Ever

THE Guest Holidays ended yesterday, and Blackpool is now eagerly anticipating the season proper.

What sort of a season is Blackpool going to have? That is the question everyone is asking.

The feeling in the town is one of optimism. The revival in trade, the weather prospects, and the big entertainment and conference programmes all point to the attraction of visitors to Blackpool in big numbers.

Hotel and boarding-house keepers express satisfaction with advance bookings and bigger-than-ever railway arrangements point to increased traffic from all parts.

THIS BUSY WEEK-END

Although the Wakes periods have not yet begun—Bolton and seven other Lancashire towns will lead the way in this respect next Saturday—this week-end promises to be exceptionally busy.

Trains numbering 130 are expected to-morrow, and a big rush by road is also certain.

Excursion trains will come from all parts of the country. A number are from London, arriving this morning and leaving on their return journey in the early hours of to-morrow.

A "Gazette & Herald" reporter last night asked representative people in Blackpool for their views on the prospects of the season.

Here is what they said:—

Mr. Harry Hall,
General Manager and Director, Tower and Winter Gardens Companies.

Blackpool will maintain its position as the leading seaside resort in Europe. The general revival of trade means that people will have more money to spend, and the entertainment houses and everyone else in Blackpool should benefit greatly.

The ambitious nature of Blackpool's theatrical, circus, film, and other attractions plays its part, I am convinced, in bringing visitors to the town.

So far as our own companies are concerned, we have gone out this summer to provide something better than any other season.

At the Opera House we are reviving spectacular revue-ballet as a resident attraction; Gracie Fields is coming to the Grand Theatre for a month, and other big stars there and at the Palace, a fine circus programme, and pre-release films at the picture theatres all figure in the season's attractions.

Blackpool Gazette 1934

Edinburgh Evening News 1934

GLORIOUS DEVON & CORNWALL

S.M.T.
EXTENDED TOURS
To all SCOTLAND, ENGLAND, & WALES
FROM THE MOUND, PRINCES STREET.

LOCH LOMOND, OBAN, AND FIVE HIGHLAND LOCHS. 2 Days— 8.15 a.m. Every Saturday	£3
GRAMPIANS, ROYAL DEE, AND PITLOCHRY. 2 Days— 8.15 a.m. Every Monday	£3
OBAN, FIVE HIGHLAND LOCHS, AND IONA. 3 Days— 8 a.m., Every Wednesday	£5 10/-
ABERDEEN, LOCH NESS, AND GLENCOE. 4 Days— 8 a.m., Every Monday	£7
GRAND HIGHLAND TOUR. 5 Days— 8 a.m., Every Monday	£9 10/-
OBAN, IONA, MULL, AND ARGYLL. 5 Days— 8 a.m., July 2, 9, and 23; August 6 and 20	£10
WESTERN HIGHLANDS AND ISLE OF SKYE. 5 Days— 8.15 a.m., Every Monday and Wednesday	£10
GLENCOE, ULLAPOOL, AND NORTH-WEST HIGHLANDS. 5 Days— 8.15 a.m., Every Monday	£9 10/-
GRAMPIANS, JOHN O' GROATS, LOCH NESS, AND GLENCOE. 6 Days, 9 a.m., Every Monday	£11 10/-
BRAEMAR AND JOHN O' GROATS. 6 Days— 8 a.m., Every Saturday	£15
ENGLISH LAKES. 4 Days— 8.30 a.m., Every Monday	£6
ENGLISH LAKES. 6 Days— 8.30 a.m., July 16 and 30; August 13 and 27	£9
DEVON AND CORNWALL. 13 Days— 8 a.m., July 2, 16, and 30; August 13	£24
SOUTH COAST AND EASTERN COUNTIES. 13 Days— 8 a.m., July 9 and 23; August 6 and 20	£22
WYE VALLEY AND WELSH MOUNTAINS. 8 Days— 8 a.m., July 7 and 21; August 4 and 18; September 1	£16
LONDON. 6 Days. 8 a.m., Every Thursday	£10 10/-
LONDON. 6 Days. 8.30 a.m., Every Friday	£10 10/-
LONDON. 6 Days. 8 a.m., Every Saturday	£10 10/-
LONDON. 7 Days. 8.30 a.m., Every Monday	£11 10/-

FULL PARTICULARS AND ILLUSTRATED BROCHURE ON APPLICATION TO :

SCOTTISH MOTOR TRACTION CO. LTD.
63 PRINCES STREET, EDINBURGH ——————— 'Phone 22881.
45 PRINCES STREET, EDINBURGH ——————— 'Phone 24831.

RAMSGATE, where a GREAT HISTORICAL PAGEANT and a WEEK OF CELEBRATIONS will take place early in July.

RAMSGATE

Some Events in 1934

SPORTS CALENDAR
on page 9.

May 14th–17th—THANET COMPETITIVE MUSICAL FESTIVAL, at Ramsgate.
June—ROYAL TEMPLE YACHT CLUB REGATTA.
July 13th–14th—VETERAN CAR CLUB.
July 14th—CONCOURS D'ELEGANCE.
May 21st (Whit Monday)—NATIONAL FIRE BRIGADES ASSOCIATION (S.E. DISTRICT) ANNUAL TOURNAMENT.
August 13th–25th—KENT SUMMER SCHOOL FOR TEACHERS.

RAMSGATE HISTORICAL PAGEANT
and
CHARTER JUBILEE CELEBRATIONS
to take place during the week
JULY 16TH TO 21ST, 1934.

1) A GREAT HISTORICAL PAGEANT, portraying outstanding episodes in the History of Ramsgate and District will include, it is proposed, the following:—
Julius Caesar and the Early Britons.
The Landing of Hengist and Horsa.
The Coming of St. Augustine.
The Presentation of a Village Fair as held at St. Laurence, which is the oldest portion of the Borough, during the Tudor period.
The following incidents connected with the Napoleonic Wars:—
  (a) The Review of Troops by William Pitt.
  (b) The Reception of the Duke of Wellington after Waterloo.
  (c) The Return of George IV from a visit to Hanover.
Scene from Dickens, e.g., " The Tuggses at Ramsgate."
The Victorian Season.
The Celebration of the 100th birthday of the noted benefactor, Sir Moses Montefiore, Bart., and the presentation by him of the Mayoral Chain in 1884.
And others.
(It is intended to make the representation of the Historical Episodes in every way worthy of the best traditions and equal, if not superior, to any Pageant which has yet been presented in the United Kingdon.)
(2) AN EDUCATIONAL, HISTORICAL AND INDUSTRIAL EXHIBITION.
(3) CARNIVAL, HORSE GYMKHANA, TORCHLIGHT SPECTACLE AND TATTOO.
(4) MASSED PHYSICAL TRAINING DISPLAY.
(5) FOLK AND CLASSICAL DANCING, BATTLE OF FLOWERS, COMMUNITY SINGING, ETC.
(6) CONCOURS D'ELEGANCE, and
SPECIAL SERVICES IN THE CHURCHES OF ALL DENOMINATIONS.

There are always countless thrills at MERRIE ENGLAND, Ramsgate's great Amusement Park, a step from the sands.
Continental Cafes, Dancing, Entertainments and a good time always at the RAMSGATE MARINA, open all day in the season.
FLYING—Ramsgate Council have decided to establish a Municipal Aerodrome at Rumfields, a short distance from the town.

A glimpse of Ramsgate Harbour.

Holiday News **1934**

Train Cruising In June.

—o—

The Latest In Travel For The Summer Holidays.

With a new itinerary which covers 2,000 miles of travel through some of the most beautiful and picturesque parts of this country, four train cruises, each limited to sixty people, are being prepared to start on their "voyages" in five weeks time, taking advantage of the longer daylight hours in the Scottish Highlands in June. A special train which is to be employed for these cruises consists entirely of first-class carriages and first-class sleeping cars weighing 500 tons altogether.

The re-appearance of the Loch Ness Monster within the last few days has caused the London and North-Eastern Railway to alter the itinerary of their cruising train. A special motor tour of the Loch will be made covering the lair of the monster.

The number of the travellers is limited so that a window seat is booked for each passenger and a numbered and reserved seat in the restaurant carriage is to be allotted in addition to an exclusive bedroom equipped with hot and cold running water, large mirrors, electric fan, heater and reading lamp. Public rooms on the train will include lounge saloon, buffet, ladies retiring room and hairdressing saloon, and there will also be shower bath compartments and a "wardrobe" coach where passengers' luggage will be kept separate and readily accessible throughout the cruise.

Newspapers, stamps, cigarettes, tobacco and toilet requisites will be sold on board and stewards and stewardesses will be available throughout the tour to attend to passengers' needs.

The cruise train will leave King's Cross for its first 1934 voyage on Friday evening, June 1st, subsequent departures being on the 8th, 22nd and 29th.

The country to be visited includes Harrogate, Ripon and the Yorkshire Moors; Penrith, Keswick and the Lakes; Edinburgh; Aberdeen and Deeside; Loch Lomond, Mulling and the Western Highlands; the Clyde and the Kyles of Bute. Eight motor coach tours and two steamship trips are included in the week's itinerary. The cost per passenger, including all meals, early morning tea, first-class accommodation and all "shore" excursions will be £20; a number of berths have already been booked but there are still vacancies for each date.

West London and Chelsea Gazette
1934

British Ship Seized

By Chinese Pirates.

Vessel Afterwards Abandoned.

Warships Rush to Rescue.

Two Russian Guards Killed.

Four British warships dashed to the rescue yesterday of the China Navigation Company's steamer Tungchow, which, with 70 English school-children on board, had been seized by pirates in the China Sea.

It was found, however, that the pirates had abandoned the vessel without hostages and that none of the children had been molested.

It was evident that the ship's guards had put up a fierce fight. Two of them—Russians—were killed, another wounded, and the second engineer (K. M'Donald, of Stornoway) was also wounded. All the others are safe.

The Tungchow was found not far from Bias Bay, the notorious lair some fifty miles from Hong Kong, where British victims of many previous kidnappings have been carried into hiding for ransom.

The warships which rushed to the rescue were H.M.S. Suffolk, the sloop Sandwich, the aircraft - carrier Hermes, and a destroyer.

They have taken charge of the Tungchow, and she is steaming back to Hong Kong, the ship's officers still being in charge.

The steamer was taking the children back to the China Inland Mission School at Chefoo after a holiday in Shanghai.

Of the 70 children, 14 boys and 10 girls are over twelve years of age and 28 boys and 18 girls are under twelve years old. They were escorted by one man and four women.

Hong Kong, Friday. — The pirated steamer Tungchow has dropped anchor here.

None of the 70 children aboard has suffered any harm.

Londonderry Sentinel 1935

YACHT MYSTERY

Adrift in the Firth of Forth

EDINBURGH police last night were still investigating the mystery surrounding the finding of an abandoned motor yacht in the Firth of Forth. The boat, stated to be valued at £700, was last seen by its owner, Mr W. Henderson Phillimore, of Redford, Polmont, on Sunday, and two days later, the boat, the Mornside, was found by a fishing vessel floating adrift two or three miles south-east of the island of Inchkeith.

The captain of the fishing vessel, Mr John Reid, took the motor yacht in tow as salvage. It was taken to Cockenzie Harbour, where he handed it over to the Receiver of Wrecks.

This is the third time that the motor yacht has been found missing from its moorings in the east harbour of Granton.

The Scotsman 1934

LINER'S QUICK TURN ROUND

Over 1000 passengers and all their luggage landed and cleared in two hours is evidence of good organisation. This is what happened when the Anchor liner Caledonia arrived at Yorkhill Quay on Monday afternoon with the Scottish Clans of America. After that began the work of storing the ship and getting the accommodation ready for another voyage to New York. With the Transylvania and California cruising from New York just now, a quick turn round at both ends of the run is necessary to keep the schedule. The Caledonia sails again at one o'clock to-day.

Edinburgh Evening News 1934

EAST, WEST—WESTERN WELSH IS BEST.

Everybody is looking forward to the first holidays. A very long winter is coming to an end, and Easter will see us all escaping from office and shop to again taste the delight of travelling to favourite haunts, or discovering anew some of the beauty spots which await exploration on all hands. In another column will be found detailed some of the cheap, but charming excursions offered by the Western Welsh Omnibuses. Stratford-upon-Avon, the Wye Valley, the Forest of Dean, and other places are calling. And as we all want to respond joyously, it is advisable to book early to avoid disappointment.

Cardiff and Suburban News 1935

THE FAMILY ON HOLIDAY.

I.—THE CHILDREN.
By Dr. Alice M. Hutchinson, M.D.
Children's Physician at the Institute of Medical Psychology.

Anything worth having is worth a little trouble, and the subject of holidays certainly deserves more consideration than it receives from many people. Whereas everyone realises that a holiday should be a period of re-stocking the body and fortifying it against a spell of future drainage, it is surprising how some persons completely disregard the well-established rules to such an end.

Perhaps the most common mistake made by parents of young children at holiday times is that of allowing a child to overdo things at the outset. At such a time, people are apt to let fall the reins and, in a spirit of mistaken kindness, allow the child to overtire itself. Far better allow a little one to become gradually accustomed to the new conditions. Regulate the period of physical exertion during the first few days, though later the restrictions can be largely withdrawn. It is significant that many children lose weight during a holiday.

Most well-tended children nowadays are compelled to rest after the mid-day meal. This rule should be observed at holiday times when the little body is more busily active than usual. If the child is of the sort that can sleep peacefully on a noisy sea shore, so much the better; but if it is easily disturbed, better take it indoors. With somewhat older children, a book may be allowed but rest is essential—and it should be of about an hour's duration.

Paddling Joys and—

Paddling is so lovely a thrill and so full of joy that prohibition is unthinkable, but in no direction is the need for precaution more important. Let the child have just as long as seems reasonable, and no more. There must be no risk of chill from too long immersion in the cold water, for in that way the resistance of the body is lowered, and lowered resistance gives latent illness an opportunity to develop.

Lucky the boy or girl with healthy ears and nose at holiday time. For them is the joy of bathing. But for the less fortunate child, with tendency to ear trouble, the greatest care is needed. Dirty bathing pools should be ruled out altogether, and even in clean water it is advisable to guard against infection by plugging the ears and nostrils with cotton wool.

While on the subject of swimming and water play generally, a word of warning may be given as to the folly of forcing a child to enter the sea. Instead of helping, which is the real desire of the grown-up, it is actually impeding; it is postponing the day when the young person will make the element his own and enjoy the delicious joy of sporting on the waves. Far more helpful to allow a boy or girl to play in a fairly shallow pool till confidence comes naturally.

Thirst and Sunburn.

Certain precautions must be taken if full benefit is to be obtained and the children are to be happy—for happiness should be an absolute 'must' on such occasions. Take, for example, the obvious factor of thirst. A child playing on the beach, digging in the salt impregnated sand and splashed by the spray, soon begins to feel the need of a drink. This is immediately satisfied and the whining stopped if a cool drink is available. Mother, before leaving home, should make it a rule to slip a bottle of water or lemon squash into her sewing bag. It seems obvious, but how often is this obvious duty overlooked.

Another matter which people are inclined to forget is the discomfort that can be caused by sunburn. For a child, the early part of a summer holiday can be completely ruined by neglect of simple precautions in this respect. A piece of muslin thrown over the shoulders will allow the little one to become acclimatised; and, as a further precaution, it might be as well to smear the child's shoulders and arms with one of those ointments that are made up for such a purpose. There can be no risk of burning while browning to the desired shade can still be obtained.

Actually, of course, rules and regulations are foreign to the holiday spirit, and a child should be left to enjoy the maximum of freedom. This is particularly desirable in the case of older children, who must be allowed to plan their own amusements. Left to themselves, they have opportunity of making decisions in new circumstances, and to this end organized outings with the family as a whole ought to be few and far between.

Cardiff and Suburban News 1935

WANTED—A Long Green Trail

BY TOM STEPHENSON

"We are still blessed with many a mile of mountain track"

WHEN two American girls wrote asking advice about a tramping holiday in England, I wondered what they would think of our island, particularly of the restrictions placed in the way of those who wished to see some of our most captivating scenery.

If, at the end of their tour, these visitors from across the Atlantic are over-loud in their praises of their native "Land of Liberty," who shall blame them?

They mention their acquaintance with the Appalachian Trail, a footpath that runs for 2,000 miles through the Eastern States from Maine to Georgia; established by tramping, mountaineering and other open-air organisations, and generously aided by the Government and State authorities.

⋆ ⋆ ⋆

NOW this path has been eclipsed by the John Muir Trail which reaches from the Canadian border through Washington, Oregon and California to Mexico. For 2,500 miles without any slogging on hard roads, one may follow this track over lofty peaks, by deep-cleft canyons and through great National Parks and reserves saved for all time from spoliation by unplanned and irresponsible building.

After allowing for difference in geographical scale, what can we in England offer to compare with these enterprises?

Many have been closed, but new ones are unknown.

What will our visitors think of one of the most prevalent features in our landscape. "Trespassers Will Be Prosecuted"?

⋆ ⋆ ⋆

WHEREVER they go, from Kent to Cornwall, from Sussex to the Solway, they will see these wooden liars; on the edge of many a tempting wood they will be confronted with the blatant warning. By the banks of luring rivers, on bare downlands and shaggy moors they will read "Strictly Private."

They will discover that though walking is a most popular pastime with thousands of devotees, yet neither nationally nor locally has there been any serious effort to meet the needs of the growing army of young folk attracted to the healthiest form of recreation.

True enough we are still blessed with many a mile of alluring paths and downland and mountain tracks, but these form but a small fraction of our original heritage, for a century ago probably no country in the world had such a wealth of pedestrian ways. For four centuries the Romans were busy driving their straight roads across the country. Some of these are the foundations of our modern roads, some linger as grass-grown tracks, others have vanished beneath cultivation or the spread of towns. Medieval pilgrims and traders have left their imprint. Drovers, pack-horses, shepherds, landworkers and miners have left their complement to the crisscross pattern, once well etched in the face of the land, but now often obliterated or only faintly visible.

Many of these ancient ways fell into oblivion, and many more have been deliberately closed to the public, sometimes after expensive litigation and often enough, for the lack of a village Hampden, without legal sanction. Others have only been retained by bitter and costly struggles and though the Rights of Way Act has simplified the procedure, it is still necessary to be ever on the watch to prevent further encroachments.

Nowhere in Britain are the restrictions so rigid, and paths so few as in the Peak District of Derbyshire.

⋆ ⋆ ⋆

NO wonder the Manchester and Sheffield Ramblers continue to press for the passing of the Access to Mountains Bill, a measure which would provide that "No owner or occupier of uncultivated mountain or moorland shall be able to exclude any person from walking or being on such land for the purposes of recreation, or scientific or artistic study or to molest him in so walking or being."

Anyone doubting the existence of a demand for such legislation only needs take a trip to Castleton, in Derbyshire on Sunday week. Early in the morning he will see a host of trampers pouring into the dale from all sides, and in the afternoon he will be swept with the marching throng into the imposing limestone ravine of the Winnats, where 10,000 Ramblers will collect to reiterate their annual demand for the freedom of the hills.

Without sacrificing the ideal why should we not press for something akin to the Appalachian Trail—a Pennine Way from the Peak to the Cheviots?

This need be no Euclidean line, but a meandering way deviating as needs be to include the best of that long range of moor and fell; no concrete or asphalt track, but just a faint line on the Ordnance Maps which the feet of grateful pilgrims would, with the passing years, engrave on the face of the land.

⋆ ⋆ ⋆

OUT of the moor-rimmed bowl of Edale the track would mount to the rock-bound plateau of Kinder Scout, and from that bare plateau start northwards to the distant border, through 150 miles of lonely entrancing country.

Picture carefree youngsters setting out on such a trail of health and beauty. By Ashop Head and thence to Bleaklow, across Longdendale and by the Laddow Rocks and Black Chew Head, they would turn across the Saddleworth Moors to Stanedge, and on to Blackstone Edge, where Roman chariot wheels bit into the native bedrock.

Then, steering between the industrial blackspots, on beyond the vale of Cliviger, they would stand on Boulsworth, and behold, on the one hand, the level brow of Pendle, where Lancashire witches held satanic revels, and, on the other, the dark moors which inspired the Brontës.

Across the green lowlands of Craven they would reach the grim portals of Gordale, and then over Fountains Fell and the dome of Penyghent they would strike the packhorse trail into Wensleydale.

The magic dell of Hardraw, with its plunging beck, would be visited en route for the far recesses of Upper Swaledale. From Keld they would turn to Tan Hill with its little whitewashed inn on a windswept moor with the authority of the Ordnance Survey to refute the claims of would-be rivals as the highest licensed house in England.

⋆ ⋆ ⋆

Traveller's Gazette 1936

Daily Herald 1935

Empire Flying-boats.

NEW flying-boats are being built for the Empire services of Imperial Airways. Recently, by invitation of Imperial Airways, a party of visitors was shown over the works of Messrs. Short Bros., Ltd., at Rochester, where the flying-boats —twenty-eight in all—are being built. The machines are monoplanes of all-metal construction and will weigh, when fully loaded, nearly eighteen tons. Each will be equipped with four engines, and will be capable of a speed of about 200 miles an hour. They are being fitted with sleeping-berths—the first British air liners to be so fitted—and there will be accommodation for sixteen passengers by night and an additional eight passengers by day. Three tons of mails can be carried.

OXO LTD. SPORTS

Oxo Ltd.'s spacious sports ground presented a gay sight on Saturday, June 10th, on the occasion of their Annual Athletic Meeting.

Over five hundred entries were received from the company's factory, warehouse and wharf staffs, and the many exciting events were watched by a large and enthusiastic crowd.

The prizes were presented by Mrs K. M. Carlisle, wife of the President of the Club and Chairman of Oxo Ltd.

Caithness Courier 1938

PEER'S DAUGHTER FOUND IN SPAIN

THE search for the Hon. Jessica Freeman-Mitford, daughter of Lord and Lady Redesdale, who, it was reported, intended marrying her cousin, Mr. Esmond Romilly, ended yesterday when a message reached Lord Redesdale that she had arrived at Bilbao, the Red outpost in North-east Spain.

Mr. Romilly, who after a recent visit to London returned to Spain, where he had fought with the International Column, is also stated to be at Bilbao.

He is aged 18, and Miss Freeman-Mitford 19.

Lord Redesdale authorised this statement to *The Daily Mail*, which was made by his son-in-law, the Hon. Peter Rodd:

"Great Relief"

"Jessica is safe. The news is a great relief to her parents, who had not heard from her since she wrote from Bordeaux towards the end of last week indicating that she was going into Spain.

"The suggestion that she has gone there to marry Mr. Romilly is scouted by the family. They are cousins, and we are sure they have no idea of marrying.

"She seems to have gone to Spain in search of excitement.

"Lord Redesdale has written gently reproaching her and telling her that it is time she came back home."

Daily Mail 1937

Local Intelligence.

ON BEN NEVIS.—Hundreds of holiday-makers who attempted to climb to the summit of Ben Nevis on Saturday were caught in the rainstorm. Only a few succeeded in reaching the top. The majority were trapped in the mist when only half-way up, and had difficulty in making the return journey to the base. Campers in Glen Nevis were flooded out.

FATAL STING.—An insect sting on a walking holiday in the Highlands has led to the death of Miss Molly Strachan, aged 22, daughter of Mr John L. Strachan, farmer, West Pilmore, Longforgan, near Dundee. With a friend, Miss Strachan set out a fortnight ago on a walking tour in Sutherland and the North, staying at youth hostels. On Monday last at Ullapool she was stung on the lip by a cleg. Distressing symptoms developed, and her friend returned with her to Dundee, where she died in a nursing home yesterday.

Banffshire Journal 1936

Congresses in Oslo.

SOME very attractive tours in Norway have been arranged in connection with four important coming meetings in Oslo—the World's Sunday School Convention (July 6-12), the International Mathematical Congress (July 13-18), the International Congress of Agriculture (July 27-29), and the International Congress of Pre-Historic and Proto-Historic Sciences (August 3-9). The tours are suitable for individuals travelling alone and range in duration from a single day to a week from Oslo back to Oslo. Special sight-seeing arrangements in and around Oslo itself have been made by Wagons-Lits/Cook, who have been appointed Official Agents for the Sunday School Convention and for the Agricultural Congress, and who will have a representative in attendance in the Mathematical Congress building.

The concluding meeting of the Agricultural Congress will take place at Lillehammer on July 30.

Congresses in Copenhagen.

THE International Association of Seed Crushers will have an unusually impressive setting for their Congress in Copenhagen on June 16, 17 and 18, for the meetings are to be held in Christiansborg Castle. Wagons-Lits/Cook have been appointed Official Agents for the event and will have an office in the Castle during the period of the Congress. The official Travel Agency for the International Congresses of Scientific Philosophy and Experimental Cytology, to be held in Copenhagen from June 21 to 26 and from August 10 to 15 respectively, have also been vested in Wagons-Lits/Cook.

Traveller's Gazette
1936

A catering halt in a tiny village encountered on a Scottish tour.

MEALS

Which You Buy

BY THE WAY

Try Local Dishes on Your Holidays

Says
MARY MACLEAN

AUGUST is the month when we usually go a-journeying. Try this year to give yourself not only a change of air, but a change of food. Look around in districts visited and find for yourself meals to which you are unaccustomed. You will be surprised at the appetites of your party.

In Yorkshire try a hock of unsmoked bacon, " green " it is generally known as up there ; boil it gently and serve it hot for supper with broad beans and a white sauce. There will be plenty cold for breakfast with boiled eggs or for lunch with new potatoes and a salad. When near the bone dice the odd bits for omelettes (directions for making these were given last month).

Farmers in Yorkshire are usually plagued by rooks, and often in a poulterer's they are found for sale at about fourpence each, plucked and trimmed ready for cooking. Only the breast and legs are edible. Don't despise the little nigger birds. A tasty way of cooking them is to casserole them or to stew them gently for an hour. Boil some rice in plenty of water for ten or twelve minutes and strain. Pile this in the centre of a deep dish, thicken the gravy, place the birds round the rice and pour the gravy over them. The smell alone will be tempting.

An appetising dish is rook pie. Simmer the birds first for about half an hour with some young carrots or runner beans before putting them into a pie-dish with the crust over.

Pigeon pie is another uncommon dish. The pigeons should be split in half and stewed slowly for about an hour before making the pie. Pigeons casseroled with young turnips and carrots are also good. Again they should be split in half before cooking.

The Scots are famous for their haddocks, which are already boned and smoked. Boil some for about ten minutes in milk, or milk and water, and drain well. Spread a lump of butter over each piece. In the South Scotch haddock is often served with poached eggs on top, but in the North they serve it with fried rashers of bacon, and somehow these alter the flavour altogether.

Good salmon is easily obtainable in many touring districts. Cut the salmon into steaks about one-inch thick, dip in beaten egg, roll in breadcrumbs and fry. Serve with parsley sauce or mayonnaise.

Cooking fish in a van is often avoided on account of the smell,

Caravan World 1937

THE BUDGET

Adding up railway fares, hotel expenses, cost of taxis and drinks, and many irresistible purchases of ivory, cloth-of-gold, enamel work and native curios, the cost would be approximately £2 10s. a day, or £75 for thirty days. The two-months journey to India, therefore, would cost between £125 to £145, and it would take you to some of the most fascinating places of India, whence the European is certain to take home unforgettable impressions. The grand total of expenditure, however, can be very considerably reduced if, instead of one or two persons, ten or twelve travel together. For such a group not only all costs are greatly reduced, but many of the drawbacks of European life in India are removed. One cab will do for four people as well as for two. One servant, one guide will be paid out of many purses. Actual reductions are made by railways and hotels if the trip is properly prepared. In fact, the tourist of modest means will probably never come to India in any considerable numbers until arrangements for group travelling, such as have become popular for trips to European countries, are made for journeys to India. Then the daily average per head will come, not to £2 10s., but to less than £2. The whole trip, therefore, can be done for a hundred pounds. That is, I believe, a sum well worth saving up for a holiday trip incomparably more interesting, more novel, and more enlightening than any that Europe can offer.

Travels
1937

"PROSPERITY SUMMER" FOR BRITAIN

RECORD YEAR FOR TOURIST TRAFFIC

U.S. VISITORS MAKE LONGER STAYS

FROM A SPECIAL CORRESPONDENT

The Coronation, coupled with the return of prosperity, produced by far the finest tourist season that Britain has experienced for eight years. Hotels, travel agencies and shipping companies are still enjoying a boom unequalled since the years before 1929.

In some ways Britain's Coronation summer is the best since 1919.

Last year the total of foreign holiday tourists visiting Britain was 267,305. Foreign business visitors totalled 102,369. These were the highest figures of any year since the war, the previous highest for holiday tourists being 245,865 in 1930.

Figures for 1936 showed an increase over 1935, Jubilee Year, of 39,537 holiday tourists and 14,379 business visitors. Indications are that last year's totals will be eclipsed this year.

Arrivals of foreign visitors each month since the Coronation "invasion" started last spring until the end of July have been:

March, 21,606	June, 33,883
April, 26,932	July, 77,349
May, 34,332	

The July total was 3,089 above the record figure for July, 1936. The total for five months was 194,102.

AUGUST RECORD LIKELY

These figures exclude Dominions visitors and the week-end and day excursionists from France and Belgium, who would account for many thousands more. The number of Americans who visited Britain from March to July was 57,214.

In August last year 52,471 foreigners came to Britain, and in September 33,957. Totals for August and September this year will, it is anticipated, at least equal, and probably surpass, last year's.

An official of the Hotels and Restaurants Association of Great Britain said: "Hotels, especially those in the West End and many other parts of London, have had a very good season indeed. They have benefited greatly by the increase in the number of foreign visitors and the increased spending power noticeable.

"The fact that the Coronation was early in the season has made this prosperity summer an especially long one. Americans are making prolonged stays. Repeatedly when it was thought that the arrivals were about to slacken there has been a fresh wave of bookings."

NO ROOM IN LINERS

The Cunard-White Star Co. is finding that a season which began in April will last until the end of October, and perhaps even later. Prolonging the already late season will be the pilgrimage to the French battlefields of 6,000 American Legionnaires. They start to come to Europe at the end of this month and will stay for some time.

Many American visitors to Britain, it was stated yesterday by a travel agency, have been "caught" by the heavy traffic. Anticipating easy liner bookings in August and September, they now find that there is no return accommodation available for several weeks to come.

Among the many delights of London which are keeping Americans here in large numbers are trips on the Thames. An increasing number of tourists make "water visits" to Oxford and other places on the river.

Daily Telegraph 1937

GIRL'S SECRET NIGHT SWIM

Daily Telegraph 1937

DEFIED CURRENTS & DARKNESS

SOUTHSEA TO RYDE CROSSING

An Austrian parlourmaid, staying with her mistress at Hayling Island, swam unaccompanied on Wednesday night from Southsea to Ryde, Isle of Wight.

She covered the four miles in five hours, defying strong currents.

The girl is Miss Louise Horna, 21, employed by Mrs. Roland Gander Dower, of Palace-gate, Kensington, W., and she made her swim secretly.

She came ashore at Ryde just before midnight and walked across the sands to the promenade in her bathing costume. Stopping a taxi she said to the driver: "I have just swum from Southsea alone" and then collapsed.

"The girl was very cold and suffering badly from cramp," said the taxi-driver yesterday "I drove her to a milk bar for hot refreshment and she recovered. She surprised me by producing a 10s note from a pocket in her bathing costume."

Later the girl was taken to the police station, and returned to Hayling Island in the morning.

Miss Horna said yesterday: "I always wanted to do the swim. I left my clothes at the Clarence Pier, Southsea, and told the attendant I was going for a short swim. This was at 6.30, and I swam on until reaching Ryde.

"Once a steamer narrowly missed me, and the current changed frequently."

Mr. Gander Dower said he and his family had been very worried as the girl did not return the same evening. He knew that she was a strong swimmer. On a previous occasion she tried to swim to the Isle of Wight, but was stopped near the forts by a police launch.

Banffshire Journal 1936

Brigadier-General A. C. Critchley, C.M.G., D.S.O., newly elected president of the British Caravanners Club, with his children and their Curtis Aerocar

Caravan World 1938

Cheltenham Spa—
in Shakespeare's England

■ ALL my life I have had a soft place in my heart for Cheltenham. I came to know it first as an undergraduate. In those days we explored the Cotswolds on foot and discovered the fact that for architectural loveliness nothing can compare with the villages among the stone-wall uplands and treeless valleys.

If I had my way I should meet all American visitors to our country at Southampton and Plymouth and try to entice them first to visit Burford, Broadway, Chipping Campden, the Slaughters, and Stow-on-the-Wold, and I should tell them that they should make Cheltenham their centre.

They would see the true England of Shakespeare in the villages, and in the Cheltenham hotels they would be made to feel that the happiness of their visitors is the staffs' main concern.

Americans are used to good hotels, so one must be careful where one tells them to go. I have always felt that the Cheltenham hotels really do cater for the comfort of their clients, and I have a strong feeling that they must have changed considerably since Cobbett's day, for, as you remember, he describes the town as " a resort of the lame and the lazy, the gormandising and guzzling, the bilious and the nervous."

All I can say about that is that if one comes to Cheltenham lame one leaves it whole, if lazy one leaves it vigorous. Nerves are soothed, and physical disorders cured forthwith.

Cobbett may have been right about the gormandising. I find that Cheltenham air gives me an appetite that is not altogether satisfied by aesthetic delight. After a day on the hill-tops I descend at eventide to eat prodigious meals.

Cheltenham has the tremendous advantage of being in touch with London by means of the *Cheltenham Flyer* and the aeroplane, and in touch with the really remote countryside.

The Cotswolds separate her on the east from any possible contamination of suburbanisation, while on the west lies the romantic valley of the Severn, and beyond it lie the Welsh Marches and the border.

There are certain fundamental qualities required in a modern health resort or spa to make it acceptable to visitors as well as residents.

It must be cheerful, lively, beautiful, accessible, up-to-date in itself—quite apart from being within easy reach of the country that is beautiful and varied.

To one type of mind the word Cheltenham will call up visions of the largest girls' school and one of the most robust boys' schools in the land. Educationally it certainly stands almost alone.

To another type of mind the word conjures up visions of the National Hunt Steeplechase, of point-to-point courses, and hunting with the Heythrop and Cotswold packs. The foxhunter will certainly find more varied country in this area than anywhere else.

Again, to the lover of our native literature and natural beauties, it will conjure up visions made imperishable by the poetry of John Masefield and A. E. Housman, the prose of Compton Mackenzie and Arthur Gibbs.

Tourist 1938

Cecil Beaton's study of the Duchess of Kent (Princess Marina), dressed as for a *fête-champêtre*,1938.

Empire Day Rally.

Youth Entertained at Derrygore

The Scouts, Wolf Cubs, Girl Guides and Brownies of Enniskillen celebrated Empire Day by spending Saturday afternoon at Derrygore. The members of the local Association of Scouts and Guides kindly provided the hearty tea, which was much appreciated by all present, and they also took part in the games.

The 1st Enniskillen Guides were under Mrs. Cooke, captain; the Brownies under Brown Owl, Mrs. J. Baker; the 2nd Enniskillen (Girls' Collegiate School), under Capt. E. Jackson; 1st Enniskillen Scouts, under Group Scoutmaster D. Fallis; Cubs under Cubmaster R. H. Saunderson; 1st Ballinamallard, under District Commissioner H. Burke.

Amongst the many helpers were:—Mrs. Teele, Mrs. Smith (Collegiate School), Mrs. Davis, Mrs. Simpson, Mr. and Mrs. Burkitt. The following very kindly drove backwards and forwards, bringing and taking back Scouts and Guides:—Mrs. Gardiner, Capt. Charlton, Hon. Cecil L. Corry, J.P.; Capt. W. Teele, M.C.; Mrs. Wadsworth, Mr. Simpson (Model School).

During the afternoon many games and relay races took place, and these were much enjoyed by the young people present.

A special word of praise is due to Mr. and Mrs. H. M. Irwin for very kindly arranging this annual outing.

Impartial Reporter 1938

Paris Jottings

BY FLANEUR

■ THE recent anniversary of Verlaine's death again brings to the fore a curious café frequented by the poet. When British tourists visit the establishment, let them remember that it was founded under Louis XIV by Francesco Procopio on the spot it occupies to-day. Since the seventeenth century the " Procope " has retained its popularity.

Situated opposite the budding Comédie Française, Rue des Fossés St. Germain, it was frequented by Voltaire, Rousseau and Helvétius, but reached its zenith in 1895 when Verlaine was its leading light.

The Parisienne—as most of us are aware—requires a new perfume or two every season. She has been admirably catered for in this respect by Maggy Rouff, in " Exentric, " a scent as subtle as a charming personality, presented in white boxes relieved with a touch of pink and glistening foliage ; in " Etincelle, " a delightful extract of exotic flowers reflecting youth and exuberance, in black boxes likewise adorned with pink and foliage.

In theatreland there is *Madame La Folie*, a revue at the Folies Bergère, with Mistinguett and Jeanne Aubert as chief exponents, wherein English visitors will be amused at a scene representing Emma Hamilton and Nelson under a novel aspect ; *La Dame de chez Maxim* (Georges Feydeau's three-act comedy) at the Odéon.

Tourist 1939

It's all so New on the Continent

Strange food, foreign tongues, fresh surroundings

EVERYTHING is new and different from workaday things. Even the ships, the sounds and the sights in the Pool of London are different as you start your holiday early one Saturday morning. The voyage itself is intensely interesting as you glide down the Thames between rows of giant factories whose products are household words, between huge docks where the world's shipping discharges goods from every country.

The ships that travel across the Channel direct from London are specially built for the job ; they are constructed to provide the utmost comfort for passengers. Excellent meals are served on board and the time of crossing passes all too quickly, for this voyage is so much a part of the holiday that you are loth to say farewell to the ship.

Gaiety the Keynote

As the *Royal Sovereign, Queen of the Channel* or *Royal Daffodil* approaches Ostend you will see the imposing line of hotels along the front and a big building—the Casino-Kursaal—where gaiety is the keynote and every night sees there a scintillating society playing games of chance or coming to hear the famous orchestras and artistes that the management provide for their entertainment.

The ship approaches Ostend Pier and soon ties up at a special jetty, bronzed seamen in blue shirts push up gangways, and soon we are streaming over the side ready for the Customs, who, with little formality, let us through. Now you are in a foreign land and all the novel things that you have done to-day seem to culminate in this moment. You may not be able to put your finger on the reasons why it is so different, but yet you know it is. Your ears are assailed by the strange sounds of a foreign tongue and you may be puzzled sometimes to know whether it is French or Flemish you are hearing. But don't listen too intently when you are crossing a road or you may be taken by surprise by a car or taxi driving on what you think is the wrong side of the road (but you are wrong, for on the Continent the traffic keeps to the right). The policemen, too, have a strange look with their white helmets and white gloves. But you will find them both courteous and efficient should you ever need their help.

You've Been Abroad !

By the time you are ready to board the ship again on the next day at about 2 o'clock you will have spent a night abroad, bathed, seen the Battlefields, gambled, eaten tasteful foreign food, enjoyed foreign wines. You will have done what you have always promised yourself to do—gone abroad. See how inexpensive the fares are on page 16.

Holiday News 1939

1940
1949

AN EXPEDITION TO LAPLAND

SCHOOLBOYS' ADVENTURES

Envy must have been uppermost in the minds of the young people who attended the second of the Royal Geographical Society's Christmas lectures yesterday—envy, first of all, of the 10 boys from Gordonstoun School who enjoyed the happy and boisterous adventure of an expedition to Lapland last April, and secondly, of the Lapland children themselves whose merriment in their winter games—skiing, sledging, skating, and scooting over miles of snow and ice—was recorded in the natural colour film with which the lecture was brilliantly illustrated.

The story was told fascinatingly by Mr. F. SPENCER CHAPMAN, explorer, mountaineer; and a master of Gordonstoun, who, with Mr. R. L. BICKERSTETH, a fellow-master—now both officers in The Seaforth Highlanders—led the expedition to the romantic home of the Laps and made the film, which took a full hour to show. He first went to Lapland several years ago to experiment in the driving of reindeer, but " Isaac," his first purchase, after drawing his sledge over 200 miles of difficult country, convinced him that the species, however efficient in some circumstances, was singularly unintelligent in most. His further explorations of those parts of Scandinavia in which the Laps, with their picturesque and highly coloured costumes and likeable ways, have settled made him want to return, and thus the expedition from Gordonstoun was planned.

The 10 boys who took part were not selected specially because of their physique but merely because they wanted to go. As the film recorded their progress over wide tracts of blending white, over hills and across frozen lakes and rivers, sometimes dragging and pushing their sledges and sometimes trying to cope with the strange and mulish temperament of the reindeer, the youthful audience applauded with enthusiasm.

At the end Mr. BICKERSTETH giving, as " an amateur explorer," his impressions of the enterprise, said that, going expecting to find a colourless land, he was surprised at the extraordinary prevalence of brilliant colours.

SIR FRANCIS YOUNGHUSBAND, who presided, said that the lecture and film would enable the audience to understand better the conditions under which the heroic Finns were defending their country.

The Times 1940

POOR CLERGY OF LONDON

Sir,—May we again ask for the support of your readers on behalf of the London Poor Clergy Holiday Fund ? The needs of the poor clergy at this time are, if possible, greater than ever, and the strain caused by the war is a very real one. The work of the clergy in ministering to their people is national service, but it brings with it difficulties, anxieties, and, indeed, weariness. Parishes are now understaffed, and many of the clergy are working single-handed. Of course some may not be able to get out of London, but we do all we can to give the hard worked clergy and their wives a short holiday at the seaside or in the country. Donations may be sent to the hon. secretary and treasurer, Prebendary Vincent, St. Martin's Church, Ludgate Hill, E.C.4, or to the Westminster Bank, 5, St. Paul's Churchyard, E.C.4.

We are, &c.,

ERNEST N. SHARPE, Archdeacon of London ; S. H. PHILLIMORE, Archdeacon of Middlesex ; C. E. LAMBERT, Archdeacon of Hampstead ; G. HERBERT VINCENT, Prebendary of St. Paul's, Hon. Secretary and Treasurer.

June 8.

The Times 1940

ROSE QUEEN WANTED

For an hour on Whit-Monday morning the Memorial Theatre lawn will again be trodden by Elizabethan figures, when the central figure in a miniature pageant will be the Rose Queen.

So that the pageant shall truly represent the attractive girlhood of the district, entries are invited from as many as care to come forward. In addition to the Queen, six maids-of-honour and a number of ladies of the Court are wanted. The Mayoress (Mrs. T. N. Waldron) and Mr. B. Iden Payne, director of the Shakespeare Festival Company, have again consented to act as judges and to take part in the ceremony.

Stratford upon Avon Herald 1940

A RECITAL
In aid of
THE MAYOR'S FUND
For providing comforts for men and women of Stratford-upon-Avon serving in H.M. Forces

WILL BE GIVEN IN THE TOWN HALL

MONDAY, APRIL 29th, at 8 p.m.

BETTY ANDREÆ	*Songs in Costume*
FRANCESCA PALMER	*Viol da Gamba*
MAYRE LAWSON	*Original Character Sketches*
JOHN BROUGH	*at the Piano*

TICKETS 3/6, 2/6, 1/-

Can be obtained from Messrs F. J. Spencer, High Street ; E. Daniels, Bridge Street ; and T. Beckett, Wood Street, Stratford-upon-Avon ; or the Custodian at the Town Hall.

Stratford upon Avon Herald 1940

MOTOR COACH TOURS

SUNDAY, APRIL 28th — BLOSSOM TOUR

Depart Stratford (Coach Station) 2.30 p.m.   Home 6.0 p.m.
Fare: Adults 3/-   Children 2/-

EVENING CIRCULAR DRIVE

Depart 6.30 p.m.   Home 9.0 p.m.   Fare: Adults 1/6, Children 1/-

RELIABLE PRIVATE HIRE SERVICE

YOUR ENQUIRIES SOLICITED

SPREAD yOur holidayS

APPEAL TO PASSENGERS (Rationing of Petrol).

Many of you can
Travel on Week-days—Monday to Friday
DO IT NOW!

Many of you can arrange
YOUR HOLIDAYS IN MAY, JUNE, JULY, OR SEPTEMBER.
DO IT NOW!

HELP US TO HELP YOU!

Stratford-upon-Avon Blue Motors, Ltd.
Telephones 2307 and 2020.

Stratford upon Avon Herald 1940

"STAY AT HOME" PLEA IGNORED

Scenes at Paddington

PLAYS IN LONDON PARKS

By OUR SPECIAL REPRESENTATIVE

Observer
1942

The Government's appeal to the public to make this August Bank Holiday week-end a stay-at-home affair seems to have been ignored to some extent.

Although it had been announced that Service men would receive priority, many were unable to find room. A large party of men returning to their units had to be left behind at Bristol yesterday while a train steamed out packed to the doors.

In London, people at Paddington fought not to obtain seats, but merely to get a footing in the corridors of trains leaving for seaside and country. Holiday makers lined the platforms six or eight deep waiting for trains to come in, and then followed a mad scramble to board them.

Children and old people were almost lifted off their feet in the scrimmage; in less than three minutes the trains were packed with people standing in the carriages, and clinging to the luggage racks. In the corridors they stood so closely together that they could not even turn.

THE STANDING ARMY

They were prepared to face journeys of five to six hours in this discomfort in their determination to get away. Many who were unable to squeeze in were left standing on the platform to try their luck with a later train.

Congestion was made worse by the huge crowds arriving in London. Trains drawing into the platforms at Paddington were almost as packed as those leaving. Passengers streamed down into the Underground station, where the subways rapidly became blocked.

Although many people travelled from Euston and trains leaving the the station were full, the crowds there were not nearly as great as those at Paddington. To relieve congestion the issue of all platform tickets was cancelled at Euston for the day.

As a contrast Londoners were given top marks at the three Southern termini.

NO BATTLE OF WATERLOO

"The public have responded extremely well to the no-travel appeal," an official at Waterloo stated. "Our bookings have been heavy, but no more than an unusually busy Saturday. Nothing like the Bank Holiday crowds of pre-war days."

At Victoria about 100 people were queueing for the Ramsgate train, but other platforms seemed almost deserted.

Charing Cross at 11.30 appeared to be no busier than on a normal day. An official stated: "Our bookings, though heavier than they were last year, are not more than we anticipated. For the past weeks there has been a steady increase in travel every Saturday."

Traffic at King's Cross was not excessive; there was plenty of room in the trains.

An official of the L.M.S. said that traffic in the provinces had been very heavy, especially at Birmingham, where many who attempted to catch trains on Friday had to wait until yesterday.

At night news from the resorts was mixed. Bournemouth reported: "Nothing like a peace-time August Bank Holiday week-end. Accommodation found for all." Llandudno, on the other hand, was "stiff with people."

Crowds poured into Bognor Regis all day; but Weston-super-Mare had fewer visitors than before the war and these had no trouble in getting accommodation. Southport was crowded out; many of those looking for rooms had been turned away by Blackpool's "House Full" notice.

Torquay was not crowded. "Easily the quietest August holiday we have had," said a resident.

WHAT LONDON OFFERS

In London, holidays at home may mean the river, the parks, the Zoo (the panda is back, refreshed after exile at Whipsnade), the fair on Hampstead Heath, the theatres (many with Bank Holiday matinées), the cinemas or, quite simply, a deck-chair in the garden.

At Regent's Park Mr. Robert Atkins and his company are holding the stage of the Open Air Theatre. Mr. Atkins, ready to play Shakespeare wherever there is a platform and the beginnings of an audience, has lately been showing the flag in East London—at the Coronation Gardens, Leyton—as well as in N.W.1. And before that he had an emphatic pastoral success in the parks of Manchester.

Now, while conditions permit, he is back at the Open Air Theatre, under the auspices of C.E.M.A., which has also been providing music of the best for the stay-at-homers in dozens of industrial towns.

He has cheerful memories of Leyton. "A tremendous success," he said, as he assumed the burnt-sack complexion of Sir Toby Belch. "In nine nights we played to about 11,000 people. The stage was small—not comparable with this at Regent's Park—and in Elizabethan fashion we had the audience on three sides of us.

"They were splendidly responsive. We have been asked to go back in October for a season indoors, if a suitable hall is free. So far we have given the comedies; there is a demand now for the heavier plays."

ALL WEATHERS

After working for a decade in Regent's Park, Mr. Atkins knows the London climate as well as anyone. Here, indeed, is an all-weather producer. His eagerness unabated, he contemplates a possible "King Lear" before the season is out, with himself as the King. This is not settled yet; but Mr. Atkins would like to try it, for a few evening performances at least, if the "to-and-fro conflicting wind and rain" will confine itself to the text.

Meanwhile, the holiday crowds next week will have three comedies—"The Dream" to-morrow, and, later, "The Taming of the Shrew," and, again, "Twelfth Night," with Miss Mary Martlew's grave, tender performance of Viola.

While there is Shakespeare in Regent's Park, there is ballet in Bethnal Green. The Sadler's Wells dancers, transplanted from the New, are beginning a week's season in Victoria Park to-morrow. The London County Council presents them as part of its share in the holidays-at-home campaign.

Holiday extended for picking hops

Hereford Education Committee, after some protests, confirmed the chairman's action in extending the school holidays for hop picking.

"It would do some members the world of good," said Mr. T. Powell, "to have a drop of malt and hops"

Sunday Express 1943

QUEUES FOR THE SEASIDE

TO thousands of Londoners bent on a Whitsun break at the coast or in the country, the Ministry of War Transport's injunction to travel only if they must did not mean a thing.

Forming long queues at the main line stations from early yesterday, holiday-makers ignored discomfort and the familiar query: " Is your journey really necessary? " and crowded into trains which left filled to capacity.

To them, war or no war, their journey was necessary, and reports from the principal holiday centres showed that they arrived at resorts which did somehow have food and accommodation for them, despite shortage warnings.

Paddington, Waterloo and Victoria carried the bulk of the London Whit traffic, but conditions were normal at Euston, St. Pancras and Marylebone.

One queue for a West of England train at Waterloo stretched three or more deep along nearly the whole length of the road flanking the platform. A mass of people with suitcases and bags hampered at other platform barriers those arriving for work in the City.

But—" No one has been left behind," a " People " reporter was told

Late yesterday afternoon Paddington was still handling holiday crowds mainly for Cornwall and South Devon.

" They are putting up with a great deal of discomfort, but the congestion is not so bad," said an official.

At the reception end of this great exodus, reports were practically unanimous in describing a record wartime Whitsun.

Blackpool is having its busiest season of the war. Not a room in boarding-houses within a mile of the promenade remains unbooked. Every available hotel was full weeks ago.

" The whole town is booked up until the middle of August," said Mr. J. Ratcliffe, the information bureau chief.

FOOD NOT SCARCE

And a food official said : " In spite of all the scare stories there should be no shortage of food."

Holidaymakers at Colwyn Bay had to seek police aid to find rooms, but the police could do no more than refer them to " likely " addresses.

There were queues over a hundred yards long at Llandudno cafes. Thousands of visitors have arrived since Friday.

Scarborough was " normal " in one respect—so many people went there that the street scenes were reminiscent of a normal peacetime Whitsun.

While visitors experienced little difficulty in getting to Morecambe and Heysham they had to stand in luggage vans and train corridors.

Brighton was " just full." But intending Brighton holiday-makers had a third deterrent. In addition to restricted travel and probable ration shortage, they knew they were liable to be turned back home by the authorities.

In contrast to the Northern resorts, East Coast resorts were quiet. The majority of the visitors to Gt. Yarmouth, Lowestoft and Felixstowe were cyclists, and many took their own food.

There was practically no activity on the Norfolk Broads, reopened to the public last week. Clacton-on-Sea had a fairly big crowd.

Torquay was another exception; streets were practically empty yesterday afternoon, with not a tenth of the usual crowds in the gardens and on the beaches. Evening arrivals were mostly Service people and war workers on leave.

Crowds who poured into Richmond (Surrey) for a riverside break had not travelled far from London. Boat hirers and steamers had one of their busiest Bank Holiday Saturdays. There was a " Wings " Week procession and a large old-fashioned fair on Richmond Green.

But these crowds may have come from Wales, the Midlands, Plymouth or Penzance, for a Paddington report last night said that trains from these places into London had been " very crowded."

*People
1943*

THE GUIDE

The Official Weekly Organ of the Girl Guides Association
(Incorporated by Royal Charter)

Volume XXIV.   No. 32.   August 11, 1944.

EDITORIAL OFFICES:

Girl Guide Headquarters
17-19, Buckingham Palace Road, S.W.1
Tel. No. Victoria 6001.

SUBSCRIPTIONS.—For 13 weeks, 3/3; 26 weeks, 6/6; 52 weeks, 13/ (post free). Single Copies, 3d. each (post free).

The Editor Speaks

MY dear Guides,
Such a tight pack in THE GUIDE this week that something had to be thrown overboard, and I thought, on the whole, you could do best without the " sermon." I hope you agree!

How many of you have thought of getting work on farms, or in the fields, during these holidays, to earn some money for the G.I.S.? We are thinking of having some kind of special Harvest Home this year—but I will tell you about that idea when there is more room. In any case, do remember how quickly even the longest holidays melt away, and use the time you have to get on with that tremendous job we have all tackled together. Have you earned or saved *your* ten shillings towards it yet? Remember, we are not expecting *every* Guide will be able to manage it, but just because it's a challenge, see if you can't be one of those who achieve it.

Yours,

The Editor

*The Guide
1944*

On holiday, you may be told to go home

TRAVEL AT YOUR OWN RISK

HOLIDAY-MAKERS visiting resorts in the regulated coastal belt, from the Humber to Penzance, this summer may find themselves suddenly ordered to leave a town in the middle of their holiday.

At any time the ban may be imposed.

"That is just one of the risks which people visiting places in the areas will run," an authority told the Sunday Express.

"If they attempt to remain after a ban has been imposed they will be prosecuted.

No guarantee

"It will not be possible for the Army to say in advance that any district is to be closed.

"If people take the risk of travelling to these areas they must accept the consequences.

"A ban might be imposed so suddenly that the first intimation would be the turning back of visitors at the stations.

"Every effort will be made to inform the railways as quickly as possible, but no guarantee can be given that this will be in time to prevent useless journeys."

Prospective visitors should write to the town clerk for information.

Undeterred by the possible consequences thousands of visitors flocked to Brighton yesterday.

Trains arrived all day packed with pleasure-seekers willing to take the chance.

Cinemas, dance halls and concerts were crowded, and hotels everywhere reported that they were "filling up nicely."

Police are puzzled to know what action to take if the military make Brighton a banned area.

Sunday Express **1943**

CROSS-CHANNEL STEAMER INNOVATION

An instrument known as the "Tele-talk" has been installed in the Burns and Laird Line steamer Lairdsburn so that passengers on the night crossing from Glasgow to Ireland may communicate direct from their cabins with the night stewards.

The system has been developed by the International Marine Radio Communication Company, working in conjunction with the Burns and Laird Line superintendent engineer, and the intention is to extend the system to other ships belonging to the company.

Glasgow Herald **1945**

21 days here put a sick soldier back on his feet

HUNDREDS of sick soldiers, too weak to stand up to the rigorous hardening treatment given to them in military convalescent depots in preparation for return to their units, are getting what is called a "pre-hardening" treatment at 11 Red Cross and St. John Convalescent Homes. Six of the homes are for men and five for officers.

War Office officials, anxious to have these men back on the job as soon as they are fit, have asked the Red Cross and St. John War Organisation to take them into their homes for carefully directed treatment.

In the homes the patients are under the supervision of Army doctors who advise on their treatment.

Hardening process

It usually takes 21 days of this treatment to put a soldier on his feet again and fit him for the real hardening process.

Each home has an Army physical training instructor, a masseuse, and a male occupational therapist. Patients do outdoor work—gardening, log-splitting or tree-felling. Some do carpentry.

Periods are set aside each day for organised games and walks. When the men are fit they are taken for country runs. Army education officers arrange lectures for them as well as map reading and other military training.

After three weeks of this they are ready for real Commando training.

Sunday Express **1943**

DON'T LET HOLIDAYS CAUSE A SAVINGS SLUMP!

It is natural to want as much spending money as possible for the rare week's holiday, when it comes round, but if every one of us stopped saving for a week, the loss to the country would be terrific. Whatever you do, when the holiday is over, switch back into the regular routine of so much to your savings account each week, and do not be tempted to let things slide. A little and often is the safest method to follow.

P.S.—If you are not a member of a Street Savings Group merely because nobody has asked you, what about trying to get one going yourself? There is still room for a great many more of these Savings Groups. Full details of how to form a group can be obtained from the National Savings Committee, Bouverie House, Fleet Street, London, E.C.4.

Cabinet 'breather'

There is to be a further short repent before the new session of Parliament opens. Members who argue that there is "so little time, so much to do" will be annoyed. But the Cabinet wants a "breather" in which to prepare its programme for the new session.

Sunday Express **1943**

Good Housekeeping **1943**

National Parks Planned on British Coast

By OUR PARLIAMENTARY CORRESPONDENT

NATIONAL parks running down to the sea are contemplated by the Ministry of Town and Country Planning as part of their proposals for the preservation of the British coastline.

The special coastal survey which is being made by Mr. J. A. Steers, Lecturer in Geography at Cambridge University, is expected to be ready by the spring for the Ministry's consideration. Consultations based on the report prepared by Mr. John Dower, the well-known Lake District architect, on suitable sites for future national parks, are going on between the Ministry and other Government departments.

Meanwhile, local authorities and joint town and country planning committees have been warned by the Ministry that the information gained by Mr. Steers's survey should be taken into account in any development contemplated, especially within three miles of the coast. They have been advised to "consult" the regional planning officers on any application for development.

Limited Powers

The Ministry is thus acting, as far as it can, on a recommendation of the Scott Report "that the coast of England and Wales should be considered as a whole with a view to the prevention of further spoilation." Parts of the British coastline where building is to be prevented and those where it may be allowed, under proper safeguards, are already defined on maps kept by the Ministry of Town and Country Planning. What is still lacking is effective power, in fact, to make good the plans.

An indication of these limitations was hinted at by the Minister, Mr. W. S. Morrison, in the House of Commons on Thursday. Explaining the purpose of the Steers survey, Mr. Morrison said that "sound holiday development" was to be permitted in "carefully selected places." Presumably, this would comprehend "Butlinisation," and the Minister's ability to control the development of permanent holiday camps and amusement parks remains to be seen.

Building on or near the coast, according to the Ministry's advice, would be allowed only where it could be "fitted into the landscape" and where "proper facilities can be provided." This would allow for Mr. W. E. Butlin's "entirely self-contained communities" and "up-to-date townships," since they would be big enough to justify the provision of the facilities.

Observer 1943

DO YOU REMEMBER?

WEYMOUTH

In looking back you see the future; the present is an ugly phase that will pass. The happy days when you could enjoy the beauties of the countryside and the invigorating breezes from the sea, are on the way back. And our omnibuses and coaches will be there to bring it all within your reach.

BRITISH BUSES

NEWBURY & DISTRICT
MOTOR SERVICES LTD

Newbury Weekly News 1944

The Journal 1945

FAIR! FAIR! FAIR!

HERBERT S. GRAY'S
VICTORY AMUSEMENTS

WILL VISIT

HEIGHAM STREET

(near City Station),

NORWICH

for EIGHT DAYS ONLY

FRIDAY, NOVEMBER, 2nd, to SATURDAY, NOVEMBER 10th
6.0 Each Evening, 2.30 Sats.

With the

SUPER DODG'EMS, HOOP - LAS, DARTS, SKITTLES, SHOOTERS, SWINGS and CHILDREN'S ROUNDABOUTS. All the Fun of the Fair for Young and Old.

This is the Fair which has supported the War Charities. Don't Fail to Pay Us a Visit.

Permanent address: Herbert S. Gray, 107, Norwich Road, Wisbech.

BELLS TO RING ON V DAY

THANKSGIVING SERVICE AT ST. PAUL'S

Within an hour of the declaration of victory over the Germans the bells of St. Paul's will start to ring their thanksgiving peals. It will take about an hour for the ringers, members of the Ancient Society of College Youths, to assemble in the Cathedral.

If the news comes early enough in the morning there will be a service of thanksgiving at noon. If it is announced in the afternoon the service will be in the evening. The Lord Mayor and members of the City Corporation will probably attend.

There will be a great thanksgiving service on the Sunday after Victory Day, and for this it is hoped to get the St. Paul's choir boys back from Truro, where they have been evacuated during the war.

The bells of Westminster Abbey will also ring, but the arrangements have not been finally settled.

The Times 1945

LOCAL TOPICS

VE-Day.—VE-Day, long awaited, has come and gone, and it turned out to be a quiet and rather sobering day, instead of the day of wild hilarity some had anticipated. Perhaps it was the long period of expectancy before the official announcement that cease fire had been sounded. Everyone was anxious to celebrate each in their own way, but there was an atmosphere of restraint, probably produced by the fact that it was not V-Day, only VE-Day, and Ripon men and boys were still fighting in the Far East or prisoners of war.

Ripon Gazette 1945

CHESTER HAS A "BOOM"

DAY-TRIPPERS ARRIVE IN THOUSANDS

Chester is enjoying a boom in day trippers, and every day this week the streets and riverside have been crowded in the afternoons by thousands of visitors who have arrived by train, bus and motor coach. There have been queues for the pleasure boats, and the cafés have been taxed to their utmost.

Liverpool Echo 1945

DUNDEE OFF TO GOOD START
RECORD EARLY RUSH OF HOLIDAYMAKERS

Dundonians whose holidays started on Thursday night took full advantage of yesterday—the day before the opening of Dundee holiday week—to travel by bus and rail.

Officials at West Station consider the volume of passengers to be a record, wartime or pre-war, for travel the day before the holiday week commenced. One described it as "extraordinary."

There were heavy bookings for all routes at the West, and intending passengers for the 8.20 p.m. special to Manchester, Liverpool, Preston, and Carlisle arrived at the station at five o'clock. Their time was spent in playing cards, singing, and keeping the children contented.

Tay Bridge reported the same heavy traffic. Most popular trains were the 8.10 and 8.30 in the evening for London.

Almost 2000, including wellwishers, had gathered to await the first train, and when it steamed into the station the crowd dashed to the edge of the platform. About half of them were successful in getting aboard, the residue standing back to try their luck on the next train, which is a special train only run on Monday, Friday, and Saturday.

The 8.10 left with corridors packed, and those left behind were comfortably accommodated in the 8.30. A number of coaches were run empty on both trains from Aberdeen for the benefit of Dundonians.

Approximate figures from Tay Bridge are:—London and south of London, 600; Edinburgh, 700; Aberdeen, 600; Newcastle, Montrose, Kirkcaldy, and Dunfermline, 100 each.

Peak hours at Lindsay Street bus station were between six and eight at night. All routes were well patronised, and a number of duplicates were run so that on no occasion was anyone left behind.

Tay Ferries were busy, mostly with returning Fife holidaymakers.

Dundee Courier and Advertiser 1945

OUTING FOR BLIND
Happy Time At Brampford Speke

A party of about 120 blind people from Exeter were taken by charabanc to Brampford Speke yesterday, when a most enjoyable afternoon was spent.

Tea was served in the Vicarage grounds, by permission of Rev. F. C. and Mrs. Eddy, and before leaving in the evening the visitors attended a service in the village church.

The outing was organized by Miss I. Chown, home teacher to the blind.

Exeter Express and Echo 1945

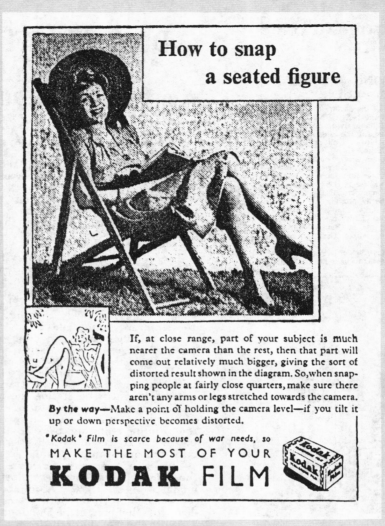

Exeter Express and Echo 1945

The Jacobite Celebrations.

SIR,—It was in August, 1745—just two hundred years ago—that "Bonnie Prince Charlie" began his gallant but (happily) unsuccessful attempt to secure the Throne again for the Stewart dynasty. The Battle of Culloden, in April, 1746, put an end to his hopes and the hopes of his followers. It also put an end to the Clan system and ensured for Scotland its Presbyterian Church.

It may be of interest to your readers to know that all along, and even to this day, prayer meetings have been held in Inverness from time to time "to give thanks to Almighty God for deliverance from the House of Stewart and from Popery." So much glamour and romance have been cast around "Prince Charlie" by various writers that one is apt to forget what it would have meant for this country in the restriction of our civil and religious liberties if his cause had prevailed.—I am, etc., PRESBYTER.

August 11. 1945.

John O'Groats Journal 1945

No Scarborough Trip for North Shields Supporters

North Shields will not be able to take supporters with them to Scarborough on Saturday for the F.A. Cup-tie as the Northern Regional Transport Commissioner has cancelled the permits for two buses which had been fully booked up. Permission has been given for a bus to carry players and officials. The news has come as a shock and caused great disappointment. Many changes have been made in the team, which will be: Johnson; Hearne, Wort; Thompson, Gledson, Smith; Jamieson, Needham, McLean, Bohills, Cooper.

Northern Echo 1945

PLANNING HOLIDAYS AGAIN

WITH SO MANY MILLIONS of us looking forward to our first peace-time holiday this year, it's certain that some of us are going to be disappointed. There simply won't be room.

For my part, I feel I've travelled enough miles during these last six years to last me a lifetime. Lots of ex-Servicemen probably feel the same way. We would be quite content to stay at home.

But then, we're not the only ones to be considered. So it looks as if we shall have to pack our bags without grumbling, when the time comes, and stagger off with them somewhere, if only to give our wives the pleasure of eating meals cooked by somebody else.

I've just been looking through a holiday guide issued by one of the travel agencies. They arrange everything for you—the tickets, the hotel, the excursions to the local sights, and even the tips—all for an inclusive charge.

They even meet you at the station, apparently, and carry your bags to the hotel, thus saving you what can be the most painful part of holiday-making. If their practice lives up to their promises, their prices are amazingly cheap.

A week at Bournemouth, for instance, including a return ticket from London and various excursions when you get there, for £9 5s. A similar week in Devon for just under £9. I doubt if you could do it much cheaper, nowadays, no matter how carefully you arranged it, however much you cut down the extras.

Personally, I've never tried a "conducted" trip. Half the fun of a holiday, I always think, is the pleasure of planning it. Or, better still (in the days when you could do it) of starting off without any plan at all.

The best way to do that, of course, is on the old bike. I know of no more glorious feeling than setting out very early in the morning, with the bike well loaded fore and aft, and slipping along easily through the still-sleeping city streets, with all England and a free week before you.

John Bull 1946

Woman's Journal 1947

For summer days - her favourite beach wear changes with the fashion...

but her favourite cigarette remains, without question . . .

Player's Please

PLAYER'S NAVY CUT CIGARETTES · MEDIUM OR MILD

[NCC 6526]

THE IDEAL RESORT FOR HEALTH AND HOLIDAY

★

If the state of your health demands special treatment, why not come to Harrogate for your holidays this year? At the Royal Baths there are many natural medicinal waters and modern physio-therapeutic treatments which are proving very beneficial in cases of rheumatism and other medical conditions. Ask your Doctor about it.

★ HARROGATE

Particulars from A. R. Baxter, Information Bureau, Harrogate.

Woman's Journal 1947

Churchill Takes U.S. For Granted—
& Triumphs

NEW YORK, January 19

REGARDLESS of the political views and orientations of Americans, Mr. Churchill is undoubtedly the greatest British ambassador to the United States in history. It seems to be three-quarters purely personal. Of course, he is recognised here, as in Britain, for the superb challenger, the ringing war leader that he was.

But that is not an adequate explanation for the affection which Americans feel for him. It is the counterpart to the affection which I discovered that Britons felt for Mr. Roosevelt—discovered with peculiar poignancy at the time of his death, when I was in London. Americans do not feel that Winston Churchill is a "foreigner." When they say "Welcome," it has the aroma of "Welcome home." Probably the real basis of this remarkable phenomenon is that every American honestly believes that Mr. Churchill likes us. Perhaps Americans are somewhat like Russians in this: Despite all our much-talked-of power — mentioned by ourselves, of course, as well as by others—Americans are still, to an extent, inadequately realised by the rest of the world, a provincial people not at all sure of themselves, both sensitive and self-critical, and youthfully responsive to praise and affection.

Matter—and Manner

Mr. Churchill has given us a great deal of both, and in a manner which has convinced the man from Main Street that he means it. He has an *insouciant* way of taking America and Americans for granted, as brothers and friends. His hine visits have made it seem, even to those who have never travelled widely, as easy to go from Chicago to London as from London to Miami, and as

From Dorothy Thompson

natural and matter-of-fact. When he expresses with complete candour his dismay that America may be pulling out of Europe, he simply expresses what millions of Americans also feel. In fact, he has achieved the almost impossible: the atmosphere in which he can say anything he likes, and Americans will agree with him or disagree without asking what he is up to.

Good Taste in Climate

In Florida, where I happen to have spent four days of this week, but in the western part, far removed from Miami, the people say, "Well, it was smart of him to come here in January. From all we hear, the climate is not so good in England—in January those fogs, you know." He is regarded simply as a sensible man, with a good taste in climate, come to dwell for a time among fellow-countrymen. Thus Mr. Churchill has become a sort of peripatetic advertisement of "union now." He makes it seem easy and natural.

Cartoons in newspapers show American hands lighting his ubiquitous cigar. Floridans, with a sound Chamber of Commerce instinct, remind him that Florida, a great importer of Cuban tobacco, manufactures very good cigars. So even the cigar becomes a promotional asset of Anglo-American relations, which are the warmer when they just exist and are not too much discussed.

Observer
1946

MR. CHURCHILL ON WAY TO U.S.A.

"I THINK I HAVE EARNED A HOLIDAY"

Mr. Churchill, accompanied by Mrs. Churchill, left London yesterday on the first stage of his journey to Florida.

Among those who saw him off were his daughter, Mrs. Duncan Sandys, her husband, and their two children, and his grandson, Julian. He waved to the crowd which had waited outside his house to cheer him on the way. There were cries of "Have a good holiday."

Detective-sergeant Cyril Davis, of Scotland Yard, who has been Mr. Churchill's personal bodyguard for the last two years, accompanied him by road as far as Southampton.

Mr. Churchill greeted dock workers and troops who were leaning over the side of the liner with his famous V sign. For a few minutes he was surrounded by a large crowd of cheering dock workers, who knocked off work and gathered on the quay side.

On board he received a deputation from Southampton Conservative Association, who presented Mrs. Churchill with a bouquet. Civic greetings were extended to him by the Mayor of Southampton, Alderman H. Vincent.

At a Press conference in the liner just before she sailed Mr. Churchill said that he had few definite plans, and that he was going to make his stay in the United States a holiday. He might make a few speeches, including one at President Truman's old college, but it was definitely not a lecture tour. "I think I have earned a holiday," he said.

Mr. and Mrs. Churchill will be joined in America in about a fortnight's time by their daughter, Mrs. Oliver.

The Times 1946

The longest queues in Blackpool are for "rock"—but this "rock," though pink as ever, lacks the fascinating word "Blackpool" running down its length inside.

Then ice cream; one ice-cream interest has just been sold for £70,000, and that means three tons of "slide" a day. Today, there are ten "live" shows on the boards and 650 resident players. Biggest attraction is "Jolly Alice the Fattest Lady," who, when riding home to become Mrs. Spicer, always stands in the bus so as not to be charged for two seats.

In the £250,000 Opera House, Dr. Malcolm Sargent sometimes beats it out, and George Formby appears there for £1,000 a week.

One fish-and-chip shop sometimes uses as many as twenty sacks of potatoes in one night. Side-shows boom in spite of a pre-war war on freaks in which the Armless Wonder Girl, the American Freak of Nature, the Human Pincushion and the Indiarubber Man were involved. And when it's all finished, there are enough streamlined buses and trams to carry away 100,000,000 people a year.

Well, that is all my aunt wants to hear about Blackpool.

Some Dress For Dinner

POSSIBLY my aunt would feel more at home if only I could get her to Torquay and particularly to the Imperial Hotel, where many people dress for dinner. At this hotel, says young Mr. Chapman, the managing director, business has gone up from £41,000 to £212,000 a year.

There certainly seems to be money at Torquay. For ten minutes in a 30 m.p.h. speed-boat, my aunt would have to pay 5s.—which, I feel sure, she would not do.

Perhaps, my dear aunt, you had better take the rest of your holiday at one of those inland spas which used to be so respectable and which are still uncontaminated by the atmosphere that seems to permeate the seaside.

But even at Harrogate there are serious changes. Still growing vegetables on the Stray! And an all-in "cure ticket" (doctor and water included) is only 7 guineas. As for Buxton, they're actually going to have a factory to send the Spa water all over the world. *My dear Aunt, take my advice. Forget all about* 1900. *Then you'll enjoy* 1946.

Leader **1946**

"I wonder how much his life's savings are?"

Blighty 1946

Leader 1947

Observer 1947

Tourist Trade Unaffected By The Fuel Crisis

By Charles Reid

THE half million photo-gravure posters of landscape and townscape which the Travel Association is circulating abroad observe a decent textual reticence. Slogan and salesmanship are snubbed. There is a uniform, one-word caption: BRITAIN. It has been left to the views themselves to beckon prospective tourists. This they do consummately.

Whatever Britain offers of beauty by loch and lea, meadow and minster, is epitomised in these 50 pictures by expert photographers. Blossom hangs its pattern against Tudor half-timber. Spires rise against cloud dapplings amid immemorial timber. Mist softens the perspective of Oxford High. Ladders of sunlight lean in the Pantiles. And inevitably, Beefeaters parade ruff and halberd against the hoar stone of the Tower.

Are these things enough to draw the dollar? Does not the tourist from abroad yearn as well for the plenties and pleasures of ancient times? Most important question of all: Will not the tourist be scared away from Britain by the fuel crisis and its likely aftermaths? On this last issue the organisers of British "tourism" are unperturbed. The Travel Association even qualifies its original estimate as a cautious and conservative one. It still expects that 250,000 tourists and business visitors from abroad will be over here during 1947.

There are ships and passenger planes for approximately that number. If there were twice the travel accommodation there would be anything up to twice the visitors, it considers.

£100 a Head

The Government's newly-founded Tourist and Holidays Board in no way dissents from the Travel Association estimate. Of the year's 250,000 visitors the Board hopes that 150,000, including 60,000 from the United States, will be on holiday here during the 20-week season beginning at the end of April. The average length of stay, taking into account short visits by people from France and the Low Countries, will probably be two to three weeks; average spending £100 a head, giving a total of £15,000,000 in foreign exchange. Our consulates and other agencies abroad have, of course, warned inquirers that they must, before sailing or flying, book return passage and make certain of hotel reservation or private hospitality on this side.

For months the Travel Association has been receiving 600 to 1,000 letters weekly from people abroad who contemplate holidaying in Britain sooner or later. There has been no falling off, since the fuel crisis began.

Looking over the Association's correspondence file—yesterday I gathered that swarms of demobilised U.S. soldiers and those of many other United Nations are bent on renewing friendships made while they were training in British camps or serving on British airfields. Far from deterring them, our post-war asceticism is likely to rank as a further attraction.

Happy Memories

They want once more sympathetically to admire us in the act and art of taking it. "During the war I lived for almost two and a half years in London, and I'm afraid that now I shall always be homesick on both sides of the Atlantic." So writes a nostalgic ex-infantryman from Washington. "I shall be very happy to return in your beautiful country. I keep of it a very good remember" is the artless compliment of a demobilised N.C.O. back in his home village on the Loire.

A boy in Battle Creek, Michigan, is still under the spell of the London Underground: how quickly one could get around! A New Zealander who has lived in 27 countries sees in England something no other country has got: not surprising she is always spoken of on the other side of the world as Home, or Mother Country. There is a note on pink paper from a youth in Paris. In 1941, then 17, he escaped from France in a little boat with four schoolmates, joined the Free French Forces, fought his way home from Bir Hakeim, through Italy and southern France. His dearest wish now is to sniff once more the air of London streets and see the green of English fields. There are letters from Holland, Belgium, Czechoslovakia, Canada, South Africa, Australia, all burning with an admiration which is none the less eloquent for being naively expressed in some cases.

Is tourist the right word for such people? Better call them friends. The dollar account is incidental.

Edinburgh Evening News 1947

Tourist Board Thinks in Millions

(By a "News" Reporter)

The worth of the tourist traffic to Scotland is no longer being calculated in mere thousands. Facts and figures now being analysed by the Scottish Tourist Board show, beyond a doubt, that a fully developed tourist programme can bring millions of pounds to the Scottish till.

The results of a detailed examination of the potentialities of tourism are to be announced within a few days by Mr William A. Nicholson, the Board's manager and secretary, who believes that Scotland can draw at least £20,000,000 from tourists annually. The figures will present for the first time a detailed analysis of what specified counties can realise from holidaymakers alone. "But," says Mr Nicholson, "if we are to deal in millions, we must know exactly how much accommodation we have for visitors, and be able to produce facts about any area at short notice."

Bulky Mail

To supply the necessary information when and where it is required, the Board are completing one of their biggest tasks, the compilation of an accommodation register covering every hotel and boarding house in every part of Scotland. Mr Nicholson believes the results will astonish even those who think they know something about our hotel and holiday industry. Working in close co-operation with Ministries and Government departments, the Board have assisted in securing 1060 licences, representing a value of £945,075, for the rehabilitation of hotels, while hoteliers who come to the Board with bedsheet and other problems find the way smoothed to the Board of Trade.

Most of the inquiries reaching the Board's offices in York Place, Edinburgh, come, of course, from prospective customers to the hotels and boarding houses. That side of the mail is a bulky one. In one day recently 1500 replies were sent out answering a diversity of inquiries. Some discussed projected visits by large parties of Scots from overseas; others replied to individual inquiries about rooms, trains, and buses; where to fish "and where can we have food by the roadside?"

Most of the inquiries are inspired by the Board's publications. "Take Note," a pamphlet of the month's events in Scotland, has a circulation of over 20,000, which will be raised to 50,000 when paper supplies permit. Also increasing in popularity is the recently inaugurated "Clan News," designed to unite as many as possible of the 20,000,000 people of Scottish birth or descent overseas. Giving news of men and happenings in Scotland, it goes to many Scottish societies, is quoted by newspapers in the Dominions and elsewhere, and is stimulating hitherto dormant desires to visit the homeland.

The overseas demand for Scottish literature, posters, pamphlets, etc., is phenomenal. Brochures describing particular parts of Scotland in word and picture will eventually have an issue of several million copies each year, while the story of Scotland's tourist campaign will be continued on posters, luggage labels, and calendars, designs for which will be invited from art students and Scottish artists next month.

Edinburgh Film

"Give us more and more films about Scotland" is the message constantly being received from overseas (a Scottish film sent by the Board to New York this year has already been seen by over 100,000 persons), and so the film is reinforcing the appeal of poster and printed word. A camera unit started a few days ago on "Highland Saga," to be produced in colour for world distribution under the auspices of the Board, and an Edinburgh film, it is hoped, will include shots to be made during the Festival period.

And when Mr Thomas Johnston, the Board's chairman, and Mr Nicholson travel to Canada and U.S.A. next month at the invitation of Scottish societies, they will take with them 10,000 pieces of tourist literature and samples of Scottish souvenirs calculated to make an impression on our many friends across the Atlantic.

World Tributes To Festival

Visitors Like Our Hospitality

Congratulatory messages on a magnificent effort are "pouring into" Edinburgh's International Festival Club in George Street.

Edinburgh Evening News 1947

An "Evening News" reporter was told to-day that congratulations to all associated with the Festival and the Club are being delivered personally by delighted visitors and by letter and telephone.

A large number of the congratulatory messages are being received by Lord Provost Sir John Falconer and the Lady Provost, Miss Diana Falconer. Many messages are also going to the City Chambers.

At the Club this afternoon Councillor W. Earsman, Convener of the Catering Committee, said that he and the others responsible for the organisation of the Club were the recipients of an astonishing number of congratulations. The Councillor said that he personally had been overwhelmed with invitations from people from all parts of the world who wished to do something by way of returning the kindness, courtesy, and hospitality being displayed by the citizens of Edinburgh.

Ministry ban on festival revival plans

IN view of the importance of the Malvern Drama Festival in attracting overseas visitors, Malvern Urban Council yesterday decided to press the Ministry of Health to reconsider its refusal to permit extensions to the Festival Theatre costing £25,150.

A letter from the Ministry had suggested postponement of the revival of the Festival (scheduled for August, 1948) and added that over-riding priority given by the Government to fuel and power and other services had caused a decrease in the department's allocation of steel and other materials.

They could not authorise the use of these materials unless it was for an essential purpose.

The development committee expressed concern at the Ministry's view and also about the fate of the Festival.

Birmingham Gazette 1947

Our Manners

GIOVANNI P—, an English teacher from Rome, has come to this country to visit some friends who used to stay with him before the war. He doesn't think much of our climate, our architecture, or our food. ("It's not the rations, it's the cooks.")

Nevertheless Giovanni would like to settle down here. Why? "Your honesty and your manners. It staggers me. Milk bottles left on the doorsteps and no one helps himself. Then, in the 'bus yesterday, I was sitting by the door when a man gives me fourpence. I looked astonished. He says: ' The conductor is upstairs. From Piccadilly,' and disappears. My neighbour explains : I am to give it to the conductor. At home, everybody is glad if he gets out of paying. And if the first passenger happened to be an Englishman and gave someone else the fare, that one would pocket it.

"And then evening papers. You put a penny down even when no one is looking. The newspaper man said he doesn't lose a penny a night. And now, with your new Social Security system, you even take a pensioner's word for it when he says he doesn't earn more than a pound and therefore qualifies for the full pension.

"But," he concludes, "I'd rather have more sun."

Leader 1948

The Potala — official residence of the Dalai Lama at Lhasa. Nine hundred feet long, the Potala is a fortress palace of white and crimson, with golden domes higher than St. Paul's.

(Heinemann)

IN SECRET TIBET

NO student of the Occult can seriously believe in the inherent inferiority of women. Three of the most gifted and dynamic personalities in the history of modern esotericism have been women—women who in force of character and intelligence far outdistanced the common run of mortals of both sexes. I refer to Helena Petrovna Blavatsky, Annie Besant and Louise Marie Alexandra David-Neel.

Of these three the last-named is, happily, still with us. A year ago I had the privilege of meeting her, and her adopted son, the Tulku Lama Yongden, in Paris, whence they had returned after an absence of ten years in Tibet, China and Mongolia.

To thousands of readers all over the world Madame David-Neel is celebrated as the author of " With Mystics and Magicians in Tibet " and " My Journey to Lhasa " in which she relates, among other things, the story of her epic journey from Yunnan, in China, to the Holy City of Lhasa, disguised as a Tibetan mendicant.

Since 1890, when she made her first journey to the East, Madame David-Neel has spent the greater part of her life in the remote places of the earth. She has studied under Zen Masters in Japan, journeyed all over China and Mongolia, and Tibet, crossed the Gobi and Sahara deserts, visited Africa, India, Russia and Europe.

HER physical powers of endurance might well shame the strongest man. On one occasion while crossing the 19,000-ft. Deo Pass into Tibet she tramped, heavily loaded, for nineteen hours, knee-deep in snow without stopping for refreshments of any kind.

But it is her explorations across the little-known and dangerous frontiers of the mind that will perhaps most interest readers of PREDICTION.

Madame David-Neel is a trained Occultist, a mystic whose knowledge has come from thirty years close association with what is perhaps the world's last stronghold of the true esoteric tradition—Tibet.

Sooner or later all travellers on the narrow path of awareness turn their steps, literally or in spirit, towards the towering peaks of the Himalayas.

Alexandra David-Neel in the dress of a Tibetan hermit.

Prediction
1948

ENSA tour of the Middle East, 1947: taking a break by the Pyramids.

THE WAY I SEE IT . . . BY
Monica Dickens

The British Tourist was a menace

BEFORE the war, the British abroad fell into two types. One was the loud, insular tripper, who was going to have none of your foreign ways, darn you, and "you'll have to shout at the man, my dear. All foreigners are deaf."

They strode through the Continent in their tweeds and brogues, wearing plus-fours in Venice and garden party frocks in mountain huts, demanding eggs and bacon for breakfast, sight-seeing loudly in churches during a service, prodding beggars with shooting sticks to see whether they were real, or just put there for local colour, fretting for the post that brought the English papers.

Their progress was marked by a trail of empty mineral water bottles, for they *knew* that no water was drinkable, *anywhere* except in England.

Going native

THE other type of traveller was the sort that used to hurl itself full tilt into local colour. 'Going native,' they called it. It involved wearing long peasant skirts and raffia hats, sandals, leather shorts, striped jerseys, and growing a beard if male. Their accent was more Italian than the Italian and more French than the French. They trilled "*Bel-l-l-iss-ssimo*," and gargled on 'r' sounds that should have been mute.

In waterfront cafés, they stuffed themselves with native offal-fish, unripe local fruit and raw and fiery wine, and often ended their quest for local colour in hospital with food poisoning.

The British abroad. You could spot either type a mile off. But that seems to have changed now. I suppose it's the result of a world war and throwing in our lot with foreign allies that has made us so much less insular. You'll notice, if you blew your thirty-five pounds abroad this year, that British travellers seem to have learned that the best way to enjoy another country is to 'do as Rome does,' no more, no less.

After the years of being confined to English hotels and boarding houses, the mere fact of going abroad is excitement enough. One is prepared to enjoy everything, to accept the most unsettling native customs as a welcome change.

No one wants to see the English papers. The respite from the morning's dollop of bad news is one of the best parts of the holiday. No one shouts for bacon and eggs—our stomachs have long ago forgotten about them, and who, from England, could ask better than white rolls and butter and coffee with lashings of milk.

Woman's Own 1948

Everything from air lines to golf courses

By ERIC BENNETT

PAIGNTON (Devon), Saturday.

BIG business men are starting to invest their resources in the hotel business, which, they believe, may make a fortune for them after the war.

A group of Midland industrialists have already sunk more than £100,000 in property investments in Paignton which they are determined to develop as one of Britain's foremost holiday resorts.

Only a few hours ago one syndicate of these Birmingham business men completed a deal for the Palace Hotel at a price of £33,000. The Palace Hotel has 70 bedrooms and stands in its own grounds. Members of the same syndicate already own the other leading hotel—the Redcliffe, which has more than 70 bedrooms.

I understand that the price this group paid for the Redcliffe, which was erected and equipped at a cost of £75,000 in 1932, was £45,000.

Other properties controlled by the same group are the Grosvenor Hotel (25 bedrooms) and the Café de Paris Restaurant. The ownership of these prominent hotel properties gives the Birmingham group a controlling interest in Paignton as a holiday and entertainment resort.

'Run everything'

Further properties for public entertainment purposes may be acquired shortly.

Mr. G. Roland Dawes, chartered accountant and director of Neville Industrial Securities, Ltd., Birmingham, who, together with Mr. S. G. Morgan, of the Concentric Manufacturing Co., Aston, leads the syndicate, assured me today that his associates are prepared to spend £500,000 on developing their properties here.

They are prepared to run everything from airlines to golf courses, from pleasure steamers to private hotel crèches for children on the Paignton sands.

Birmingham Gazette 1947

A CULTURAL TRIUMPH

EDINBURGH FESTIVAL

From Our Scottish Correspondent

The International Festival inaugurated in Edinburgh last Sunday with a magnificent service of praise and dedication at St. Giles' Cathedral is an event the repercussions of which may well have a decisive influence on Scotland for many years to come.

There has been no lack of those willing to belittle the festival's significance and purpose; there are the alleged nationalists who claim that Scotland's arts are insufficiently represented; others who see in the whole stupendous undertaking a shopkeepers' ramp. But what criticism there has been is quite swallowed up in the growing enthusiasm which has attended the gradual understanding of what this festival is going to mean.

It is emphatically an international festival. In the streets, in the hotels and hostels of Edinburgh large numbers of foreigners and gathered. They bring with them, whether amateur or professional, listener or executant, something that, for the time being, puts politics in their place and causes the grosser features of nationalism to disappear. There is in Edinburgh these days a high sense of beauty, in the streets and gardens, in the splendid, towering Castle Rock, in the Usher Hall, in the theatres and picture galleries. Nothing could be more inspiriting, and to those engaged in education, formal or informal, it is a moving experience.

In terms of adult education the festival is a revelation of what man can do for himself in the cultivation of those aspects of human life where the reward is without price and devoid of all sordidness. We in Scotland have tended in the past to think rather too much in terms of the relationships of education to economics, to career making, to the ultimate utility of the educational process in whatever form it may take. But here, for a short three weeks, is the spectacle of men and women supremely devoted to their art, seeking only to give of their best and to interpret in all its fullness the genius that resides in great literature, music, drama, and painting.

The release from the ordinary, compelling preoccupations of the daily round is immense. Not only Edinburgh but all Scotland shares in the sense that this is an experience which will percolate to the schools and colleges in the days to come. The progenitors of this great enterprise will have built greater than they knew and, for once in a way, our thoughts as educationists are removed from those grimmer aspects of the scene among which life normally demands that we dwell.

Times Educational Supplement **1947**

" Oh, look, here come Mrs. Gibson's skis, empty again."

Woman's Journal **1947**

Well Held, Ma'am!

"With her right wrist supported by a sling, Mrs. Churchill caught the Golden Arrow at Victoria to-day."

Picture caption in evening paper.

Punch **1949**

SATURDAY SHOPPING IN GLASGOW

An interesting reversal of the trend towards idle week-ends has been noted in Glasgow, where some of the Glasgow dealers are now opening all day Saturday. For some time managements have been inclined to the viewpoint that mid-day closing on Saturday did not influence sales, while it was obviously completely successful from the viewpoint of assistants. They received the longer week-end with evident satisfaction.

Among the firms now announcing all-day opening is Paterson, Sons & Co., Ltd., of Buchanan Street, Glasgow. This very well-known house adopted the policy from October 1st, and anticipates that its adoption will prove of value to the many out-of-town visitors who find Saturday afternoon the most suitable.

Pianomaker **1949**

CHRISTMAS & NEW YEAR HOLIDAYS

Our Christmas and New Year Parties have always been good fun and many of us have pleasant memories of Cranleigh, Dockenfield, Hillside and Barfield. This year there will be two parties—one at **GAVESTON HALL, NUTHURST, NEAR HORSHAM, SUSSEX,** where we had a very successful party last Easter. This party will be from **December 24th to January 3rd**; the other party will be at **GT. BALLARDS, CORDWALLIS, CAMBERLEY, SURREY,** from **December 23rd to December 28th** (or longer). Both are comfortable Boarding Schools I have rented for the occasion.

My Christmas parties are always run in a very informal way. Accommodation will be partly in single and double rooms and partly in larger rooms. There are more single and double rooms at Gt. Ballards than at Gaveston Hall. We usually do ourselves very well at Christmas—our turkeys are growing up near Ipswich and friends from all over the world are sending parcels with raisins, nuts and dates for our Christmas puddings! We will have the usual Christmas festivities, dancing, games, a drink at a country inn. People who come on my Christmas parties like to contribute in one way or the other to their success—someone produces a bottle of port, others decorate the rooms and the Christmas tree or arrange games.

There will be staff to look after the domestic side of the parties; we will see to it that the house is warm and that there is plenty of hot water and good food, but I am not proposing to run these parties in the manner of luxury hotels. You will find good company and a friendly atmosphere but no porters, waiters or chamber-maids! As usual, I shall try and put together in each party people who have something in common and are likely to enjoy each other's company. When you book for one or the other party, please state your preference—Gaveston Hall or Gt. Ballards—but let me suggest to you which party I think you would most enjoy. If possible, try and come along to talk this over.

There will be a special *New Year Party at Gaveston Hall* and we shall make a week-end of it (December 30th to January 3rd or shorter stays).

Deposit : **£1.0.0.** Please send this when booking and deduct it when paying the balance 10 days before the holiday starts. Deposits are not returnable in case of cancellation.

CHRISTMAS				NEW YEAR			
Cost : 11 days	—	……	…… £9.0.0	4 days	……	……	…… £4.0.0
7 days	—	……	…… £6.10.0	3 days	……	……	…… £3.3.0
6 days	—	……	…… £6.0.0	New Year's Eve and Night			£1.5.0
5 days	—	……	…… £5.5.0				
4 days	—	……	…… £4.15.0				

(Shorter stays if room available : £1.5.0 per day.)

Erna Low Christmas Arrangements **1948**

HEALTH, SANITATION, AND FIRST AID

LATRINES

Change of air, food or water tends to affect most people adversely at first. Camp constipation is a very common result, and a very real trouble. It is, however, most often caused by nervousness or bashfulness in the face of new and unexpected conditions. The first essential, therefore, is to provide *complete privacy* in latrines. They should also have an unobtrusive approach since many campers hesitate to be seen going to the latrine. Proper siting is of real importance.

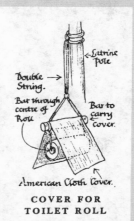

COVER FOR TOILET ROLL

Organised Camping, **Ministry of Education 1948**

The head chef at Skegness shares a joke with the ladies, c. 1948.

SHOPHOUND'S HIGHLAND FLING

EDITOR'S NOTE: *Scotland is much in the news, with the Edinburgh Festival, the Scottish Industries Exhibition at Glasgow, and many holidaymakers. Shophound, who has been visiting her native heath, tells readers about her finds.*

EDINBURGH

SHOPHOUND started her Scottish survey with Edinburgh. Good hotels—you will need to book as far ahead as possible—are the Caledonian, North British, Royal British, Royal Hotel, and the Roxburghe in Charlotte Square (very County). A little way out of Edinburgh you will find good food and good service and charming surroundings at Grey Walls at Gullane, the Open Arms, Dirleton (20 miles from Edinburgh), and the Marine Hotel at North Berwick. Attached to the Marine is St. Anns Children's Hotel, where children can stay with governess or nannie or in the charge of the hotel's fully trained staff.

Edinburgh abounds in tea rooms, but best known of them all is Macvittie's at the west end of Princes Street. For lunch or drinks try L'Apéritif, a gay little place in Frederick Street, either at the snack bar or in the adjoining dining-room or at one of the tête-à-tête alcove tables in the corridor. The food is good and not too expensive. Hound enjoyed a delectable dry sherry, noodle soup, grilled sea trout, raspberries and cream, and coffee for 10s. 6d. L'Apéritif is open till 11 p.m.

Another good place is the Beehive Inn in the Grassmarket locality, and its old Edinburgh atmosphere (the old execution place can be seen from its windows) makes it a good starting point for a raid on the famous antique shops. The Beehive is well patronized by visiting stage stars, and Hound has pleasant memories of its dry Martinis.

For a pleasant dinner in elegant surroundings go to the Albyn in Queen Street where you will find good food, good wines and excellent service. On your way in, stop and admire the crystal chandelier and its vista of twinkling reflections in the mirrors.

Another good place of the same type is Ricky's, Fountainbridge; and if you want oysters there is Harry's Oyster Bar, 85 Leith Street, décor by Basil Spence. Sea food is also the speciality of Crammond Inn—a little farther afield, overlooking the Forth and the Almond rivers—with its rope floor and barrel seats.

Dine and dance at the De Guise Restaurant, an important part of the Caledonian Hotel, which is good but expensive; or, if you like Bohemian company, Hound suggests the Café Royal in West Register Street, once the haunt of the Ettrick Shepherd.

Jenners of Princes Street is a household name in Scotland. Wandering round its well-planned departments, Hound saw innumerable temptations. The hats were a happily chosen collection, the costume jewellery slap up to date—scatterpins, pearl ropes and all—and the number of jerseys and cardigans quite fantastic to wool-starved eyes. Of special interest to overseas visitors is their own special shop in Jenners. Anything bought here and sent direct to ship, plane or overseas address is free of purchase tax. We, too, can send these things to friends abroad with a limit of £5 value.

VOGUE'S EYE VIEW
of BEACH IDEAS

There's a sense of fun in beach fashion . . . the ideas that prompt it have a sea-salt tang of wit; the casual is conjured into the unexpected, the familiar takes on a new and charming freshness . . . Left: This month's cover transforms a fisherman's creel (by G. W. Scott at Harvey Nichols) into a picnic basket, or perhaps a carrier for bathing suits. Shoes of buttermilk leather, by Brevitt at Pinet, are sandal-cool and slipper-soft; unblocked for summer comfort, flatheeled for easy walking over cobbles, pebbles, or sweeps of sand . . . The make-up is Leichner's Island Tan. Below: Inspiration from another source . . . middy blouse precisely as worn by Mary Martin in New York's successful musical, *South Pacific.* Made of blue denim, it has a pullover neck, no buttons, no placket; find it, and the shorts too, at Marshall & Snelgrove

NORMAN PARKINSON

Vogue 1949

RAWLINGS

*Perthshire
Advertiser
1950*

As a souvenir of her visit to Perth on Thursday, Greer Garson, the film actress, accepted a MacGregor tartan rug from Miss G. M'Hardy, secretary of the Scottish Shorthorn Breeders' Association. Mr Frank Harding, Chicago, looks on.

★BRITAIN'S latest limousine weighing two tons, left Dover the other day on a 1,300-mile drive to the airport at Belgrade. Today week, Coventry's mayor, Councillor Harry Weston, will arrive at the airport by air and then drive to the City headquarters. There the car, the exact replica of a Humber 27 h.p. Pullman, built recently for the Mayor of Coventry will be handed over to Belgrade's mayor. Belgrade is sending 9,000 tons of timber to build a new theatre and Coventry is sending the car in return.

Car and Car Topics 1952

"See Europe from an armchair" with MOTORWAYS

When we say "See Europe from an Armchair" we really mean it. All you do is to put yourself in our hands, our experts do the rest. From the time you leave London until you return, you travel solely by Motor Pullman. In a series of leisurely tours we unfold before you the magic carpet of Europe, with all its beauty, history and legends. Each night in a hand picked hotel where good food and choice wines are set before you in pre-war abundance. An experienced Courier is always at your disposal to smooth any problem that may arise.

We are operating a new fleet of British Motor Pullmans (21 individual armchair seaters). Inclusive tours visiting France, Switzerland, Germany, Belgium, Scandinavia, Italy, Austria and Spain.

Apply for beautifully illustrated Brochure (ready Dec.) and agency terms.

MOTORWAYS
(OVERSEAS) LTD.
71 Knightsbridge, London, S.W.1
Telephone : SLO. 7123 6

Travel Topics 1950

Star's Ten Crowded Hours

Film star Greer Garson made a crowded 10-hour visit to Perthshire on Thursday to inspect the eight white Shorthorns which were purchased for her at Tuesday's sale in Perth.

The star completed her studio work in London on Wednesday night, and caught the late night Scottish train with only minutes to spare. She arrived in Perth at 10 a.m., and motored to Crieff after breakfasting in the Station Hotel. At Crieff, Miss Garson visited Millhills Farm, where her seven heifers and one bull are being quartered until transport arrangements have been made.

At 4 p.m., the actress returned to Perth and was cheered into the City Chambers by several hundred housewives and a sprinkling of men, who had waited in the high winds for more than an hour despite the counter attraction in the nearby City Hall, where Sir Stafford Cripps was speaking.

Miss Garson was met at the Chambers by Lord Provost J. Ure Primrose, who had invited her to visit Perth after hearing of her purchases. After signing the visitors' book, Miss Garson told a "P.A." reporter that she was delighted with her purchases, and hoped that they would stand the trans-Atlantic journey. "I would have attended the sales myself," she said, "but I only finished filming last night. The film is 'The Miniver Story,' and it has been a very pleasant piece of Anglo-American co-operation." She added that she thought a White Shorthorn herd would "look lovely" against the red background of her New Mexico ranch.

After being shown several prints of photographs taken by a "P.A." photographer earlier in the day, the star jokingly commened: "I never looked lovelier; wait till Walter Pidgeon sees them."

At 8.15 p.m.—just over ten hours after her arrival—Miss Garson was London-bound again in the Perth-Euston train.

the lizard...

She loves the sun—and *how* she loves it. So do lots of
girls—but they'd be well advised to do their sunbathing
a little farther from the water, and to keep down the length of
each full-scale sunbath to ten minutes at first. *This* lizard's lucky;
she has three weeks' holiday—and she
managed, in the first two weeks, to acquire a gradual, even
tan. She's still wearing a protective cream, though, and every night
she uses skinfood to prevent dryness.
That two-piece swim-suit looks fine on her long,
slim figure—but it's not for the girl who's dumpy or curvy.
A pert little flared-skirt suit is the one for her.
Our lizard would be wiser, though, to
wear sun-glasses—she's bound to start screwing up her eyes as
soon as she opens them—and that's the quickest way to acquire tiny
wrinkles. But perhaps she never *does* open her eyes!
Now that *would* be a pity. No use having a film-star
figure if you don't wake up and sparkle sometimes!

Woman
1950

AIR-TRAVEL LUGGAGE, by Clarke's, in Tygan woven plastic with poly-
styrene hangers and duralumin folding-frames: Tygan designed by
Margaret Leischner; lining by Enid Marx; fittings by John Waterer

Design in the Festival
1951

The shipbuilding pavilion at the
Festival of Britain, 1951.

ORCHESTRAL CONCERTS

New Era Concert Society

LONDON SYMPHONY ORCHESTRA

Royal Festival Hall...............................15, 29 May

    Conductors...............RICHARD AUSTIN
                           CONSTANT LAMBERT

Royal Philharmonic Society

ROYAL PHILHARMONIC ORCHESTRA

Royal Albert Hall...........11, 16, 21, 27 May, 4, 17 June

    Conductors...............SIR THOMAS BEECHAM, BT.
                           LEOPOLD STOKOWSKI

Henry Wood Concert Society

LONDON SYMPHONY ORCHESTRA

Royal Albert Hall...............................28 May

    Conductor...............SIR MALCOLM SARGENT

PHILHARMONIA ORCHESTRA

Royal Festival Hall...............................25, 28 June

    Conductor...............To be announced

FOR LEAFLET GIVING PROGRAMME DETAILS OF ALL ORCHESTRAL
CONCERTS ANNOUNCED IN THIS FOLDER SEE BACK PAGE UNDER
"INQUIRIES AND BOOKINGS".

Celebrated orchestras from outside London are preparing
festival programmes for the London Season and include:

BOURNEMOUTH MUNICIPAL ORCHESTRA

Royal Festival Hall...............................26, 27 June

    Conductor...............RUDOLF SCHWARZ

CITY OF BIRMINGHAM SYMPHONY ORCHESTRA

Royal Festival Hall...............................20, 21 June

    Conductor...............GEORGE WELDON

Festival of Britain programme 1951

Abram Games's design for the Festival of Britain logo, 1951.

THE WEATHER CLERKS

By PAUL JENNINGS

IN these days, more and more pleasant little places in the Home Counties are being chosen as sites for terrible scientific establishments, so that their cosy pubs resemble the opening of a British spy film, with high-domed geniuses eyed uneasily by local rustics. It was therefore pleasant to read, this week, a Central Office of Information booklet* mainly about Dunstable. For this little town, with its tea-rooms and its sober, gentlemen-farmers' hotels, a Green Line terminus and turning-off place for Whipsnade Zoo, also houses scientists; but they are engaged in the vast, airy, rambling and entirely beneficial occupation of weather prediction. Dunstable, in fact, is the home of the Central Forecasting Office.

Sea-Clouds

It seems an eminently suitable place for them. Every time I have been through Dunstable it has been an extraordinarily weathery day, with enormous ragged-edged clouds lumbering up from Northamptonshire, and appalling black thunderstorms that look as if they reach up to Scotland but suddenly give way to sunshine, the kind of weather that makes you remember that we are on an island, covered by surprised sea-clouds not yet used to a stable land mass.

Dunstable is at the middle of our weather; and although the booklet tells us it is one corner of an international information system (the other three being Paris, Rome and, surprisingly, Moscow) we are not surprised to learn that most of our weather comes from the west (always, excepting, of course, the Cold Air from Siberia).

When, on some fairly calm night, we listen, with mild surprise, to the B.B.C. (who, of course, get it from

* Called, rather paternally, Your Weather Service (H.M. Stationery Office, Kingsway, W.C.2, 1s. 3d. post free).

Dunstable) telling us of gale warnings in Areas Bailey and Rockall, it appeals to our seafaring, Atlantic instinct. We scent the wild rain and the dark seas, even as we sit in our warm, lighted rooms. We have no idea where Bailey and Rockall are, but they sound magnificently bleak, and we picture to ourselves lonely black cliffs and screaming gulls.

Balloons

The booklet gives plenty of technical information, but it doesn't answer my own, doubtless, rather naïve, difficulty, which is this: if a depression is an area with low pressure in the middle, why doesn't all the air rush inwards from the outside, where it's high pressure, and equalise things? And vice versa with an anti-cyclone, which is the other way round? In the booklet it just says that the winds blow counter-clockwise round a depression.

Nevertheless, there is nothing intimidating about these scientists. (It is significant that the only harmless scientific figure in folklore is the Weather Clerk. One can fear medicine men, witches and sorcerers, but not a Clerk whom one imagines, for some reason, as wearing a top hat.) For one thing, they are always sending up balloons. When the balloon bursts the radio equipment comes down by parachute, with labels offering a reward for return; and it is astonishing to hear that they get most of them back. I've never had a transmitter drop in my garden. This is evidently the kind of thing that only happens to Other People, like being Gallup Polled.

Although there is much talk of aircraft, one has the feeling that somehow these weather men are concerned with a simpler, innocent, agricultural community, for the booklet is always talking about

"farmers, sailors and fishermen." The whole thing is reminiscent of anthropologists like Le Play, who is quoted by Christopher Dawson as saying, in Les Ouvriers Européens, that " these fundamental types are six in number; first, the hunters and food-gatherers; secondly, the pastoral peoples; thirdly, the fishermen of the sea coasts; fourthly, the agriculturalists; fifthly, the foresters, and sixthly, the miners." It would be pleasant to hear the B.B.C. say, " Here is a wet weather warning for hunters and food-gatherers."

Yet they are intensely concerned with our everyday life, too. It is comforting to an Englishman, beginning to doubt his hardihood, to be told that after all " Cambridge is a distinctly colder place in winter than Lerwick in the Shetlands." And, now we have the curious information that " the driest known place is Great Wakering, near Shoeburyness." we may expect all the campers in England to descend on the Thames Estuary.

Village Forecast

It is even more splendid and surprising to learn that the services of this giant organisation are available to anyone. " A forecast for a village fête is as much a technical problem for the forecasters," it says, " as one for a Royal progress through London." All you have to do is send a prepaid telegram. I should love to see a typical reply: DEPRESSION OVER LITTLE BUMPING STOP COLD AIR FROM SWINTON SPREADING WEST STOP SHOWERS FINE INTERVALS CHURCH FIELD STOP

And what could be more human than the admission that their sources of information at Dunstable include not only aircraft and weather ships in the Atlantic but also " a village postmistress in the Pennines " ?

Observer
1951

Hove in danger from gay Brighton

HOVE, with its location as a seaside town near Brighton, has to think especially of protection work. Miss Joyce D. Whatton told members of Hove Deanery branch of the Chichester Moral Welfare Association. " Lots of people come for gaiety, to relax, to make money, not always in the right way.

The irresponsible come to get away from people they know, people who expect them to observe certain standards," she said. Youngsters came to hotels and guest houses, knowing nobody, having quite a lot of time on their hands. Foreign students living in London were attracted to the coast. Loneliness and the longing for something intimate

like home life led people into danger.

Miss B. F. Friend, treasurer, reported a large drop in subscriptions. " We had support for a long time from a number of elderly people, but they are gradually dying. Now we are very much down and just struggling along. In fact we have a small overdraft." she said.

Brighton Evening Argus 1952

MUSIC IN SIENA
by F♯

"SIENA remains the most perfectly mediaeval of all the larger cities of Tuscany. Its narrow streets, its spacious Gothic palaces and churches, the three hills upon which it rises enthroned, with the curiously picturesque valleys between them, are still enclosed in frowning walls of the fourteenth century." That is how Edmund G. Gardner began *The Story of Siena* in Dent's Mediaeval Town Series.

Because my companions had not seen this perfect mediaeval city we were motoring from Bagni di Lucca on what turned out to be the wrong road, very rough and dusty (by Empoli when it should have been the Florence highway), to spend the night of Sunday, April 22nd, 1951, at a *pensione* which, about fifty years ago, was the haunt of nice English families. There they could lodge for 5 to 6 lire a day a head, all found. This would be a little less than twopence now. The drive had been disappointing altogether, for the heavenly Tuscan landscape was almost colourless under a shrouded sky. But we were not expecting real Italian Spring weather. We had not had it for two months; the sun could not be trusted for a single day. So long as it did not rain . . .

Gramophone 1951

ODDLY ENOUGH
By PAUL JENNINGS

AN entertaining marginal feature of the Festival Gardens at Battersea is the uneasy alliance between the official designers, erecting their gay and tasteful pavilions and their fantastical cane and wire works with light and airy sophistication, and the Showmen, emerging in the spring from winter quarters on obscure grounds in the Midlands.

It is easy to imagine the official eyebrows raised at the Showmen's headboards, with vivid paintings of the Italian lakes and lions and female cyclists, at the steam organs with their lay figures in three-cornered hats, stiffly clashing cymbals and beating drums. And it is easy to imagine the Showmen's bewilderment, for they are already seriously compassed about by such menaces to traditional, unplanned fun as the Town and Country Planning Act. One Showman, arriving at Battersea this year and studying the plan, which is full of elegant words like "piazza" and "colonnade," is known to have asked for Mr. Piazza.

✻

NOT that all Showmen are of Italian extraction, like Mr. Punch. Far from it. They have a paper, called *The World's Fair*, which is published in Oldham. It is full of serious accounts of meetings of the Showmen's Guild, held in various Great Eastern and Railway Hotels. In one way, to read *The World's Fair* is to feel again the disillusionment of the adult, that began the first time one became conscious, in the light of common day, of that sad area on the fringe of the magic fair, among the mud and clinkers and guy ropes behind the Wall of Death, overlooked by the sad evening windows of the nearest houses, where one realised, for the first time, that it is ordinary men, with ordinary

Observer 1951

wives and wirelesses in their caravans, who make fairs. It is the last straw to find *they* have a union, too.

✻

AND yet, and yet. As one reads on in this fascinating paper, one becomes more and more aware that the Showmen do have contact with some mysterious, magic world completely beyond the control of the State machine. They range the country, visiting fairs with queer, archaic, George Borrowish names like Kirkheaton Rant; Greasborough Feast, Lumphinnans Games, Tilsley Wakes. Rationing does not worry them, for, says one advertisement, they may buy "an entirely new American novelty machine for producing REAL FLUFFY SNOWBALLS ENROBED IN RICH FRUIT SYRUPS," or a "CHOC ENROBER (3,000-4,000) chocs an hour. Perfect. Seen working)."

The World's Fair contains many advertisements inserted by fabuloussounding warehouses at Leeds and other serious towns, crammed with such items as Fur Monkeys, Edible Spanish Cigarettes, Lot of 10,000 Shubunkins, 100,000 Land Tortoises, Stink Bombs, Rock, Joke Beetles, Plate Lifters, Wobbly Joke Pencils, Dribbling Scent Bottles, Blowouts with Voice. The reader is offered "Knock Men's Hat Off or Kelly's Wedding (10 Figures, universal motor)" or 1 Rhinoceros; or "1 Octopus, complete with gate and paybox" (it seems curious, this zoo-size paybox and all the rest of it, just for one Octopus. It costs £2,000, which seems odd. It also has "centre fitted with pneumatics;", which seems odder still. However); or "A Limited Number of Reconditioned Mechanical Elephants."

More or less strenuous amusements at Battersea.

The Festival of Britain 1951

Few complaints but much praise from tourists

By A Sunday Times Correspondent

AS 750,000 visitors from abroad are expected in Britain this year, and it is estimated that they will spend about £120 million, including their passage money in British liners, it is important to know what tourists think of us. The Travel and Holidays Association has an excellent system for finding out. Questionnaires are given to visitors asking such questions as "Will you come back soon?" and "Did you find anything less expensive than you expected?"

These are returned in considerable quantities. In addition a prepaid card asking for general comments is also handed out. It comes back in great numbers.

It might be expected that complaints would outweigh compliments. They do not. Compliments become almost fulsomely monotonous after an hour with the cards. Complaints are much more interesting.

Take food. A Swede scrawled in large letters over one card "Much more food wanted," but an American wrote "You are too generous with food, give tourists less and your own people more."

Taking it from a different angle, a Frenchman wrote "The price of beer should be reduced, the price of tea should be increased, and boiled cabbage should not be served in restaurants." An American wanted all restaurants "placed under French or Italian management, cheapen all liquor, abolish licensing hours, and make bad coffee a capital offence."

Railways criticised

Everybody — Italians, Armenians, French, American, Dutch, Norwegian and Spanish—wanted something done about our liquor laws. It was left to a Dutchman to utter the final comment from the heart, "We loved England. Food is not the only thing in life."

The railways come in for their usual criticism. The opinion of the Continent on Harwich Station, its dirt, its inconvenience, its porters, matches the Continent's opinion of the trains from Harwich to London.

Visitors find our officials mostly courteous and kind, but official delays, especially with Customs and Immigration, are regarded as abominable. They regret that everybody speaks only English at points where foreigners are in greatest numbers; and, though they find our police wonderful, there is just a suspicion of doubt creeping in. One tourist said that all members of the Metropolitan Police should carry street guides because "some young constables do not know the way!"

A lot of foreigners want our traffic shifted to the right. The motorists among them want our cyclists to ride in single file, and our towns to be better signposted and routes out of London more clearly marked. Saddest of all, they want the hedges on our Devon roads cut down because they make it "impossible to see the view."

Picture hung too high

They want matters of extraordinary detail also. One woman wanted her favourite Fragonard at the Wallace Collection changed back to a remembered position because it is now "too high."

And there are a remarkable number of wails about the impossibility of buying stamps anywhere except at post offices coupled with the relative invisibility of post offices. Taxi drivers are (a) rude, (b) courteous, (c) never have change, and (d) rook foreigners in the small hours.

It would not be seemly to give the nationality of the man who said he enjoyed his visit, "but I wish you would get some nicer-looking hostesses."

From all of which it is clear that foreigners are remarkably like us.

Sunday Times 1952

THE FULL-WIDTH FRONT is accepted without compromise in this touring coach by Windovers Ltd on an AEC chassis

---

Holiday week ends in gales and downpour

GALES, torrential rain, storm-swept beaches and temperatures well below normal—that was the tale of yesterday's dismal end to a raincoat-and-umbrella August Bank Holiday week.

From North to South and from East to West came reports of storms, drenched and chilled crowds, pounded beaches and cancellation of regattas and other outdoor events.

Lifeboats were called out at Margate, Southend, Bembridge, and Yarmouth (Isle of Wight) and Bridlington, Yorkshire.

48 hours on sandbank

The Margate lifeboat towed into Whitstable the barge-yacht Spurgeon, in which four men and three women had been stranded on a sandbank without sleep for 48 hours. The owner, Mr. A. N. Booker, of Holland Park Avenue, London, W., with his wife and friends, had set out on Thursday to return to Queenborough from Brightlingsea.

Eight yachts taking part in the race from Brixham, Devon, to Santander, Spain, had to turn back because of the weather. This 400-mile event is the premier ocean yacht race of the year.

The Portsmouth-Fishbourne (Isle of Wight) car ferry service was suspended, leaving about 80 cars and their occupants at Portsmouth and a similar number on the island. About 70 cars were said to be left at Yarmouth when the last ferry left for Lymington with strong winds blowing and there were about 30 left at Lymington.

The Queen and Duke stay indoors

From Our Own Representative
ABERDEEN, Saturday.

Deeside had one of its wettest summer days in history for the first day of the Royal Family's holiday. It rained heavily from dawn till dusk, and the Royal Standard hung limp from the tower of Balmoral Castle, where the Queen and the Duke of Edinburgh spent the day indoors. During the afternoon Queen Elizabeth the Queen Mother and Princess Margaret motored to Birkhall, where the Queen Mother will take up residence on August 20.

At Allt na Guibhsiach shooting lodge, near Loch Muick, where the Duchess of Kent and her family have arrived on holiday, conditions were just as bad, but the heavy rain did not keep the Duke of Kent, Princess Alexandra and Prince Michael at home. They went shopping in Ballater.

Sunday Times 1952

*Design in the Festival
1951*

holiday fares
NOT
increased

To the country... to the sea... go where you will. It's only 1¾d. a mile by rail—a hundred care-free miles for under 15/-! And when you arrive at your holiday centre there are usually cheap Runabout tickets to help you explore the district for a week to your heart's content. Can't wait till holiday time? Then treat yourself to the many attractive day trips being run now. They are very cheap — and it's so much quicker by rail!

BRITISH RAILWAYS

Daily Express 1952

A Volunteer Agricultural Holiday

My husband and I would like to go on a volunteer agricultural holiday. Can you give us some general information about this?—MRS. K. (Ipswich).

THESE agricultural holidays are great fun and as you are paid for the work you do, out of pocket expenses are very small.

One drawback, as far as you are concerned, is that married quarters cannot be provided. You do not say if you have any children, but youngsters under seventeen cannot be admitted to the camps.

You'll earn 1s. 9d. for each hour worked (2s. if you go in October or November) and the charge for accommodation ranges from 37s. to 42s. weekly, depending on the time of the year you go.

You will be expected to work at least 36–40 hours a week, weather permitting, and you should take old clothes for the job, including stout shoes and an old mackintosh. A hat and a long-sleeved blouse should be taken to keep off the sun.

If you decide to go on one of these holidays, not only will you have a grand time in good company, but you'll be helping your country as well. Write to me, mentioning the part of the country you wish to visit, and I will give you details of where to write.

Woman's World
1952

Daily Express 1952

Trippers are marooned on 'Dipper'

MARGATE was blacked out last night by an electricity failure, and—

Couples were marooned in basket-seats on the Big Wheel in Dreamland amusement park;

Two trainloads of trippers were caught high up on the "Dipper" scenic railway;

The cast of "Show Time" at the Hippodrome took candles on to the stage to carry on.

At a cinema 2,000 people sat in darkness singing "We're going to get lit up when the lights go up in Margate."

It was two hours before they did.

Daily Express 1952

HAVE A GOOD TIME!
says BILLY BUTLIN

JUST a few more days to Whitsun—and the opening of another holiday season. I'm off for a last-minute "look-round" of my six holiday camps—one a day for the whole of next week—to make sure that all is ready for the many thousands of people who have entrusted their comfort and happiness to me.

If you are among them may I bid you welcome in advance and say that I and thousands of loyal staff will do all in our power to make your holiday memorable and enjoyable. If you have made other plans for this year then I wish you the best of weather and —have a good time, anyway!

* *Note — to those still undecided. There are a few vacancies at Butlin's for the next few weeks.*

FREE BROCHURE from:
439, OXFORD STREET, LONDON, W.1

Hoteliers' Hopes Rise As Crowds Flock Into North Norfolk Resorts

CROMER'S Bank Holiday week-end established a post-war record. There were more people in the town than at any time since 1939 and probably before, and few people remember the beaches so packed as they were on August Monday.

What is more, for the first time since the war the weather was right. The three days—Saturday to Monday—produced 30.1 hours of sunshine and temperatures which were comfortable—63 to 69 degrees—but not too high.

On Monday there were cars and buses everywhere. Car parks were full, side and main streets crammed and one had to drive round for some time before a place offered itself for parking. People crowded the town streets and hotels were not only full, but many were turned away. The Advertising Association had a busy time trying to accommodate people who arrived without making reservations and sent one party as far away as Fakenham because no accommodation was available nearer.

Many Turned Away

One hotelier to whom a reporter spoke remarked: "I could have done with an india-rubber hotel this week. I turned no end of people away and although I rang up other hotels to try and get accommodation for them, they were full also. It certainly is the best August holiday I have had since I came to Cromer. If I had had twice the accommodation I could have filled it."

This kind of remark was fairly typical of the hoteliers who were interviewed.

Caterers also had a good week-end and the promise of August is such that Cromer can expect to be full for the remainder of it.

Most of the hotels are fully booked up and are turning away requests and report that things are a great deal better now than they dreamed possible after the disastrous gales and damage of January.

The railways have been busy bringing in thousands of people—period visitors and trippers—and both stations report "heavy traffic." Among these were more from the Midlands than usual.

What has been most noticeable this week is that the true "holiday spirit" has returned. Comenting on this, a hotelier said: "People seem to be saying 'The Coronation is over. Now let's have a real holiday.'"

made it impossible for a running commentary to be given.

Two simple and easy-to-understand rescues were therefore performed. In the first, Michael Pigott was the "drowning man" and the corps instructor, Mr. F. Brindley, performed the rescue. The second had Ian Randall in need of rescue and Sqn.-Ldr. Ray Chance to perform it.

Mr. Chance, whose father lives in Alexandra Road, is studying law in London and was on holiday in Sheringham. He spent a night in a dinghy when his bomber crashed and this experience led to his joining the lifeguards.

North Norfolk News 1955

Summer Holidays in the British Isles 1952

The FIRST POST-WAR BRITISH CRUISE from GREECE to the ISLANDS of the ÆGEAN accompanied by four lecturers

The following classical scholars will conduct the lectures given throughout the Cruise:

F. KINCHIN SMITH, M.A. Oxon:
Head of the Department of Classics, University of London Institute of Education, who will personally direct the Cruise and will be in charge of the lecturing arrangements both on board and at the sites

PROF. A. ANDREWES, M.A. Oxon:
Wykenham Professor of Ancient History, University of Oxford.

PROF. H. D. F. KITTO, M.A. Cantab.:
Professor of Greek, University of Bristol.

W. G. G. FORREST, M.A. Oxon:
Fellow and Lecturer in Ancient History at Wadham College, University of Oxford.

M/S MIAOULIS

The M.S. *Miaoulis* has been chartered for the first post-war British Cruise from Piraeus to the Greek Islands. This vessel was built in Italy in 1952 and is owned by the well-known Nomikos Line of Piraeus, who have a very good reputation for the cuisine and high standard of service on board their ships.

The M.S. *Miaoulis* operates on the normal service between Venice and Piraeus and must be considered a suitable ship for this type of Cruise from Piraeus through the small Greek Islands. The vessel normally carries first, second and tourist class passengers, but on the Cruise she will be a one class vessel and all cruise passengers will have the use of the whole of the ship as far as deck space, lounges, etc., are concerned. Between Venice and Piraeus and return a number of deck class passengers will be carried in the 3rd class portion of the ship, which is separate and self-contained and is not shown on the centre page plan.

There are three Dining Saloons on board, and passengers accommodated in the 6-berth cabins on "B" Deck will feed in Dining Saloon "C"; other passengers will feed in the Dining Saloons "A" and "B" on the Main Deck. There will be one sitting for meals. Except in the case of Dining Saloon "C" individual tables for four to eight persons are provided.

The ship normally carries 217 persons in cabins, but in order to ensure the maximum possible comfort only 163 passengers will be carried on the Cruise from Piraeus which is approximately 75% of the capacity of the ship.

All Public Rooms are Air Conditioned and all Cabins have forced draught system ventilators.

Swan Hellenic Cruises 1954

COMFY COACHES

EXCURSIONS

Sunday, June 5th. — WORTHING & BRIGHTON, 8/-. EASTBOURNE, outward via Brighton and Newhaven, return via Haywards Heath, 10/9.
Monday, June 6th.—WORTHING & BRIGHTON, 8/-.
Tuesday, June 7th.—SOUTHSEA, 7/6. BOURNEMOUTH, 10/9.
Wednesday, June 8th.—WORTHING & BRIGHTON, 8/-. LEE-ON-SOLENT, depart 1.30 p.m., 7/6.
Thursday, June 9th.—BOGNOR & LITTLEHAMPTON, 8/-. Afternoon Excursion to WINDSOR, 4/9.
Friday, June 10th.—WORTHING & BRIGHTON, 8/-. Afternoon Mystery Tour No. 7, 3/-.
Sunday, June 12th.—WORTHING & BRIGHTON, 8/-. SOUTHSEA, 7/6. Afternoon Circular Excursion to Bekonscot Model Village, 6/6.
Tuesday 14th, Wednesday 15th, Thursday 16th, Friday, 17th June.— Ascot Races, 6/9.

THREE-DAY TOURS OF NORTH DEVON AND SOUTH DEVON
Full details now available from our Booking Offices.
Booking Offices: Lower Bourne, Tel. Farnham 5610; and 5a, Castle Street, Tel. Farnham 4535; and usual Village Agents.

Farnham Herald 1955

● One of the biggest hits in Town, this delightful show, a Bristol Old Vic production, directed by Denis Carey, with book and lyrics by Dorothy Reynolds and Julian Slade and music by Julian Slade, is presented by Linnit and Dunfee Ltd. and Jack Hylton.

"Salad Days"
at the Vaudeville

Right:

Newton Blick, the tramp, owner of the magic piano, hands over this remarkable instrument to Jane and Timothy (Eleanor Drew and John Warner), two young ex-students of the University, who have decided to get married. They are to have the piano for a month, and the scene is one of London's parks.

Pictures by Denis de Marney

Theatre World 1954

LOBBY LUD BLUSHED AT THE FLOWERS

From LOBBY LUD: LITTLEHAMPTON, Sunday.

EVEN a hunted man may blush sometimes. I did yesterday. Whisper it softly. Don't tell a soul—but Littlehampton welcomed me with flowers.

"Lobby Lud bouquets," the notice read in a nursery garden on Arundel Road. Glorious gladioli, dahlias by the dozen! Such a gesture deserved at least a 10s card. I left one on the hedge nearby.

But first, a visit to the Southdown coach station to ask about excursions to Bournemouth and to slip a card under a box of eggs on the inquiry counter.

Bognor can pick up £20

NOW comes the turn of people in BOGNOR REGIS. Lobby Lud is at large there. Anyone who identifies him and challenges him correctly today will win £20.

Remember to have with you an I-SPY badge or-book, and challenge Lobby thus:

"I-SPY Mr. Lobby Lud and claim the News Chronicle prize."

Description: Age about 25, height 5 feet 9 inches, hair fair, eyes brown, build slight, clean shaven.

Guide to his whereabouts:

10.15-11.30.— London Road, High Street and pier head area.

11.30-12.45.—On the front west of pier.

2.0-3.0 p.m.—Hotham Park.

TOMORROW:
BOURNEMOUTH

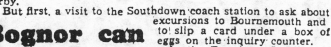

Lobby Lud

In the Broadway I called at J. Wheeler and Sons' furniture shop and in exchange for a bottle of woodworm killer tucked my third card behind a glass-fronted bookcase.

In the church

Seeking sanctuary on my way to the front, I left yet another card—in the parish church : 10s. for the box that holds sums for altar flowers.

I met King Carnival, in the guise of a town crier, ringing his way down High Street and followed him. But no one spotted me.

Gladly would I have given a pretty bride with roses pink and bridesmaid blue a wedding gift of £15. But outside the Congregational church after lunch, though people spoke my name, they had no eyes for me.

I danced on my way beneath carnival flags to the front and flowers again; a show near Butlin's wheels and roundabouts. They were raffling three pots of honey. To help them along I took ticket No. 15, then left another card against the third prize ticket for the cos lettuce class. The winner was Mr. R. A. Godwin, of 19, Terminus Road.

By now the hunt was up—and not one challenger.

Strange Customs

During the whole route through Syria we were pestered with Customs Officers at little outposts along the road; we had to be on the constant lookout for a rushing khaki figure, bursting with ego, hailing us from simply anywhere. When we finally pulled to a halt thirty yards down the road an angry puffing body would climb aboard, ready to invade every nook and cranny he could find. We would smilingly invite him in, and in a moment he would become absorbed with the novelty of our "portable box", beaming and nodding "Good, Goo—ood", the only English word he would know. He would eventually leave smiling happily, having forgotten to open a single cupboard door! It has amazed us that throughout Europe and the Middle East we have not yet been searched—so we still retain the Crown jewels !

Caravan 1954

News Chronicle
1954

Recapturing the magic smell of the seaside

INQUIRING noses are exploring the atmosphere of the Promenade at Cleethorpes. Their investigations have been prompted by a letter from a man in London, who had read that the Hotel and Boarding House Association at Cleethorpes was trying to discover a suitable scent with which to perfume cards. The idea is that next summer's visitors will take them home as reminders of the seaside during the winter.

"Many years ago, before the First World War, I lived at Cleethorpes," says the writer of the letter. "What always seemed peculiar to me even at a very early age was an indefinable and very pleasant odour about the front. It seemed to be a mixture of cockles and mussels, seaside rock, candy floss and all the other things associated with a seaside resort. I have wandered far since those early days but I have never been able to recapture that magic smell.

"One day I knew I would return, and I wondered if that smell would prove to be only a delusion of my childhood days or if it really did exist. After more than 30 years' absence, I did recently revisit Cleethorpes and I was thrilled to find again that magic smell. You, too, may know of this odour. If not, I advise you to walk along the Promenade and discover it for yourselves."

He adds that if they can get it on to a card, they will have achieved something worth while.

Yorkshire Post
1955

Picture Post
1955

Don't shoot the proprietor: he is probably doing his best under difficulties. Few go into hotelkeeping now for easy money or an easy life, and the general standard of British hotels is undoubtedly improving. Remember the hotelier cannot refuse to buy eggs if the price goes up; cannot eke out his pans and linen for quite as long as you can; competes for staff against overfull employment and a well-meant but inflexible Catering Wages Act; is restricted in extending and practically debarred from building. As long as he gives you a square deal and a smile, have sympathy for him.

Daily Mail 1955

How to Avoid Those Haunted Holidays

LEAVING a home empty for two or three weeks' holiday seems quite a hazard for those who are doing so for the first time. If you take sensible precautions before you go, you will enjoy yourselves without perpetual nagging doubts about fire, flood, or burglary.

The ideal arrangement is to leave the keys with a neighbour or your daily help. She can come in every day and make sure everything is all right also prepare your home for your return.

★

Failing this, remember the following suggestions:

NEWSPAPERS and Milk.—Give written instructions about stopping and starting them.

Pets should be boarded out with friends who are genuine animal lovers, or with kennels.

Plants should also be "boarded out" if possible. Otherwise apply the old but successful water - by - suction method. Put all the plants on a large tray on the kitchen floor, place vessels of water round. Plug lengths of thick twine or wool into the roots of the plants and trail the other ends in the water. Enough moisture to keep them going will creep up the lines.

Food that is perishable must not be left. One banana in the kitchen will produce clouds of tiny flies.

★

PACKING.—For some time before the holiday make lists of your personal requirements and the things you really need to take. Don't waste holiday money on toothpaste, talc, and mending materials when you have plenty at home. Take one or two simple pastimes, books, and toys for the children to amuse them in off moments or a rainy day; also remedies for tummy upset, mosquito bites and sunburn.

Pack tea flasks and plastic cups for picnics. Take an old rug or dark blanket for the beach; use it as an extra hold-all by folding beach towels, raincoats, and odd jackets in it and fastening with straps.

★

BEAT the burglar.—Bank valuables if possible. Don't lock drawers and cupboards. If thieves come, they will only force them and damage your furniture.

Be sure that every window is latched securely. If a catch is out of order have it mended. An excellent protection is to bore small holes through the window frames, not taking that in the outside frame right through.

Cut stout metal meat skewers to required length, push through the holes. This prevents the sashes from being opened from the outside. Push a piece of heavy furniture against a french window.

★

CURTAINS.—Don't pull them. The dead look of completely curtained windows is a give-away. Instead cover furniture and carpets with newspapers where the sun may strike too brightly.

Bring all ladders and step-ladders into the house, close and lock back doors and back gates.

Double-lock the front door in the presence of the family, so that there will be no nonsense about "Did I or didn't I?" Now enjoy yourself!

A.S.

HOLIDAYS BY ROAD MAY COST MORE

Express Staff Reporter: Ostend, Wednesday

HOLIDAY coach tours in Belgium may cost visiting Britons more. A court decision in Ostend today will prevent British travel firms using their own vehicles on Belgian soil.

For years local motor-coach owners have been objecting to coaches registered and licensed in England picking up passengers and carrying them on Continental tours.

They claimed that the British were taking trade from Belgians.

On a complaint filed by the Belgian National Railways, three English drivers, Herbert Less, Sydney Barlow, and Cecil Skelton, were fined in their absence for operating motor coaches without a Belgian commercial licence.

PRICES UP

With Lewis Leroy, head of the Lewis Touring Company in Tunbridge Wells, they were ordered to pay costs and damages to the Belgian State.

The spokesman of the Belgian National Tourist Office said to-night: "This means that British travel companies running all-in Continental tours will have to employ Belgian coaches in Belgium and put their prices up in consequence.

"After all, we would have had the same outcry if Belgian travel firms attempted to station coaches in Britain."

Mr. Leroy said in Tunbridge Wells last night: "Immediately we realised we had committed an offence we got a licence to operate English coaches from Ostend.

"We have always been on the best of terms with the Belgian authorities."

My Weekly 1956

Doctor on Value of Longer Holidays

"The demands of industry to-day merit at least one month's holiday a year for everyone," Dr. G. A. Powell-Tuck, of Dorridge, says in to-day's issue of the *British Medical Journal*. He is concerned at the increasing number of patients with anxiety and tension states and symptoms of psychosomatic illness. "Many of them are physically and mentally exhausted, not only by the ever-increasing tempo of modern life, but in large measure because of the inadequate annual holiday period, which appears to average about two weeks."

Birmingham Post 1956

A spade is a spade, but a bucket is—taxed

Mrs. Jean Mann (Lab., Coatbridge) asked the Chancellor of the Exchequer why purchase tax is imposed on seaside buckets but not on spades.

His reply yesterday "Seaside buckets are a toy and taxable as such, but for Customs purposes we call any spade a spade."

Daily Herald 1953

Television challenge to seaside entertainers

AT most of Britain's seaside resorts the curtain has gone up on the summer shows that every year provide a large slice of fun and frolics for millions of holiday-makers. From now until the end of September, comics will deliver their gags, sopranos will reach stratospheric "C's," and dainty dancers will flash their eyes and kick their shapely legs to give mum, dad, and the kids, big sister and her boy friend, a full share of mirth, melody, and happiness.

For more than half a century, resident seaside entertainers have been an essential part of holiday routine, as traditional as fish-and-chips, lobster nets, and of slot machines. And Joe Public and his family have been steadfastly loyal in their support.

Today, that loyalty is threatened. The 1955 seaside entertainers face a challenge unthought of in the days of pierrots and white coons—the challenge of television. It is a challenge which no artiste or producer can afford to ignore, for TV now covers practically the whole country.

With few exceptions, hotels of every class and grade have installed sets. And it is quite a common thing to see the word "television" pasted on the name plates outside boarding houses as an added inducement to patrons.

The cathode ray tube that brings top-line talent into people's homes can also take it to them on holiday. It is a sobering thought.

One man among the regular providers of seaside entertainment who is fully alive to the stern challenge of TV is Greatrex Newman. He has been providing summer shows around the coasts of Britain for more than 30 years, he tells me. This year, at Scarborough, Yorkshire, he establishes a record—it will be his 28th resident season.

Exeter Express and Echo 1955

GRETNA RACKET

DAILY SKETCH PARLIAMENTARY CORRESPONDENT

CHANCES of the runaway marriage racket at Gretna being ended soon are slim. The law is in such a tangle that a major operation would be needed to sort it out—even if the Government could see how to go about the job.

Campaigners against these over-the-Border weddings by teenagers thought they had found a way of, at least, reducing the scandal.

They hoped the Government might sponsor a Bill to make a Scottish wedding between a couple below the age of consent invalid in England if English justices had refused to allow the marriage.

Mrs. Jean Mann, Socialist M.P. for Coatbridge and Airdrie, put the proposal to Sir Reginald Manningham-Buller, the Attorney-General, in the Commons last night.

Sir Reginald could give her no hope. He assured her the problem is being studied.

"But," he said, "there are very real difficulties about making invalid in England a marriage which is valid according to the law of Scotland."

Daily Sketch 1956

India impression... drawn by Michael Peyton. The last stage of the journey is through Australia.

Caravan 1954

Now drive-to-bed tours

Daily Sketch
1956

reach Britain

THIS year Britons get their first chance to go holidaymaking like the Americans do —touring by day and spending the night in motels.

Motel? That's a hotel where you drive to bed.

There are eight of them across Britain so far. Others are planned.

Britain's first motels were planned to catch American tourist dollars. But they have caught British holidaymakers' imagination, too.

It looks like being the next revolution in the holiday business.

For a motel holiday is one without fuss. It's not too dear, you get service at any time of the night. There are no rules and you come and go when you like.

The cost is from £1 to 30s. a night.

You drive into a garage, leave the car and walk through a door into your bedroom.

You want your suit pressing? You hang it in

by PETER MARSHALL

the wardrobe. The job is done by morning.

You can get a meal and a drink any time you want it.

Graham Lyon, Dover hotel proprietor, looks like becoming Britain's King of the Motels.

He pioneered motels here, and his favourite way has been to buy an old pub and build his motel alongside.

In each of his motels' bedrooms are twin beds, radio and telephone. Each, too, has a private bathroom.

And Graham Lyon has a dream of 100 motels spread across Britain.

Remember—if you plan a motel holiday—that you can only stay for one night. That's to keep them for travellers only.

And you pay your bill in advance, so you can leave whenever you like with no time wasted.

Where will you find motels? There's one in Kenilworth, Worcs., one in Lympne, Kent, at Southampton, and near Exeter, Devon.

Scotland has two — at Aviemore, Inverness-shire, and Elgin, Morayshire.

Others are planned for Bath, Oxfordshire, and London Airport.

That's only a small beginning when you think that America has 53,000 motels, all doing big business.

But people who stay at the smart new British motels are saying the idea is going to catch on like mad.

Retford, Worksop News 1957

Young Farmers Talk of Holidays

A vivid description of their holiday last year when they visited several countries in Europe with other Lindsey members of Young Farmers' Clubs was given by three young men at last week's meeting of Gainsborough Y.F.C.

They were Malcolm Wood, Richard Williamson and Richard Dickinson who illustrated their talk with photographs and slides of the countries and towns they saw, including Switzerland, Rome and Venice.

During the business part of the evening, arrangements were made for the panto' trip and also for the area elimination rounds of the public speaking contest to be staged at Sturton on January 18th.

At this week's meeting Mr. Newton-Loynes, secretary of Lincoln County branch of the N.F.U., gave club members good advice on the "Art of public speaking." His lecture was doubly welcome in view of the Sturton competition.

Mr. Malcolm Wood proposed a vote of thanks using the technique recommended by Mr. Loynes.

WRAC recruitment brochure 1956

They wanted to kill August Bank Holiday!

Daily Herald
1956

Holiday task—2

AND while Cambridge students are in darkest Africa, eight men from Oxford will run all the way from Land's End to John o' Groats

They are all members of a club known as The Tortoises.

Each man will run 10 miles, then travel by car for 70 miles and rest until the time comes for him to run another 10 miles.

"It's not a stunt or a student's rag," Jeremy Saville, 21-year-old captain of The Tortoises, claimed.

Apparently, they want to find out what exactly happens when an athlete gets very, very tired.

News Chronicle 1957

Who made our summer break August Bank Holiday? And why call it BANK Holiday?—*Brian Meeghan, Bitterne Park, Southampton.*

SIR JOHN LUBBOCK (later Lord Avebury) was mainly responsible in 1871. It was even suggested that the holiday should be known as St. Lubbock's Day.

The name BANK Holiday was adopted to dodge the killjoys who considered that the working man had enough time off already.

They did not realise that an official bank closing day would lead to a widespread shut-down!

It was partly because of its deliberately disarming title that Lubbock succeeded in getting his Bank Holiday Bill passed.

If it had been called the National Holiday Bill, he said: "I doubt not it would have been widely opposed; but the modest name of 'Bank Holiday' attracted no attention."

Don't let 'summer tiredness' spoil your holiday!

TAKE CARE OF YOURSELF at holiday time—because that's when you take more out of yourself than ever. Make sure you're absolutely fit. Many things can get in the way of full enjoyment—long tiring journeys by train, by coach or by car, settling the children in strange surroundings, the mere excitement of being away. But these same things can be a source of pleasure if you avoid the summer tiredness that results from nervous strain in warmer weather. That's the time when Yeast-Vite is invaluable, soothing away irritation while it builds up your energy reserves. Slip a bottle of Yeast-Vite into your handbag or pocket—carry it wherever you go, and be sure of enjoying your holiday!

YEAST-VITE
The Lightning Pick-me-up

TABLETS
1/9 and 4/-

'Yeast-Vite' is a registered trade mark

Why YEAST-VITE acts so fast

Yeast-Vite contains three vital ingredients, phenacetin, to soothe nerves and disperse headaches; caffeine, to give an immediate 'lift', and, to build up vitality, yeast—the perfect natural source of Vitamin B.

Daily Herald 1956

Holiday task—1

SIX young Cambridge students will spend their summer vacation tramping through the jungles and pygmy country of French Equatorial Africa and the Belgian Congo, searching for the Honey-Guide.

This is a bird which is reputed to lead men to wild-bee hives by hopping from tree to tree in front of them. The bird likes to eat the wax that is left when a hive is broken up.

Michael Holderness, 22, a medical student from Caius College, told me yesterday: "None of us has ever been to Africa or the tropics before. Nor have we ever done any exploring.

News Chronicle 1957

Holiday Hats
Come Home to Roost!

Think of all the sun hats that looked so gay on holiday beaches from Blackpool to Biarritz, Carnoustie to the Côte d'Azur. Think of them now wilting dejectedly in hall cupboards and the top of wardrobes.

Why not turn them into something useful and remind ourselves all winter long of happy days under the sun!

Most of our hats fall into two classes—the coolie and the sombrero. Here's an idea for making gay and charming use of each of these types.

Olé! as they say in Spain. Three cheers for the wide-brimmed sombrero that's become a spectacularly original hanging-plant basket.

Sling it upside down on thick dressing-gown cord, reinforced with stout wire for safety, line the crown with aluminium foil to stop an odd drip coming through and put a deeply-potted house plant in it.

If your hat is too deep for your plant pot, pack the crown with cottonwool to bring the pot up to the required height.

A coolie hat is practically a ready-made lamp shade. Just pop it over any fixed-wire lampshade fitment, and the deed is done.

You needn't even remove the cord or ribbon you tied under your chin! Take these up inside the hat, push them through at the top point and tie them there in a perky little bow: after all a bit of nonsense is a cheerful thing to have about the house!

My Weekly 1956

Tossa, "Lily of the Sea"

YES, indeed ! Tossa is described as the " Pearl of the Costa Brava," and well it may be ! After having had time to consider the matter, both my husband and I agree that our holiday in this delightful spot was the best that we have ever spent.

Was it the geographical position of the village which makes it, even in these days, somewhat isolated ?

Was it the perfect weather, or the magnificent mountains by which Tossa is surrounded ?

Was it the blue Mediterranean, the music which greeted one at every turn, or the truly charming people who live there ?

In my own case, and with my Spanish ancestry, perhaps it was the people and their way of life which interested me most of all.

What fun it was, on our first evening, to find the small cafés, frequented by the " locals," rather than to stay in the " tourist " bars. Here it was that one met the fishermen—the Peters and the Josephs, and was invited to meet them coming in with their catch in the early morning—and what a joy it was to see these proud and simple people, who live from day to day, bringing in the fish which they had caught.

It was in one of these cafés that we were chatting to the proprietress, over a lunch-time apéritif, when she informed us that Señor, her husband, is Mayor of Tossa. It was here that we were taken into the kitchen to see a typical Spanish family luncheon being prepared. It was here, also, that we were shown, with great pride, a small boy's new suit for his first communion.

What fun it was, in the evenings, to be invited to sing to the wonderful guitar accompaniments, and to be allowed to try the castenets. It was just like a jolly family party !

I have not mentioned the wonderful sea-bathing, the delightful Spanish food or the fascinating shops of Tossa. These are the features which one expects or hopes to have on any seaside holiday.

Rather, it was the unexpectedness of Tossa which appealed to us.

ETHEL HELLABY,

Townswoman 1956

WHERE SHALL WE GO? (*Continued from page 29.*)

A FIRST VISIT TO SCOTLAND

My husband and I have heard so much about the beauty of Scotland that we feel we really must see it for ourselves this year. We thought a coach tour which stopped at a different place each night might prove a little tiring for us and would really like to stay somewhere that would make a good centre.

THERE are excellent weekly tours of Scotland which do not involve the continual packing and unpacking of your suitcase in order to move on from place to place each night. These tours operate from centres in different parts of Scotland and you stay at the same hotel at the centre throughout the tour, sight-seeing by coach in the daytime and returning to the hotel each night.

If it is your first visit to Scotland, you may find it difficult to choose which part of the country you would like to see first. The tour centred on Edinburgh is very popular, for the Scottish capital is acknowledged as one of the world's most beautiful cities. As well as sightseeing in Edinburgh itself, you can see something of both Highlands and Lowlands—the tour visits the peaceful pastureland and quiet valleys of the Scott country, the famous Forth Bridge and the haunting loveliness of the Trossachs and Loch Katrine.

Even more tempting, perhaps, is the tour of the Western Highlands and Islands, with headquarters in Oban—a lovely town built on the shores of a sheltered bay and within the shadow of majestic Ben Cruachan. Loch Lomond, Ben Nevis, the Great Glen, Loch Ness and Glencoe are among the places visited on this tour. And one whole day is devoted to a cruise through the Sound of Mull to the lonely islands of Staffa, where Fingal's Cave is to be found, and Iona, from whence in the sixth century St. Colomba sent forth his missionaries to spread Christianity to the mainland.

And Aberdeen is the centre to choose if you would like to visit Royal Deeside, Balmoral Castle and Braemar.

Some tours are more expensive than others, but the average price of a week's tour is about £13.

A CARAVAN HOLIDAY

We have often thought of trying a caravan holiday but could not afford the expense of buying a caravan. Do you know of any caravan sites where the caravans are available for hire?

A CARAVAN holiday makes an adventurous change from everyday routine and there are quite a number of sites in various parts of Great Britain where the caravans may be hired—the National Caravan Council, of 8, Clarges Street, London, W.1, publishes a list of approved sites. (If you write for the list, please enclose a stamped, self-addressed envelope.)

ISLAND IN THE SUN

My sister and I have been to France, Italy and Switzerland on past holidays and this year we want to go somewhere new.

Can you give us any ideas—but somewhere warm please !

HAVE you thought of going to Palma in Mallorca—an enchanting holiday-town on a dream island where olive-covered mountains slope gently down to the warm blue sea, where palm trees and gay café awnings shade the streets and where the sub-tropical climate encourages you to be lazy ?

The famous Gothic cathedral overlooking the harbour, the richly decorated Moorish palace of Almudaina, the bull-fight arena, shops and glittering night-clubs offer you plenty to see and do when you are tired of lazing in the sun. Further afield you can visit many other interesting places—the mountain monastery at Valdemosa where Chopin stayed, for instance, or Porto Cristo and the intriguing Dragon Caves.

You can make the journey from London to Palma by rail and sea via Paris and Barcelona, or direct to Palma by air.

CHILDREN WELCOME !

We have three young children between the ages of two-and-a-half and ten years and when trying to book accommodation for our summer holiday last year we were disappointed to find that some hotels we wrote to were not keen on accepting children as guests. It would be such a help if there were a list of addresses of the places where children are welcome.

MANY hotels and guest houses are only too delighted to accept bookings from families with children and often go out of their way to make special arrangements for them. Parents who have met with disappointment over bookings in the past will welcome the publication of a very helpful guide to these hotels, guest houses, farms and holiday camps which cater for families with children of all ages.

Addresses throughout Great Britain are included—and range from the farms in Devonshire which have their own dairy and garden produce to the hotels in popular resorts which offer play-rooms, special washing and ironing facilities and the services of a baby-sitter in the evenings.

The guide, appropriately called " Children Welcome ! " is published by the Herald Advisory Services, of 3, Teevan Road, Croydon, Surrey, at 3s. 6d. (postage 3d. extra).

NOTE : *In view of the international situation and the shortage of petrol supplies some alterations may be necessary in the tour routes and the prices quoted above.*

Woman and Home 1957

NORA AND TILLY GO ON HOLIDAY

*

The train journey down to Cornwall to stay with their uncle is most exciting

*

Nora and Tilly have gone to stay at their Uncle Ben's farm down in Cornwall.
Do you hate having to go on a long train ride, sitting bolt upright, not being allowed to fidget, or draw pictures on the steamy windows with your fingers? Of course you do, and so do Nora and Tilly.
But their journey wasn't a bit like that : they enjoyed it, and here's why.

After Mummy had put them on the train she asked the guard to keep his eye on them, in between blowing his whistle and waving his green flag. The only other people in the carriage were two jolly little boys who were travelling with their mother, but as luck would have it, she was very nice and gave no trouble at all.
Naturally they were all a bit shy at first but with our friend Tilly on board it wasn't long before the atmosphere became friendly and the stiffness wore off. You'd be surprised what the exchange of a piece of chocolate for a couple of Liquorice Allsorts can do towards breaking the ice.
They soon found out that the boys' names were Brian and Patrick. (Brian was six, Patrick eight.)

After they had made friends, all four children settled down comfortably to have a good read at their books and papers, the Mummy being very unselfish and letting each of them have a corner seat while she sat in the middle and got out her knitting. "Too peaceful to last," thought she, and how right she was, for just then Master Brian felt the time was ripe for a fidget.
"Why don't you all play some games?" said his mother. "Something you can play sitting down, if I may make so bold."
"I know," said Tilly. "What about a spelling bee?" "Oh yes," said Nora, spelling being one of her strong points. So they had an amusing time spelling out quite long words, but after a while they got a bit bored with it because Nora kept on winning and the boys didn't get a look in.
So they switched to a more exciting game with pencils and paper, seeing who was the quickest at spotting the trains as they roared past, and writing down the numbers of engines. Our Tilly was as sharp as a needle at it but she wasn't able to beat Patrick who really was an expert. "Oh, well, I've played it for years," he said modestly. (It's wonderful what experience these old gentlemen of eight have had.)

Well, the time simply flew, and after they had all eaten their lunch their Mummy put the flasks away and made the boys tidy up. "Mustn't leave an untidy carriage for other people to sit in," she said, as they got out at Plymouth.
Nora and Tilly waved goodbye and were quite sorry to part with their nice little companions.

BUILD A BOAT—FOR £10

For £10 you can buy a build-it-yourself three-seater rowing dinghy. For £7,500 you can buy a luxury 30ft. sloop which carries six people. These are two of the exhibits on view at the National Boat Show, sponsored by the Daily Express, which is open at Olympia until January 12.

Daily Mirror 1957

Woman and Home 1957

Where Are Southsea's Missing Visitors?

WHAT has happened to many of the visitors who normally, in these first two weeks of July, fill the hotels and boarding houses and throng the beaches and sea front in Southsea and elsewhere on the coast?

This is a question which is

Portsmouth Evening News 1957

being asked by many of those concerned in the Southsea holiday industry. For there are not so many holidaymakers as last year.

Hotels and boarding houses are not so full. They are, however, fully booked for the peak weeks from July 27 to August 10.

One hotelier felt that the shortage of visitors was the result of the period of petrol rationing, when many decided not to book up for these present two weeks. She felt, too, that because of increases in hotel rates and expensive railway fares, many people had decided to seek holidays abroad where some attractive terms are being offered.

The question of expensive

fares was stressed by Mr. Alex Kinnear, General Manager of Portsmouth Piers, Beach, and Publicity Department.

He said: "Heavy railway charges are a great concern to us in holiday resorts. People in the Midlands have to pay about as much for fares to resorts as they spend on board and lodging when they arrive."

He said that the predominant factor about holidays in British resorts was the sun. Last year the weather during the summer was so bad that hundreds of people said, "Never again."

"So many are following the sun to the Continent this year," he added.

From Southsea's viewpoint, however, there is one bright factor: June was this year the best for visitors and business which the resort has experienced for many years.

"South Africa

gives you
the holiday of a lifetime!"

SAYS THE CAPTAIN OF THE FLAGSHIP

We carry a large number of passengers who come to South Africa to escape the winter and to enjoy a holiday you won't find anywhere else in the world.

South Africa offers a welcome change from a European holiday. There is so much to do and to see that is completely and fascinatingly different. Where else can you study wild animals in their natural surroundings and do it safely from a car? Where else will you see Native life in all its colour and quaintness? And when you've travelled around and seen and enjoyed all the marvels of this amazing land, there are quiet resorts where you can relax — or fashionable plages where you may join in a gay social round.

But it's the sunshine that makes everything so marvellous. There it is, shining on you every day...bright, beautiful and heartening. South Africa gives you the finest holiday you'll find anywhere in the world.

The youngsters take a look around.

A fashionable night club in Johannesburg.

South Africa

LAND OF SUNNY CONTRASTS

 The South African Tourist Office is at your service for free, friendly and helpful advice. *For detailed information on transport, accommodation and costs consult your Travel Agent or South African Railways Travel Bureau, South Africa House, Trafalgar Square, London, W.C.2.*

SOUTH AFRICAN TOURIST CORPORATION

70, PICCADILLY, LONDON, W.I. Tel : *Grosvenor* 6235. 475, FIFTH AVENUE, NEW YORK, 17

Some Extracts from Letters of Appreciation

Below we give some extracts from passengers who travelled on our 1958 Cruises

. . . I remember with great pleasure the delightful holiday in Greece. I knew from the reputation of Swans that it would be most efficiently organised—but I did not expect the "bit over" which made so much difference to our pleasure.   *Bourne End.*

. . . A belated note to say how very much I enjoyed my cruise with you. My admiration for your organisation is enormous, as was my pleasure in its results.   *London, S.W.7.*

. . . I just *dream* about the wonderful trip you gave us. Haven't been able to "come down to earth" at all. Thanks again for making it so perfect.   *New York.*

. . . I would like to add that my wife and I enjoyed the Cruise very much indeed, and we were deeply interested in all we saw and heard. I would also like to congratulate you upon the excellent organisation; and especially do we want to comment upon the excellence of the team of lecturers.   *Canterbury.*

. . As a member of the April Hellenic Cruise I should like to put on record my appreciation of all that went towards its success. It was, undoubtedly, more than a holiday; it was a wonderful introduction to Greece and Turkey, if, inevitably somewhat compressed.
Lytham, Lancs.

. . . We would like to express our thanks for the excellent organisation of the cruise which we found very enjoyable and stimulating. One could have wished that there had been more time to digest the varied impressions. We especially appreciated the very fine team of lecturers. We also appreciated the help and courtesy of your couriers and the contribution made by the Greek Guides.   *Haslemere.*

. . . May I take this opportunity of thanking you for the splendid trip which you organised, and for the great care as to detail which marked every feature. I certainly hope to avail myself again of the advantages offered in a Hellenic Cruise.   *Brighton.*

. . . I enjoyed the Hellenic Cruise enormously and do thank you for the marvellous organisation and care of detail, which made this such a stimulating and happy experience.   *St. Helens, Lancs.*

Swan's Hellenic Cruises 1957

Westmorland Gazette 1959

Portsmouth Evening News 1957

Teddy Boys "Menace to Camps"

TEDDY BOYS are a menace to the reputation of holiday camps, said Mr. C. Copus, of Hayling Island, at the annual conference of the National Federation of Holiday Camps, Ltd., at Folkestone yesterday.

Mr. T. Porter (Devon) said that the Federation had considered compiling a black list, but there were legal difficulties.

Individually, owners did make their own lists, however, and were watching bookings closely.

Mr. Copus said that they were always willing to be friendly with Teddy boys, but near the end of the holiday, discretion was thrown to the winds. The system of checking bookings was not foolproof.

Mr. E. B. Hutchinson (Folkestone) said that strong-arm methods were the best way to deal with Teddy boys.

Delegates were divided on the question of allowing rock 'n' roll in the ballrooms of their camps.

Some favoured a half-hour session each evening, others a mixed dance, while some said that a separate night a week for modern dancing was more suitable.

Mr. J. Bishop said that rock 'n' roll was here to stay. It had become a national sport, and they had to cater adequately for it.

Hygiene and Health :—*Visitors to the principal centres have no more reason to fear sickness than at home.* Medical aid is at hand upon the voyage, and English-speaking physicians practise in all the more important cities, where there are also hospitals equipped with all the refinements of medical science. Druggists' shops are numerous, and all the leading English and American preparations can be bought. Public sanitation has made such strides that epidemic diseases have been brought within really manageable proportions. The temperate parts of South America are quite as healthy as England, and in the tropics ill-health is more frequently caused by heedlessness than by inevitable causes.

Precautions in the *tropics* are very simple, but they should be observed. Some travellers have themselves inoculated against typhoid fever before starting the journey ; this is a wise precaution. To prevent malaria, a five-grain tablet or capsule of quinine should be taken every night—say a hundred capsules for a three-months' trip. A small bottle of chlorodyne as a remedy for dysentery is occasionally useful. A supply of purgative medicine (pills or salts) is also essential.

Travellers should make a special point of never sitting in damp clothes, even for five minutes ; a complete change should be made after a hot journey at the first opportunity. Also avoid drinking the water of the country—not that it is invariably bad, but it may be. Always wear a hat. Do not take chilling showers. Be careful of your food. It is a very good plan never to drink anything but bottled water, never to eat surface vegetables or unpeeled fruits, and to eat meals only when they are well cooked and served at a reliable hotel. Pork should always be avoided. Perhaps the best single rule is to accept the advice of English and American families that have lived a long time in the tropics.

South American Handbook 1958

This is the life!

A CUNARDER IS AN ENCHANTED WORLD OF GLAMOUR AND LUXURY

As soon as you go aboard a Cunarder you embark on a fairy-tale world of luxury . . . gay, glamorous, carefree. Every moment is memorable. Every menu is worthy of a frame. You're in the mood to be entertained? You feel energetic? You just want to laze? At all times and in all parts of every Cunard ship there is a sense of being well looked after. The shopping centre with its nearby hairdressing and beauty salons is a fascinating rendezvous . . . Mayfair in mid-Atlantic! Swift, attentive yet unobtrusive service is an essential part of the Cunard way of life.

Remember, you are entitled to the new £100 dollar allowance for U.S.A. and Canada. Why not take advantage of it. Ocean fares, shipboard expenses and American and Canadian rail fares are all payable in sterling. It also makes possible the attractive prospect of visiting the United States or Canada en route to Australia, New Zealand and the Far East.

TRAVEL IN A BIG WAY – TO USA AND CANADA

Cunard

Harper's Bazaar **1958**

Coach Touring on the Continent

continued from page 3

There are three or four different types of coach tours ; those which actually start in this country, those that you pick up in Calais or Paris after you have travelled by train and boat from your starting point, and those which start right in the region you are going to explore, having reached there by specially chartered plane. Other variations include touring for a week and staying in one place for a week, as well as what is known as a fantail arrangement, whereby you stay in one place all the time and go out each day on drives to different places of interest. Some tours, especially those which are quite short duration, are not accompanied by a tour manager. They are usually somewhat cheaper.

When you arrive at a place and have enjoyed a good dinner, resist that temptation to spend an hour in the lounge and go to bed early. You will be missing so much. Spend as little time as possible in the hotel, and go out and explore on foot as much as you can. You may not be interested in old churches, but there is always a market in the early morning, the quaint cellar café where you can watch local life in the evening. The shops themselves are always fascinating, particularly when you can move away from the more obvious tourist boutiques. Round the back streets, in the shop kept by the little old lady in black, you may buy just that pot which you want to take back, or that silk square which will still remain undimmed under northern skies. If you take this advice you will come back feeling that you have enjoyed every moment of your coach tour and hoping that next summer you will be able to go again.

Highway Holidays **1959**

We Fly

B.O.A.C.

To Beirut

THE beautiful Britannia took us there in 8 hours' flying-time. We left London on a cold grey day and touched down in midsummer weather into the pulsating, cosmopolitan scene of Beirut airport from which planes go on to Australia, India and other points East. Our plane was big enough to divide into 1st class and Tourist: 1st class seats tip up, leave ample space to stretch the legs. Beirut is at once ancient and modern, occidental and exotic: skyscraper apartment buildings, air-conditioned hotels, souks and tunnelled alleyways; women balancing jars (or petrol cans) on their heads trudge past sheik-like Arab gentlemen in Cadillacs, and Coca-Cola signs are everywhere. There are sandy beaches all around, hot enough for sun-bathing. Night life is gay in Beirut: you can see the *danse de ventre* at one club and Spanish dancing or a French cabaret at the next. But most wonderful were the excursions we made to the fabulous cities of the Lebanon—to Baalbek with its honey coloured temples, and to prehistoric Byblos, which was first inhabited in neolithic times—see pictures on the following pages.

Harper's Bazaar **1958**

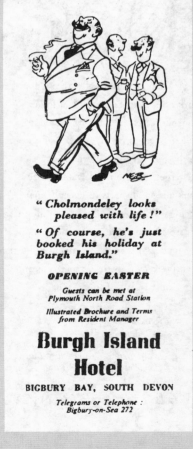

Woman's Weekly **1960**

Woman's Weekly **1960**

THESE ISLANDS HAVE A SPECIAL CHARM

Spectacular coastlines, a temperate climate, and a refreshingly half-foreign air make the Channel Islands a favourite holiday playground

HOLIDAYS AFLOAT

FOR everyone who enjoys boats—and we always make the proviso that they should be able to swim well—water holidays have tremendous appeal. You can hire a cruiser on the Norfolk Broads or the upper reaches of the Thames. You can go hostel-boating on Britain's inland waterways. You can go luxury cruising in the Mediterranean, or cargo-cruising to Scandinavia or the Canary Isles. Or you can go on a cruising holiday with a difference—a week on the French Riviera and a five-day sea voyage home, or a week on Venice Lido and four days' cruising in the Adriatic.

7 days on the Norfolk Broads from £8 per person
13-day Mediterranean cruise from £45
14-day Adriatic cruise with week in Venice from 42 gns.

Woman's Weekly **1960**

The wide sweep of fine sands at St. Brelade's Bay, Jersey, delights the visitor.

Woman's Weekly **1960**

THEY lie in the clear, deep blue Atlantic off the north-west coast of France. The people speak a French patois. Their place-names—Grandes Roques, Bonne Nuit Bay, Corbière—leave no doubt about their French origins. And for centuries they have maintained their native bonds with Normandy and Brittany.

Yet the Channel Islands are British. You do not need a passport to go there. Nor do you need foreign currency. And you will have no language difficulties. They are the perfect choice for those in search of a holiday with a Continental atmosphere without actually going abroad.

The islands are endowed with some spectacularly lovely scenery—rugged, cliff-bound coasts, golden beaches, secluded coves and green hills. Their temperate climate gives them warm, invigorating days from April until October.

Horses—between shafts and on course

It was a horsedrawn week for me, beginning with a cross-country pony-cart jaunt from Wantage to Duxford (11 miles) for a barn dance, the beginnings of the coming-out of Miss **Candida Betjeman** (*pictures on previous page*). She's a raving beauty of the younger generation, and the daughter of Mr. **John & the Hon. Mrs. Betjeman**. The barn dance, at Mr. & Mrs. **John Florey's** farm, was fun, and the drive even more so.

Mrs. Betjeman, driving a skewbald mare to a four-wheeled wagonette (borrowed from Lady Agnes Easton), led the procession, but not for long. The **Hon. Christopher Chetwode**, egged on by his passengers, started pushing up to the front. "Christopher, you poopstick!" called out Mrs. Betjeman crossly.

"Don't you know that it's terribly bad form to canter if you're in a cart?" A severe reprimand, but in the circumstances I am sure that her father, the late Field-Marshal Lord Chetwode (once C.-in-C., India), would have given an approving nod.

We jig-jogged along. **Lord Chetwode** (in blue-and-white ski-sweater and deerstalker) was driving a two-wheeler, the Hon. **"Bobbie" Corbett** a smart red-and-black wagonette, and Miss Betjeman her two-seater Ralli.

Their passengers included Miss **Victoria Heber-Percy**, Lady **"Buffy" Charteris** (usefully able to supply the bit of expert horse and carriage knowledge when needed), Mr. **Henry Berens**, Mr. **"Mike" Taylor** (son of the Headmaster at Repton), Mr. **Henry Harrod**, and Mr. **Simon Lennox-Boyd**, the red-headed son of the former Colonial Secretary, who proved nimble at running along in front when we needed a pointsman at cross-roads.

Tatler 1960

LOCH LEVEN

ALTHOUGH there have been the occasional off-days sport has continued on a reasonably good level, some anglers being fortunate or skilful enough to bring in two-figured catches of trout averaging 1 lb., with some double that weight or more.

When the fish are taking it pays to fish almost anywhere on the loch provided the drifts are suitable, but at this time of the season most Loch Leven anglers make for the Shallows where great hatches of natural flies invariably occur.

During several outings to the loch in late May and early June the writer had capital sport with a wet fly cast comprising Peter Ross (tail), Grouse and Green, Burleigh and Bloody Butcher (on the bob). More than half the fish taken on these outings were taken on the Burleigh and Bloody Butcher.

Other anglers have fared well with Grouse and Claret (yellow tail), Wickham's Fancy, Kingfisher Butcher, Dunkeld, and yellow tailed Greenwell's Glory.

My own fish were taken on small doubles (size 16) and were hooked when fish were making "shark fin" rises in near-calm conditions.

It is always a good policy to watch out for rises when you are fishing Loch Leven. Get the flies over the surface breaks quickly and quietly and it's practically a certainty that a fish will come up for one of your flies.

Quite a lot of the trout taken from the loch, however, are caught by deep sinking the flies and a sudden bump is the first inkling that a fish is on. All the same I much prefer to see the fish coming for the fly near the surface and for this reason I rely a lot on the top-dropper flies.

It will be obvious from the fact that such flies as Dunkeld, Hardy's Gold Butcher, Cinnamon and Gold, Kingfisher Butcher and Wickham's Fancy kill so many trout at Loch Leven that a gold-tinselled fly should never be absent from the cast. Equally, it is worth remembering that green-bodied flies also do well.

But one should not be too fastidious in the matter of patterns. It pays to try the unorthodox. During a national competition at the loch a couple of seasons ago I was in a boat with a Glasgow angler who "nailed" a dozen fish on a cast composed entirely of Clyde flies, so small and skimpily-dressed that it was a matter for wonder that the fish even saw them!

On another occasion the writer has killed nearly a score of trout on a day's fishing with a badly-mangled split-winged Greenwell — and the fly was still killing trout when its hackle was streaming behind it!

Evening fishers always do well this month so if you cannot get a boat during the day try and get out in the evening.

Contrary to expectations, considering that the conditions were very bright, catches in the Scottish national championships were very good. Seventy anglers took part and the total catch was 279 (weighing slightly over 294 lb.). Dr. J. Cuthbert (Bothwell and Blantyne A.C.) had 15 of these fish (15 lb.) to win the event. — KINGFISHER.

Trout and Salmon 1960

Sun and sand at VIAREGGIO

from £24.5s.

VIAREGGIO is a large resort with cafés and shops in plenty, mile after mile of broad beaches, and a good deal of sunshine. In the evenings the resort is humming with excitement: night-clubs, cafés, theatres and even the streets themselves are crowded with gay people out to make the most of their holiday. Why not join in the fun? We've selected the right places for you to stay at—in particular, the Grand Hotel and Royal where our Hostess is ready to arrange local sightseeing excursions for you, or to suggest evening entertainment. It's all so easy—and enjoyable—if you plan your holiday through us!

Holidaymaking 1960

Holiday legacy left by bank manager

A retired Middlesbrough bank manager, who died in November, has left a legacy of £500 to his old branch with instructions that the income from it should be used to provide an annual holiday for a member of the staff. Lots are to be drawn at the bank's head office to decide the lucky holidaymaker, he stipulated.

The bequest has been made by Mr. Harold Rowland Barker, who lived in The Crescent, Nunthorpe, near Middlesborough, and who was manager of the Linthorpe Road, Middlesbrough, branch of Martins Bank. He left £5,328 net (Duty paid £160).

Yorkshire Post 1961

For Sand, Sun and Scenery
VENTNOR
THE WONDERLAND OF THE ISLE OF WIGHT

A glorious holiday awaits you and your family by the warm blue sea. Official Guide 9d. in stamps.

Direct train ferry Service from Waterloo

TOWN CLERK (W.W.), VENTNOR, ISLE OF WIGHT

SCOTLAND
FROM £10·0·0 WEEKLY

POST COUPON TODAY for *FREE* TARTAN BOOKLET
Please use BLOCK letters

NAME ....

ADDRESS ....

.... Dept. 'T'

CALEDONIAN TOURS LTD.
93 HOPE STREET, GLASGOW. C.2

I.P.F. Lantern Caravan

National Cripples'
Journal 1961

Your editor kindly asked me to tell you of this unique scheme, which is planned to give a family holiday to those who, because of respiratory paralysis following poliomyelitis, are dependent on machines worked by electricity.

The main caravan accommodates any equipment used in this country, including an iron lung. By courtesy of the Corporation it is located on the Portsmouth Corporation Caravan Site on the edge of Langstone Harbour with excellent views. The van will sleep up to five persons; the special bed is adjustable and movable. Luxuries include radio, television, refrigerator and telephone. Wide spread generosity ensures that we do not want for anything.

Each visitor must ensure adequate resident nursing assistance. This may include relatives or a professional nurse, who is usually giving up a week of her holiday to help. To accommodate these extra people there is a second caravan, and so there are nine beds in all. No charge is made for the use of these caravans or for gas or electricity.

The results have exceeded our highest hopes. We have already had in the caravan visitors who have been so severely paralysed that any greater affliction is not compatible with life; in other words we have successfully received the severest type of illness. We have managed to overcome fairly successfully scores of minor and a few major problems. The only difficulty about which we have some reservations is that of excessive weight and unusual height. During one such visit our new rocking bed was not functioning correctly; through no fault of our own the hoist was faulty and we did not have a bed with access to both sides. All these failings have now been remedied and I would welcome a similar visitor as I am confident that he too would have a happy visit.

Flooded river prevented boating

In one way this year's gala was unique. It was the first time in the lifetime of Mr. Erik Brown, the city's boat hire proprietor, there had been no boating on the river on the Big Day, due to the swirling waters.

Mr. Brown can look back over some 50 years. "I can recall boating being cancelled on some public holidays in the past but never on a Miners' Gala Day," he said.

Apart from removing a big entertainment feature from the day's events, the overnight rise in the river made the day a write-off from a money-making viewpoint.

Mr. Brown, who owns about 100 boats, looked ruefully at the brown surging mass of water flowing at a dangerously high speed and flooding the towpath in places.

"It wouldn't be safe to let anyone out in a boat today," he said. The river began to rise about 4 a.m. and it was estimated to be between eight and 10 feet above normal.

"I can recall many Gala Days," said Mr. Brown. "If it was fine the boats would begin to go out about nine and would continue perhaps until nine at night."

Durham County Advertiser 1961

Gala pledge to Durham miners on fuel policy

WOMEN'S cries of "Shame" greeted Mr. Hugh Gaitskell at Durham Miners' Gala on Saturday when he referred to the Labour Party's internal dispute over the defence policy.

Mr. Gaitskell, who was addressing the gala crowds from No. 1 platform, said he believed that the Party had gone a long way to settling the defence dispute which had certainly divided it over the past two years.

Durham County Advertiser 1961

In over 20 miners' galas Saturday's was the worst example of a drunken orgy on the part of teenage boys and girls he had seen, writes a correspondent, who says "the behaviour of these stupid youngsters who think they are clever was positively disgusting. He quotes one instance:

"About 6 o'clock two youths and two girls, not much more than school-leaving age, deliberately smashed bottles and glasses against the police patrol box. Standing by were a police superintendent and two other officers.

"The 'naughty children' were told to pick up the pieces—the four of them should have been frogmarched to the police station and kept in for the night. One of the girls, with an impudent gesture, drank from a bottle of beer, with a most unladylike sneer on her face.

"Twenty to 30 oddly-attired teenagers—obviously intent on trouble—sauntered through the Market Place in the direction of Claypath, shouting and gesticulating. They were ignored by the police. It reminded me with a shudder, of Nazi youth out on a looting expedition in an occupied country."

Durham County Advertiser 1961

Town 1962

Farmers on the least-'developed' islands, St Agnes and St Martins, also want a share in holiday profit. They sub-let rooms and by agreement with the Duchy can put up chalets, at most two on a holding. Despite an attempt at camouflage, the new chalets show indecently bungaloid beside cottages of rough granite, green to the door with succulents grown wild. It's also doubtful whether the tiny islands can ingest more visitors, unblighted as they are by tourist amenities. 'Please don't expect us to provide public lavatories,' said a farmer on St Agnes, 'we haven't enough water for ourselves.' Rainwater supplied them, dripping down walls white as a gull wing. In drought, everyone relied on a single well. (Tresco Estate have bored for water, so far in vain, and St Mary's should get government help to build a catchment basin.) As for electric power, everyone generated his own, rationing current until bedtime. 'We can't cope with droves of trippers,' a farmer declared flatly, 'imagine a few horrible litter bins down there,' pointing beyond the calcium lighthouse to narcissi embrasured in a steep, glossy hedge, a red slope of cattle against the carns which are now dry rock, now tumbling sea. This islander had enough tillage to live – austerely – off his daffodils and Guernsey milk. But his neighbour, with only nine acres, let the spare bedroom. He was bunching violets in a greenhouse hot and deep-scented to the verge of suffocation, impregnated by the aroma of the Sunday joint next door.

It's always useful in the trade to have a new twist occasionally—it certainly was for Roberta Suarez, daughter of the London manager of the Spanish National Tourist Office, when with her partner, Ewen Cameron, she won the twisting competition at the annual dance of the London Travel Trades Club. For their prowess (see above) they won wine and records. Winners of the two Silver City air tickets from Lydd to Le Touqet were Daphne Bradley (Rank Organisation) and Dennis Spall (PAA). There were nearly 270 members and friends present at the dance, which was held in the Royal Hotel, Woburn Place

Travel World 1962

PICTURE PRETTY

How do you fare in a snapshot? With picture-taking a part of the summer ritual, it is useful to know a few tricks that will help you look as lovely in a photograph as you are in reality.

For pictures that will preserve a happy memory of you on holiday occasions here are some DO'S and DON'TS to follow.

Prior to being snapped, DO tidy your hair, lipstick and clothes. Any sort of rumple is magnified in the filming.

While the camera is operating, DON'T slump; sit or stand tall else your figure will look dumpy. DO keep your feet together and your hands in your lap or at your sides. DON'T thrust any of these into the limelight. On camera the hands and feet grow in size unless they strike a retiring pose.

DON'T drop your head as this wrinkles the neck. DO tilt your head slightly to one side. This will enhance the features.

DON'T stare, giggle or be caught eating. In pictures these actions tend to appear silly—even ugly. DO smile with your eyes and your lips. It's fun you are having.

Bear these hints in mind, and there's little likelihood of your appearances before the camera having disappointing results.

People's Friend 1962

Thelma Smith, Scheveningen

Maureen Luke, Ulvik

Pat Davies, Ostend

Valerie Spencer, Lugano

Heather Milne,
Viareggio

Jeanne Budds, La Baule

Pat Bunce, Garmisch-Partenkirchen

Dorothy Walters, Kitzbühel

SHE is sensible, good natured, keen on her work, enthusiastic about her resort and eager to make you love every minute of your holiday there — she is a Cooks Hostess.

She will greet you soon after arrival and can tell you about everything that is going on — where to bathe, dance, walk, buy your English newspapers . . . She is an encyclopaedia of local knowledge and ready to give her friendly help whenever you need it.

Every year hundreds of people write to comment on her unobtrusive kindness and efficiency; on the way that she has made them feel at home right from the first day.

You'll appreciate having a Cooks Hostess at your resort.

Holidaymaking 1962

9.   'Eat as you Please' Arrangements

We have increased the number of bed and breakfast, demi-pension or Meal Voucher arrangements at Fieberbrunn, Soelden, Lech, Serfaus, Obergurgl and Davos to give skiers more freedom of movement or budget skiers a chance to economise.

Ski with Erna Low 1963

Where do we look for our travel centres tomorrow?

Travel World
1962

£34
FOR 10 DAYS

CANALLING

Non-energetic types, who like watching the world go by, will love cruising on one of Britain's canals on a barge. Trips go from Nottingham to Lincoln—at a lazy pace. You sleep and eat on board, but there's plenty of opportunity to go ashore if you want to stretch your legs before settling down with a book and a box of chocolates.

Where to write

Book through Cooks, who have offices all over the country. Head office is at 45 Berkeley Street, London W.1

£35
FOR 2 WEEKS

MOROCCO

For adventurous birds only. The going will be bumpy in a Land-Rover, but you'll see some fantastic country through France, Spain, via African and Moorish towns, and on the Atlantic coast of Morocco, over the Atlas Mountains to the Sahara Desert. Age limited to pioneers between 14 and 21.

Write to: Adventure Unlimited, 48 Kensington Gardens Square, London W.2. Safaris take place in May, June, September. No fancy hotels on this trip—tents only. Sleeping bags, boots, rucksacks, can be hired at 2s. 6d. per item.

37½ gns.
FOR 12 DAYS

YUGOSLAVIA

If you want to see what happens behind the Iron Curtain, fly on this organised tour to Opatija in Yugoslavia. Hotel overlooks the Bay of Kvarner, where you can swim during the day, dance at the quayside cafés at night.

Write to: Lyons Tours, Colne, Lancashire. Tours leave from Victoria Coach Station, London, and you board your plane at Manston Airport.

£79
FOR 15 DAYS

GRAND TOUR OF SOUTH EUROPE

Our ancestors used to take a couple of years for the grand tour of Italy and Greece, but today you can do it in two weeks. You fly to Venice, then visit Florence, Rome, Athens, Sofia, Belgrade, plus a weekend's cruise around the Aegean Islands. Terrific value for those who want to see absolutely everything.

Organised by Poly Travel, whose head office is at 311 Regent Street, London W.1.

Ideal Home 1963

ERNA LOW. runs her own Ski Trains

To Austria and Switzerland and Italy (Dolomites Region)

Ski with Erna Low 1963

In view of the great increase in our Winter Sports traffic, we have decided to run our own special trains this year and have secured Couchette and Seat Allocations on Special Train and Special Departure Dates as specified below. The couchette allocations and ticket stock are held at our office which means :

1. Immediate Confirmation of Couchettes.

2. Prompt Ticket Despatch.

Our Ski Specials are a very economical and quick method of reaching your destination. They are routed via the **Short Sea Route** (Dover or Folkestone/Calais) and you will reach most destinations in Austria or Switzerland in under 24 hours travelling time. There is **No Change** between the Channel Port and your Main Line Destination in Austria. For Switzerland you will change at Basle, Sargans, etc.

Modern French Rolling Stock will be used. During the day each compartment will seat 6 people and in the evening it will be transformed into sleeper compartments — with three comfortable bunks on each side ; pillow and blankets are provided. It is recommended to take sheet sleeping bags with you as sheets are not supplied.

COUCHETTES ARE
INCLUDED ON ALL
RAIL TRAVEL
CHARGES QUOTED
IN THIS BOOKLET

Holiday strike

The Sunday strike of Yeomen warders at the Tower, and museum staffs, has been extended to include Bank Holiday Monday.

The Civil Service Union, to which the staff belong, said yesterday that it would be hard to avoid a full-scale strike in the museums if the Treasury did not meet its pay claim within two weeks.

Daily Telegraph 1963

CLACTON COUNTS LOSSES FROM EASTER TEENAGE INVASION

A street scene typical of Clacton town centre over the weekend, including a police dog-handler patrolling with Alsatian.

Takings are down by £60,000:
Rates strike threat

East Essex Gazette 1964

HONG KONG: British agent tricked by Chinese model

A report from our HKTA correspondent

The activities of a British agent in Hong Kong were terminated last week after an incident involving two Chinese. The agent, Peter Studde, was last seen in their company at Kai Tak Airport where they watched his departure. Both are well-known in Hong Kong's fashionable night spots where their names were given as Mr Ho and Miss Lee.

A week in waiting

Our correspondent's investigation showed that for a week they had followed him, always in the background, but never far away. At the Royal Jockey Club in Happy Valley they viewed his gambling with oriental equanimity as they sipped jasmine tea in the shade of the club-house. On Big Wave Bay they sat in the shade of a giant parasol while he skied across the azure-blue sea, behind a powerful speed boat. Whatever he did, wherever he went they followed, eating the same exotic food in secluded restaurants, sleeping in the same luxurious hotels. By the

Travel Agency 1965

end of the week their first impressions had been confirmed. Mr Studde was an excellent athlete, an accomplished linguist and unlikely to be outwitted easily. Tuesday proved them wrong.

The day of the dragon

In a quiet back-street Miss Lee proved conclusively that he was no match for Chinese cunning. He had always found Chinese models compulsively fascinating and so he could not resist Miss Lee's invitation to enter a small secluded shop through a bead curtain. Inside they spent some time examining the carved toys, then Studde accepted Miss Lee's challenge. He picked one up cautiously. Immediately he knew he had been tricked, a huge paper dragon leapt out of the model pagoda he was holding so carefully. 'Just another of Hong Kong's surprises,' Studde commented as he joined in Miss Lee's and Mr Ho's laughter. The week had indeed been full of surprises. His hosts had shown the British travel agent as many of Hong Kong's delights as it is possible to see in a week. His investigation of Hong Kong's facilities at first hand had been one of his most enjoyable experiences. He had eaten better than anywhere else in the world, danced in the most exotic surroundings and found prices lower than he had dreamed possible. Now he was off home with a suitcase filled with hand-made suits and a wealth of first-hand experiences to relate to his clients.

PARAGUAY

—Air Services—

To **Asuncion** from London via Rio de Janeiro
  Air France operates twice weekly with Boeing 707 aircraft, taking 16¼ hours
from London direct
  Panair do Brazil operates a weekly service with Caravelle and DC-8 aircraft
  Minimum Return Fare is £314 6s. 0d.

**Full day excursion to Caacupé and San Bernardino.
Cost from £2 16s. 0d. per person.**

This tour takes the main road of the country (Mariscal Estigarribia Road), passing typical primitive markets where colourfully dressed women, smoking big cigars, offer their merchandise in "Guarani," an Indian language still spoken throughout Paraguay; thus giving to Paraguay the distinction of being the only bi-lingual country in the whole of South America. Further in the country the tour passes through the town of San Lorenzo, with its modern National School of Agronomy. In Capiatá a tour is made to the Cathedral which has remarkable works of sculpture and painting made by the Indians during the 16th century under the direction of the Jesuit Fathers. At Itauguá the tourist watches the natives patiently knitting "ñanduti," a delicate lace cloth resembling a spiders web. This type of knitting is quite tedious, a table-cloth sometimes taking two years to make. When approaching Caacupé the tourist sees the cattle plains spread out below him from the vantage point of a large hill. Dotting the countryside are small farms. In the distance is Ypacarai Lake. Experimental farms, conducted by the Inter-American Service of Agricultural Co-operation, may also be seen. On the opposite side of the hill is Caacupé, religious centre of Paraguay and neighbouring countries. Caacupé is famous for its "Virgin of Caacupé' and each December 8th there is a countryside pilgrimage to this little village. After a tour to the church and town of Caacupé we take the unpaved road to San Bernardino, a resort village and the Club Náutico, lunch at the Hotel del Lago, thereafter returning to Asunción.

Holidays by Air 1965

THE BLACK SEA DREAM

I never actually spoke with Penka. She had long brown legs, long black hair, and one of those Slav faces with high cheekbones and big smiles that make Carroll Baker look like a Peter Robinson window dummy. Life in Czechoslovakia must still be pretty tough, as all her clothes were too small – her black skirt missed the knees by three inches and the top button was missing off her white blouse. It was Sunny Beach on the Black Sea and she was the kind of girl you don't find any more in the West. The little German girls with their Dresden faces and blonded hair peeled off smooth *après-ski* pants like women who know they're being watched, and then ran into the sea squealing. Not Penka. She dropped her skirt and blouse like a girl who was all alone on a West Indian beach and knew that Bond was but a vodka away. I tried to speak to her but we couldn't find a common language. I threw in French and she offered Russian. The language barrier on the Black Sea is a great preserver of dreams.

On the beaches of Bulgaria all the nations of Europe meet. All the Penkas and Annetchkas and Marias, the Hildes and Julies and even the Ethels. Browner, barer and bolder than on the French Riviera, they lie on the white sands frying gently all day. Not all look like Penka. Communism may have solved many problems for Eastern Europe, but there's still something wrong with the diet. Hippy Hungarians and bulging Bulgarians pad along the sands squeezing their 50-year-old bodies into tiny bikinis, and couldn't care two roubles. In the Adam and Eve tents they don't even bother with the bikinis. The only time they dress up is to ride the camels and then in white sheets and handkerchiefs they play at being Peter O'Toole and prod the beast down the sands. It's a casual life with no special plages, no mattresses, the sun oil comes out of a lemonade bottle and no delicious queers bring iced martinis. But it was worth the 2,000 mile journey just to look at Penka and know what Baron Reutern meant.

Daily Telegraph 1963

TOURIST CHIEFS CRITICAL OF RAILWAY PLAN

DAILY TELEGRAPH REPORTER

SOME of the strongest criticism of Dr. Beeching's plan for British Railways came yesterday from leaders of tourist organisations. Mr. Huw Edwards, chairman of the Welsh Tourist Board, said: "These cuts will kill half the work of the board. To make mid-Wales to all intents and purposes a derelict area is a crime against the Welsh nation."

A spokesman for the Scottish board said that the proposals would be disastrous for the tourist industry when it was developing rapidly. "It will also be a disaster for Scotland and the Scottish economy."

Many industrial, manufacturing organisation welcomed the report. The Federation of British Industries spoke of "positive steps to attract traffic best suited to the railways."

A spokesman for the London Chamber of Commerce approved the measures to improve freight services. They will be of great value to commercial undertakings." he said.

Councillor Tom Barrasford, of Llandudno, chairman of the Association of Health and Pleasure Resorts, said that he did not think the report could be criticised from a business point of view.

The human element seemed to have been ignored. Some resorts relied on the railways for part of the industry on which they lived.

In Manchester, a senior police official said that if the proposals were implemented traffic in the city was likely to increase by between four and five per cent. With an annual traffic growth of seven per cent., this was expected to make an overall rise of 10 to 12 per cent.

Traffic experts were convinced that many rail users would turn to cars to travel to work. Thousands of extra vehicles would pour into the city every day.

Town 1965

HOLIDAY WIFE HAS TWINS ON NIGHT EXPRESS

By MIRROR REPORTERS

TWIN girls arrived for Mrs. Patricia Abrahams yesterday—by express delivery.

They were born on a Trans-Continental express train as it sped through France

And they were delivered by an undertaker.

Mrs. Abrahams, 27, and her 34-year-old husband Noah, were on their way back to their home in Astrey-close, Harlington, Beds.

They were expecting ONE baby in two months.

Then things began to happen. The timetable of happy events was:

3.20 A.M. The 700 passengers awoke to the cry: "Is there a doctor on the train?"

There wasn't. But along came the undertaker, Mr. Malcolm Crawford, who is also a former male nurse.

3.40 A.M. Express Delivery Number One she weighed in at 3½lb.

Gendarmes were alerted to stand by at the Gare de Lyon, Paris.

3.45 A.M. The train arrived at the station. So did the gendarmes—twenty-five of

them. "We're ready when you are, lady," one shouted. "Oh, well, that's that," said Mr. Crawford.

But it wasn't. Another shout went up: "Stand back. Another baby's on the way."

4 A.M. Express Delivery Number Two weighing in at 3½lb.

4.25 A.M. Off to hospital. Two gendarmes carried a baby each, the others helped Mrs. Abrahams to a waiting van.

And Mrs. Abrahams joked: "I hope there are no more coming..."

Last night all were reported fit and well.

And the babies were named—Esther and Ruth.

Mr. Crawford, of Hurlingham road, Birmingham, said: "What a shock. I've never delivered a baby before."

Daily Mirror 1965

Holiday Tummy

guard against it with
Entero-Vioform

Coq au vin in Brittany, Devonshire clotted cream... delicious, but not the sort of food you're used to eating every day. A change of diet, a change of water can lead to tummy upsets. Don't spoil your holiday. Pop into a chemists for Entero-Vioform, the safe, sure remedy for the family's holiday tummy troubles.

CIBA LABORATORIES LTD·HORSHAM·SUSSEX
4/5

Nova 1965

is this the day?

September 17th
October 1st
October 15th
October 29th
(or see page 172)

then why not honeymoon in romantic Majorca

Leave London (Victoria) at midnight on each of the above Saturdays and at 2 a.m. Sunday be airborne in a British United Airways BAC 1-11 jet flying direct to Palma in only 2 hours.

Special arrangements for honeymooners at no extra charge include

Limousine car to Victoria Station (radius of 20 miles only).

Best hotel room available.

Bouquet of flowers for the bride on arrival at hotel.

Bottle of Champagne in your room.

V.I.P. treatment during your stay

Holidays are for two weeks' duration with a wide choice of hotels from only

41 GNS
(FULLY INCLUSIVE)

FOR FURTHER DETAILS OF THESE SPECIAL HONEYMOON HOLIDAYS AND A COPY OF OUR FREE BROCHURE CONTACT

 WORLD WIDE AIR HOLIDAYS
A member of the Ellis Travel Group

WORLD WIDE AIR HOLIDAYS LTD. 108, New Bond Street, London, W.I. MAYfair 5944

(An Ellis Travel Group Company)

Brides 1966

TRAVELLER'S DIGEST - 5 YUGOSLAVIA

By Kenneth Westcott-Jones

HOW'S THE WEATHER

It's still summer in September all the way down the long Adriatic Coast of Yugoslavia. Only in the extreme north, at resorts such as Opatija and Lovran, and on the Slovenian Coast at Ankaran and Porotoroz, will there be any cooling off at night. The sea will stay warm, in the low 70s, most of the month. Dubrovnik is perfect at this time of year, with a slight easing of the sun's ferocity and welcome night breezes. Farther south on the Montenegro Coast it is still near-tropical. On the islands, of which Hvar, "Madeira of the Adriatic", is perhaps the most delightful, it is exceptionally mild in winter and not too hot in summer (if you go there in winter they do not charge you on any day the temperature falls to freezing point, or if it should snow). Inland, way up in Serbia and in the valley of the Drina, at Belgrade, hot clear days give way to sharply cool September nights and the first autumnal colours will show. Everywhere, though, weather should be as good as the best of an English July and you'll notice, if you stay into October, that this is the month the Scandinavian tourists prefer.

WHO'S IN POWER

Marshal Tito (born Josip Broz) is President of the Federated Yugoslav Republics and his power derives from his position as leader of the only political party, Socialist Alliance. He practises a form of 'liberal' Communism which differs from the strict Marxist and also from the Moscow Party Line. Tito enjoys definite popularity with the 19 million people making up this post-World War I creation of six states, five nations, four languages, three religions, two alphabets—and one Party. The Constitution allows a small measure of private enterprise, and foreigners can actually buy villas on the coast. Freedom of speech and worship are guaranteed, but religion is somewhat under a cloud, although Roman Catholic and Eastern Orthodox churches attract big congregations. There are many mosques. This is not a 'police state' but police in uniform are very likely to appear and confiscate your camera if you try to take pictures in areas marked by a sign showing a crossed-out camera, e.g. near frontiers, military installations and certain factories. Traffic police enforce speed limits and can levy on-the-spot parking fines.

HOW ARE THE PEOPLE

Yugoslavs are proud, independent, sturdy, reliable, extremely honest, and kind to visitors. The people of prosperous Slovenia in the North are Austrian in appearance and manner; down South the effects of 500 years of Turkish domination are still evident. The languages are a problem. Serbo-Croat is the official one—Slovenian and Macedonian, plus several minority languages, are also used. German is widely understood. Students and hotel people speak quite good English. On the coast the ordinary Latin alphabet is used but inland, especially in Serbia, the Cyrillic similar to Russian is widespread. This should be learned (it takes about two days) if you're going to tour in that region, otherwise the road signs won't be readable.

HOW MUCH

Prices are very low by our standards. You get about 3,500 Dinars to the £ and they go a long way. Remember that the average Yugoslav will only be earning about 40,000 Dinars a month. Food is very cheap, transport costs are absurdly low, but some consumer goods (bicycles, typewriters) are still costly.

HOW TO GET AROUND

The railway system is good in the north but weakens in the mountainous south and is positively tottery towards the tortuous Dalmatian Coast. The main line Ljubljana-Zagreb-Belgrade, the lines to the Kvarner Gulf, and the long branch to Split are the best for passenger traffic, with comfortable express and sleeping cars. Fares are very low even in 1st Class (recommended). 'Ekspresni Voz' is an express train in Serbo-Croat; you pay a supplement of 600 Dinars. JAT (Yugoslavian State Airlines) have useful internal services between Belgrade and most cities, especially Dubrovnik, Titograd, Sarajevo and Split. Dubrovnik's Airport is now of international standard (BEA flies there direct from London) and direct JAT flights connect it with Ljubljana and Sarajevo. Roads are steadily being improved. There is a toll motorway between Ljubljana and Belgrade via Zagreb. A new coastal road was opened to Dubrovnik from the north in May and this is being extended towards Budva and the south. Most secondary roads outside Slovenia and the more populated parts of Croatia are rough, dusty and full of pot-holes. This even applies to main roads in Macedonia and Montenegro. You can hire a car: usually a small Fiat of the type built in the country under licence.

Nova 1965

THE CELEBRATIONS

Malham Moor can never have borne a greater crowd than that assembled on 24th April to commemorate the completion of the Pennine Way. More than 2,000 people were estimated as being present. A third of them managed to crowd into a large marquee, but the others were interested enough to bear for an hour or more with an icy wind that swept across the moor.

Lord Strang, chairman of the National Parks Commission, in opening the proceedings admitted that an unconscionable time had been taken in completing the Pennine Way. This in part was due to inadequacies of the National Parks Act which he hoped would soon be reviewed and improved.

The Rt. Hon. F. T. Willey, Minister of Land and Natural Resources, who in the morning had been one of a small party which scaled Penyghent (2,273 ft.), took Lord Strang's hint. He said he hoped this year to amend the National Parks and Access to the Countryside Act, 1949. He added that he was appalled that it had taken 14 years to complete the Way.

Tom Stephenson said it was good to know the Way was now completed but he hoped some blemishes would be removed. He hoped the Commission would protect it from tarmacadam, pylons, afforestation and reservoirs. He also hoped accommodation for walkers similar to that to be opened in Longdendale would be established where needed, especially in the Cheviots.

Rucksack 1965

HOLIDAYS DURING TERM DEPLORED

BRO. ALBAN, headmaster of St. Joseph's Academy, Blackheath, London, in a circular to parents deplores the ever-increasing number of pupils who are withdrawn during term-time for holidays.

"Many parents wished to take their sons away for the full ten days allowed by the regulations," he says.

He says he is "quite appalled" at the "disruption caused both before and after the summer by absences."

He therefore gives the exact dates of all school holidays up to 1967 to give an opportunity to parents to plan, if possible, their family holidays in advance.

Universe 1965

LAKER FORMS OWN JET LINE

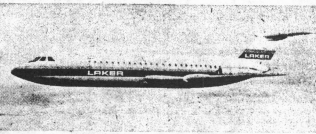

● A 1-11 in Laker livery

MR. FREDDIE LAKER — ex-British United Airways managing director — has launched his own all-jet charter airline with a fleet costing more than £4 million.

Three twin-ejt 300 series 1-11s have been ordered from the British Aircraft Corporation. They will be delivered by the end of this year and be in commercial operation by summer, 1967.

First news of Mr. Laker's plans for a new airline was revealed exclusively by *TTG* last year — only a week after his resignation from BUA (*TTG*, December 3).

The airline—Laker Airways—is designed to cater specifically for 'B' licence category traffic. It has a nominal capital of £10,000.

The three 1-11s, costing, with spares, more than £4 million, will be chartered out to tour operators on a contract hire basis for entire seasons.

Mr. Laker's 1-11 livery has been designed to leave the top of the fuselage clean for the respective tour operators' names to be painted in.

On Tuesday Mr. Laker stated that no company had yet contracted to use his 1-11s, but he was "talking to everyone."

Laker Airways will operate out of Gatwick airport, where hangar and maintenance facilities have been leased from Air Couriers.

Sole directors of Laker Airways are Mr. Laker and and his wife, Joan.

Mr. Laker revealed that initial development costs for the carrier, including crew training on BAC demonstration aircraft, would total £211,500.

"The inclusive holiday trade by air is about to explode and inclusive holiday promoters will be able to take advantage of this new specialist jet service," he maintained.

BAC's 1-11, Mr. Laker added, was a low-cost vehicle which would offer the kind of economy needed to enable tour operators to remain viable.

● See page 32

Travel Trade Gazette 1966

Swan Hellenic Cruises 1966

Alternative Itineraries in Athens and Istanbul

We are offering alternative itineraries in Athens and Istanbul specially planned for those passengers who have travelled with us previously.

Leave Piraeus by motor coach at 8.15 a.m. for Athens to visit the Kerameikos, adjacent to the walls of Athens and the Dipylon or Double Gate whence the famous Panathenaic procession proceeded every four years to the Parthenon. The Kerameikos was shared by the potters of Athens and the great Athenian cemetery which has produced such a splendid collection of pottery and of sculptured tombstones, some still *in situ*. Here were buried many of the great men of Athens. Continue to the Agora Museum, housed in the carefully rebuilt Stoa of Attalus (2nd century B.C.), which contains a remarkable collection of objects found by the American School in its extensive excavations of the near-by Agora. Continue on foot through the Roman forum to the Tower of the Winds, built in the 1st century B.C. to serve as a combined wind-indicator, sundial and water-clock, and decorated with figures symbolising the eight principal winds. Thence by coach to the Acropolis.

In the afternoon there will be an opportunity of visiting the Byzantine Museum instead of the National Museum.

Leave by motor coach at 8.15 a.m. and during the morning visit: Imperial Palace with its splendid mosaics showing vivid hunting and other scenes of the time of Justinian; Church of Sts. Sergius and Bacchus ("Little St. Sophia") built by Justinian about A.D. 530—a small precursor to the grand Cathedral of St. Sophia; Church of St. Irene built in the 4th century A.D.—one of the first Christian churches of Byzantium; the spectacular underground Basilica Cistern; Fethiye Mosque, former Church of the Pammacaristos Virgin, with its recently uncovered mosaics which are among the most important surviving examples of the Late Byzantine period; Church of St. John of Studion (Imrahor Mosque), founded in A.D. 463, with the remains of a 13th-century mosaic pavement of unusual interest.

After visiting St. Sophia in the afternoon there will be an opportunity of visiting the Archaeological Museum instead of the Seraglio.

*Shepton Mallet
Journal, City of
Wells Reporter and
County Advertiser 1966*

The Small Faces pop group who will be performing at the Mid-Somerset Show.

Petticoat 1967

The Small Faces at Shepton Show

A BREAK with tradition, but one which it is hoped will attract more young people to the Mid-Somerset Show this year, is the inclusion of a top pop group in the programme. The group is The Small Faces, whose latest record "All or nothing" is quickly becoming a best seller.

The group will give two performances in the show ring at 1.30 p.m. and 6.30 p.m. They will also make an appearance in the evening at the show dance.

The four young men from London have had considerable success in their relatively short time together as a group. Already they have had five records in the Top Twenty, one of them topping the Hit Parade.

The group is made up of Steve Marriot (lead guitar and vocals), Ronnie 'Plonk' Lane (bass guitar and vocals), Kenny Jones (drums) and Ian 'Mac' McLagan (organ, guitar and vocals). The oldest members of the group are only 20.

BREAKTHROUGH

The group's first breakthrough came in Sheffield. After a date in a working men's club, they went along to one of the city's top clubs and asked the manager if they could do a short audition appearance for him free. They finally persuaded him to let them go on and subsequently brought the house down. The audience would not let them leave the stage and the manager was so delighted he even paid them! The boys repeated the procedure at Manchester with equal success.

On returning to London the group were playing in a pub in the East End when an agent booked them to do a one-night stand at a club in Leicester Square. Their reception was such that they were immediately booked for a five week appearance. Stories of the group began to circulate and a top agent signed them up without having either seen or heard them.

URBANITES

THE Romantics don't, I find, tend to go to Spain which is perhaps a mistake. The coasts are for hedonist S-Setters but inland is a different country. It was in Salamanca I met Jill who was not only beautiful but an Urbanite. Jill, like most Urbanites, was a Place Collector, a City Wanderer. She was among the I-must-get-away-from-Nature-and-all-that-green-stuff brigade. She wasn't an architectural student but some are. It isn't that they dislike Nature but it doesn't tot up in their minds like cities and buildings and things do.

"I must see things," Jill said one day, "otherwise I'll find myself married with a kid and we'll finish up at Weymouth and I shan't know anything."

The Urbanites collect places, never staying long, always reading guide books. Jill used to put on a phony pair of glasses and look fascinated at stone walls. She said it helped her concentrate. Among her favourite places in life were Bourges Cathedral, Cnossos on Crete, Toledo, Marseilles and Istanbul. She sighed over the Parthenon at dusk, Mycenae at dawn and the Cafe Gijon in Madrid at midnight.

Urbanites don't need advising where to go. The whole world is theirs and the only problem is planning the itinerary.

DOERS

BUT Jill and her fellows are essentially lookers, just sometimes slightly looked down upon by the Doers. The ones who have got to be doing something, the I-can't-sit-here-on-this-tiny-beach-any-longer-Freda kind. The holiday has to be an adventure. Time for the beach days when you're a working housewife and you can lie there fluttering your eyes at that Italian with the super body while *he*, the one you came with, is sleeping his executive sleep.

Petticoat 1967

GARBOS

THE Garbos wouldn't be seen dead at a music festival. They seek out the unknown places, they travel in the less crowded months, go to the unfashionable countries. It was they who discovered Albufeira, Collioure, San Stefano, Antalya in the south of Turkey, Sv. Stefan in Yugoslavia, islands like Skyros or even a few years ago, Corsica. Some are real Garbos who seek solitude and hire yachts, or take over mountain shacks in the Pyrenees or settle in a lonely Schloss in an Austrian valley. I met a Garbo once on Peniscola in Spain. Her name I can't remember but we sat in the castle and looked down at the sea and she said: "Isn't it marvellous just getting away from everyone and everything?" And we watched the sea come in and cut off the castle from the mainland for another night. Perhaps that's all there is in it. Getting away from it all.

snobs

BUT the Snobs couldn't accept that. They want to be with it all, not away from it. These are a desperate few who would like so much to be fashionable and so follow the International Set as they drift from St. Moritz to Paris, to Dublin, to Sardinia, to Monte Carlo, to Biarritz, to the Bahamas. Always a year behind the rush to a fishing village at the drop of a royal hat only to find he left two months ago. I must admit that I enjoyed my week with the world's rich in Monte Carlo in the last week of July two years ago, but to keep it up must be agony. Don't bother to start.

Perhaps the most surprising thing about holidays was the survey carried out at stations and ports last year asking people if they'd enjoyed their holiday. Fifty-nine per cent said it had been disappointing. I wonder what they'd expected?

Swan Hellenic Cruises 1966

18th APRIL BEIRUT BAALBEK DAMASCUS

OPTIONAL TWO-DAY PRIVATE CAR EXCURSION TO BAALBEK AND DAMASCUS: Disembark and leave at 11.15 a.m. by private car for BAALBEK (1¾ hours). The enchanting drive over the Lebanese mountains through Aley, Bhamdoun and Sofar affords wonderful views over the Mediterranean and the whole of Beirut. After lunch at Baalbek visit the colossal Temple of Jupiter, the vast Temple of Bacchus and the charming little Temple of Venus, which are among the most impressive monuments of the Syrian School of Roman architecture to be seen today. In the quarry is a stone 68 × 14 ft. estimated to weigh over 1,500 tons; it is the largest hewn stone in the world. Late afternoon continue to DAMASCUS (2¼ hours). Dinner and night at hotel. Evening free in Damascus.

Why freeze in Britain?

Good question. Why freeze in Britain when we can take you on a 16-day sunshine holiday to the Bahamas for £176. Or 12 days in Bermuda for £109. Or 17 days in Barbados for £205. Or 17 days in Antigua for £213. Or 17 days in Jamaica for £223. And if worried about the economic freeze, don't be. All these places are in the Sterling area. There, you're feeling warmer already!

To: BOAC, Airways Terminal, London SW1

Send me your Sunshine Holidays booklet that does away with travel allowances.

NAME ....

ADDRESS ....

.... I.B.

YOU CAN RELY ON A BOAC HOLIDAY ➤ **BOAC**

Brides 1967

Cycle Training 1966

Symonds Yat

The following day we inspected the paved surface of the Roman road at Blackpool Bridge, admired the scenery around the serpentine Wye from Symonds Yat rock, and, according to our choice, either went boating on the river or meandered around Goodrich castle.

Approaching Welsh Bicknor youth hostel, fine views of the river and tree-clad hillsides gave us a fitting ending to a delightful day.

The next morning the boys were at first very quiet and withdrawn. They had suddenly realized, and regretted, that this was to be the last day of the holiday. The mood did not last once we were again on the road, as demonstrated by the lusty singing (for want of a better word!) as they pedalled happily over Kerne bridge and down the east bank of the river Wye.

The singing gradually diminished as we exerted ourselves to climb Ruardean hill, until only puffing and panting could be heard. The swooping descent into Mitcheldean was the last big one of the tour, though the remainder of the route was by no means flat as we followed the lanes past Flaxley abbey and Northwood Green, eventually to join the main road near Gloucester.

Farewells were said and the boys were soon going their separate ways: the tour finished at Gloucester as quietly as it had started. At the final parting all seemed deep in their own thoughts—but thoughts of what?

Perhaps they were wondering how soon it would be before they could once again enjoy the pleasure of cycling in quiet byways. I hope so, for we saw a lot. Yet we missed a lot, for there is always more to see . . .

Discovery by bicycle is truly an adventure.

Ardgartan campsite, with Ben Lomond in the background, c. 1965.

Don't feel obliged to look at our history, our monasteries, our frescoes, our mountains.

If you want to laze, we want you to laze. We also have sunshine, seclusion and seashore by the mile.

No need to move. Well, just an arm – to raise your glass of slivovica, or bite into that sun-ripe orange. No need to ramble through cool pine forests, go water-sporting, climb soaring mountains, sail to fascinating islands. They'd be irresistible if your sun-tan weren't coming along so well. (Have some more oil.)

Then our history. Roman and Turkish. Medieval art. Franciscan churches. You could read about it while you roast, of course. Fishing is fun. But you could just eat the catch. And the veal, the pork, the lamb, the pancakes, the paprika, the wonderful wine. There are wine-cellars, where tasters are welcome, free. Ah, you moved.

Maybe, now's the moment to mention the folk-dancing, the shops, the hotels, the low prices, the lemon trees, the flowers. And that warm, vivid sea. Float out . . . that's easy. Then flop again, and look forward to the night life – once you're sure the sun's really gone down.

As for tomorrow, the sun, seashore and seclusion will still be here. If that's still all you want.

For more facts about Yugoslavia's marvellous miles of coastline, ask your Travel Agent or clip this coupon.

YUGOSLAVIA

Yugoslav National Tourist Office,
143 Regent St, London, W1.
Telephone: 01-734-5243 or 8714
I may laze, I may look.
Please send *free* facts about
Yugoslavia anyway.
□ General information
□ Motoring □ Camping

Name _____

Address _____

_____
                          RT1

Radio Times 1967

Vogue 1968

VOGUE'S TRAVEL GUIDE

Imperial Hotel, Torquay
Revel in the five-star international reputation of The Imperial . . . the luxurious comfort of its sunny rooms, enjoy the finest foods and wines which are unequalled anywhere. Dance nightly in the ballroom or in The Commodore Night Club.

Walking Stalks

While on holiday in Jersey this year, with my parents and sister, we went on a coach tour. One of the things that stands out in my memory is seeing cabbages which were sixteen feet tall. The driver of the coach told us that walking sticks were made out of the stalks. Much to my delight, he handed one of these sticks round the party in the coach. It really was amazing to see that such a good walking stick had been made from a cabbage stalk!

—A Postal Order to David Carruthers, Carlisle, Cumberland.

Sparky 1967

Mayfair Hotel

Friendly informality, fine cuisine, air conditioned Cocktail Lounge, outdoor barbecued steaks on Saturday nights, fish and chips Wednesday and Friday Lunchtime are combined with moderate rates to make your vacation in Jamaica one to be remembered.

4 WEST KINGS HOUSE CLOSE,
KINGSTON 10, JAMAICA W.I.
TELEPHONE 69419 and 67987
CABLE MAYFAIR, JAMAICA

Revellers welcome in 1967 at Trafalgar Square.

Pensioners on the prom, 1967.

ANNE LAMBTON . . . has travelled the world and knows what to wear in different climates . . . moves around in a social world and knows what to wear for the right occasion. She will be happy to answer any reader's inquiry about a specific problem involving

What to wear where and what to do when

My husband is awfully bad at being parted from his city suit, and this year we are joining friends in Spain staying, according to you, at one of the most elegant places in Europe, Sotogrande. I'd like to know what you consider the right clothes for both of us to take.

Your husband will need two or three pairs of cotton pants, with casual shirts, and a pair of canvas sneakers—on sale at Harrods. If he plans to play golf, then two or three cashmere pullovers, as the course can be chilly in the evening, golf shoes, and socks to wear inside them. At night, he can wear either a seersucker suit, in perhaps champagne or blue, with a coloured shirt ; or, for a change, a lightweight navy blazer with grey or white pants. You both need swimwear, and something to accompany it, like a short navy blue towelling coat for your husband. And quite honestly, as far as you are concerned, the best of Pucci. By day you lie in the sun. You play golf or tennis in the evening, then dine and dance—you in pyjamas, your husband casually dressed as described. You need to take the odd very good ring and pair of earrings, have an expensive evening bag and plenty of scent, as the kind of people you will be mixing with have so much money that, although they may be relaxing and living casually by their standards, they sometimes do something eccentric like going swimming wearing an enormous square cut diamond because they have just arrived from Madrid and haven't bothered to put it away in the safe in their bedroom.

My job entails going to Portugal in August to supervise some fashion photography. As I found Torremolinos almost unbearably hot in March, I am really dreading this next trip.

Feeling the heat is partly psychological, as is feeling the cold. So, start by talking yourself into feeling cool and never do anything in a hurry. You'll notice the locals don't. See your doctor, who can give you some special vitamin pills, which help one not to get burnt by the sun, or upset by heat. Plan your wardrobe so that all your dresses are sleeveless, and lined, so that all you need to wear beneath is a tiny pair of briefs and light lace bra. Lie down and cool off after a bath, and keep your hair off the back of your neck during the day by wearing it in a plait, or up. Wear dark glasses, and don't drink any more liquid during the day than is really necessary, but prevent yourself from getting dehydrated by drinking during the cool of the evening. Wear open flat sandals or very lightweight fabric slippers.

Can one accept a formal invitation by telephone ?

No, not unless it is something like an Embassy which gives as R.S.V.P. a telephone number, in which case you speak to the second secretary and this is quite correct.

When writing to an American is it correct to address him, as we do in England, with Esq. following his name, or with Mr. in front of it, which is the way they appear to write to each other ?

It depends entirely where you are writing to the American. You write to all males, English and other nationalities included, in the accepted American way when they are in the States. When they are in England, you follow the English formula, and so on through other countries—rather as one would put *Personal* into the different languages, whatever the nationality of the receiver.

I am just not the figure for wearing pyjama suits, and I know that on my holiday I'm going to feel hopelessly out of things as we are staying with friends at Cap d'Antibes in the height of the season. Any suggestions ?

Yes, two. Buy a couple of ground length dresses in African prints—they are made by Simon Massey, and available very inexpensively in most of our leading department stores. And for best, a silk embroidered caftan. If you fancy the real thing, Simpson's in Piccadilly are importing them direct from Morocco ; if not, there are any amount of inexpensive copies around in the small boutiques in the Knightsbridge and King's Road area.

Woman's Home Journal **1968**

Was due to go to Prague

LUTON'S Borough Librarian, Mr. Frank Gardner, was in Germany yesterday, on the first stage of a Continental trip that was to have taken him into Czechoslovakia.

But as Russian troops moved into the country, Mr. Gardner was expected to change his plans and return to Luton earlier than he intended.

Enquiries at Luton's travel agencies yesterday suggest that there are no visitors from the town in Czechoslovakia, although the Beds and Herts Travel Service thought that some holiday-makers might be " passing through."

An official said : " Czechoslovakia is not in itself a popular holiday attraction, but some tours of European capitals go to Prague."

An official of Thomas Cook and Son Ltd.'s Luton office said that no-one was visiting Czechoslovakia through bookings made with Cook's.

He added : " We have a few people who want to go there later on, and I don't know whether they will decide to change their plans."

The Borough Librarian's trip to Czechoslovakia was to have been part business and part pleasure. He is in Frankfurt as one of the representatives of the British Library Association at a conference of the International Federation of Library Associations.

He intended to travel into Czechoslovakia next week for another library conference, and then stay on for a short holiday.

Mr. Gardner is due back at work in the middle of September.

Luton News and Bedford Advertiser **1968**

The Listener 1969

Bournemouth is different. It has the stodge and the greed and cunning of a Blackpool but without the vox pop, without the hurdy-gurdy. And it's got no art, no whimsy, to compensate, nothing trend-setting like Brighton. I thought about this: it's not only the image of the place as somewhere people go when they've had it —and the palm court orchestra, the fig-tree. It is partly geography. Bournemouth is too far from the metropolis for a day trip and not far enough to be foreign like Cornwall or Jersey. London does provide her with more settlers than any other indi-vidual town, but a lot of immigrants come from the North. The two principal named trains into the resort are the Bournemouth Belle from London and the Pines Express from the North.

In the winter, although the subtropical belt by the sea stays green and laced with its cooling chines, behind Bournemouth the weather gets rough. The ferocity of winters in Hardy's Wessex on those— they're almost moors—has to be felt to be appreciated. Bournemouth is in Hampshire but it's so uptight to Dorset. In some areas Bournemouth is the capital of Dorset—for police and for hospitals. Poole, Dorset, be-gins just a few yards from Bournemouth West Station. They run together, Bourne-mouth and Poole, you can't tell where one ends and the other begins. And in the middle of Poole harbour, the second-larg-est, finest natural harbour in the world, that strange Brownsea Island where Canute debauched the maidens and Baden Powell made his first boy-scout camp. England's second lakeland: a yachting centre second only to Cowes.

Greater Bournemouth has small works turning out mobile homes, boats, sports-wear and swimwear, and three great firms —Bowater finance house, Ryvita slim crisp bread makers, and Max Factor the perfume and cosmetic company. Then there are people who make machinery for hover-craft; and out at Hurn in the north, airwork services, flight refuelling, and the most powerful aerospace company in Europe— this is not their main plant but it is an important one—in the British Aircraft Corporation.

Of course Bournemouth's biggest em-ployers remain the hospitals and nursing homes, the funeral directors, hotels, the catering and domestic service, but next come the schools, and the aerospace. We often talk of nationalising the aerospace industry and of private schools. I leave you with this thought, and it would be a good investment: why don't we nationalise the whole of Greater Bournemouth?

Third Programme

BINGO . . . but not for Doris — she is too worried about her street name

SURELY the best bingo story around this week comes from our Romford correspondent.

It concerns housewife Mrs. Doris Gilbert, a keen bingo fan . . . but a fan who has often lived in fear of hitting the big jackpot.

For Mrs. Gilbert has always believed that by winning a big prize at bingo her address would be revealed to all and sundry. Not that she minds people knowing where she lives . . . just that she didn't want people to know the name of the street she lives in.

For Doris no longer wants to live in BOGS GAP LANE.

She wants something more sophisticated and sweet sounding. So with typical bingo determination she has asked the local parish council to help avoid any embarrassment and change the name of the street.

Twenty-four other residents of Bogs Gap Lane feel the same way and they think that their homes in Steeple Morden, Cambridgeshire, are due for a new address.

Doris, 46, tells us: "The name originally came years ago when this area was rather boggy. I've always felt that if my address was made public then I would be humiliated. I did not want to give up bingo and I travel about 40 miles each week to play in the big games.

"This name just doesn't do justice to this lovely area."

Doris, a mother of six children, said she had finally decided to come out in the open about the name in an all-out attempt to get it changed.

The South Cambridgeshire Rural District Council has said it will consider the request for a change of name, so let's hope Doris will soon find herself living in a more romantic street such as **Bingo Broadway, Full House Lane, Scoop Street, Jackpot Promenade** . . .

Leisure 1969

Only in England would Donne's assertion that no man is an island have seemed a paradox and not a commonplace. Son of an island, each man is himself an island, secure in the certainty of his own boundaries. Things foreign break upon him like waves. He is the world's toughest traveller. What an incredible diaspora of amateur explorers, footloose second sons, dissatisfied colonels and inquisitive ladies in hoop skirts creates and fills an Empire between Drake's accidental circumnavigation of the globe and Scott's doomed saunter toward the South Pole! The Africans called Mungo Park 'the one who travels alone', and the same term would apply to Livingstone, Lawrence, Doughty, Burton. The attraction between the British and the Arabs must rest in part on a common austerity, an ability to travel light.

The Listener 1969

Cricket in Corfu

In *Holidays Abroad* (Radio 4) Sir Ian Orr-Ewing, MP for Hendon North, spoke about the cricket matches they have in Corfu. ' One of the most attractive features of this island is their habit of playing cricket. We left here about 100 years ago, but they still keep it up and they're full of enthusiasm. We had a tremendous match last Wednesday which ended with 1,000 spectators sitting round the ground roaring their heads off at every run that was scored by the Greeks, and, of course, if the ball ever hits your pad or even your head you are immediately rewarded by a shout round the ground. Every cricketer on the ground and most of the spectators shout "Howdat" and I may say they're very well rewarded for their enthusiasm by the Greek umpires. This certainly teaches you not to play cricket with your pads. There's a strip of concrete on which matting is laid and all around—it's normally a car park—there's very rough gravel and this is very painful indeed. The Greeks are brave people. You see them dive forward to catch, and they invariably come up with kneecaps stripped and elbows bleeding. Round the ground are all the cafés, and people sit quietly in the shade drinking their ouzo—once we managed to get a six right into a bottle of wine and broke it on the table. If you haven't played cricket in Corfu you've never really played cricket.'

The Listener 1969

Daily Mail 1969

Holiday trains to West face hold-up

NEARLY 100 holiday trains to the West Country will be delayed today because of damage to the track, British Rail said last night.

Only a single line will be open between Exeter and Taunton. The damage was caused by a faulty freight wagon.

Alterations will be made today to services linking Devon and Cornwall with Paddington, Waterloo, South Wales, the Midlands and the North. Some trains tomorrow will also be affected.

Most trains linking the West with the Midlands and North via Bristol will travel over their normal route, although subject to delay.

Couple run from voice in the sky

A HOLIDAY couple were strolling along Blackpool sands yesterday when a voice from the skies asked them to move out of the way.

When Mr Joe Clarkson and his wife, Mona, looked up they saw a biplane silently sweeping towards them, its pilot waving them aside. As the couple ran, the plane made an emergency landing. Its engine had failed.

Later the pilot, Mr John Wilkinson, aged 27, of Leventhorpe Lane, Thornton, Bradford, met Mr and Mrs Clarkson, and said he hoped he had not shouted rudely. Mr Clarkson, of Leyburn Road, Masham, near Ripon, replied: "I thought you were very polite in view of the circumstances."

TENT FOR THREE

Touring with a baby was no problem for the Gills on their Continental holiday.

Angela and Reg Gill set off from Solihull last October with no special destination in mind beyond a wish to see Andorra. But, being experienced campers, they had given much thought to the well-being of Andrew, aged twenty months.

"If a baby is happy and comfortable, then it's O.K. for the parents," Angela decided, and based her plans on that philosophy.

They fitted a child's safety seat to the rear seat of their estate car; packed a push chair and the pram body taken off its wheels so Andrew could sleep in a familiar bed. They also took a trailer which converts to a tent.

"We caught the overnight Normandy Ferry from Southampton to Le Havre, and Andrew slept beautifully. We were off the boat by seven and drove to Brive, near Limoges, for our first overnight stop. Owing to a mix-up over the bill, bed and breakfast for three came to only 21s. (£1·5)!"

Reg purposely drove through the Dordogne for its fabulous scenery, then they camped two nights at Aix les Thermes. "From here we did a day trip to Andorra and were terribly disappointed. The rugged countryside around was gorgeous, but the rest was so commercialised."

They pressed on over the Pyrenees, along switchback roads towards the Costa Brava; difficult driving with sheer mountain on one side, precipitous drop on the other, but Andrew behaved marvellously.

"A British couple we met recommended a campsite three miles outside Tossa de Mar, so we went

Woman 1970

there and found it excellent—in its own secluded bay, private beach, shady pine trees, restaurant, playground, tennis, hairdresser; even a night club in season.

"It was perfect for Andrew; no fear of traffic, and the Spanish woman washroom attendant kept an eye on all the kiddies. The beach was near for us but just too far for Andrew to reach alone—a very good thing. He went in the water every day with Reg. The weather was ideal—warm enough to get sun-tanned, with cool evenings. It got dark at seven-thirty so Andrew went to sleep easily."

Photography is Reg's hobby, so the Gills took morning trips to Tossa, Blanes, Lloret and the market at Gerona, where there was plenty of scope. They lunched in the tent, spent afternoons on the beach, and after Andrew had his tea, often went to the Poseda Maria Angela, a restaurant near the castle where a four-course meal cost 12s. 6d. (62½p). "Andrew slept in the car nearby so it was easy to pop out and make sure he was all right."

The Gills took with them tinned stewed steak, spaghetti, baked beans; fourpenny packets of cereal rather than big ones which don't keep so fresh; tinned food for Andrew, and twelve packets of dolly mixtures. (He enjoyed the milk in Spain and had lots of yoghurt.)

Angela wore sweater and jeans for travelling (best, she says, when coping with children), swimsuits in camp and dresses in the evening.

Their complete holiday cost £143 15s. 6d. (£143·77½) for eighteen days and next summer they're setting their sights on Italy.

Spain 15 days from	£36	Tunisia 15 days from	£64.10
Italy 12 days from	£28.10	Turkey 15 days from	£80
Austria 10 days from	£24.10	Canary Isles 15 days from	£70.5
Yugoslavia 15 days from	£51.5	Bermuda 15 days from	£109
Majorca 15 days from	£39.5	Bahamas 15 days from	£143.19

and lots, lots more

Off-peak bonus!
Five star gift pack comes with all holidays with departures up to and including May 30th and from 9th September on!

Go Off-peak!

LUNN POLY
Dept. RT.1, 36 Edgware Rd, London, W2. 01-262 7777
Please send me 1968 Holiday Brochure.

Name_____

Address_____

Lunn-Poly is a member of the Travel Trust.

Guardian 1970

Daily Mail 1970

£50 travel limit is ended

By PHILIP WHITFIELD

OUT goes the £50 foreign travel limit. From today you can spend as much as you like as often as you like on holidays abroad.

Businessmen too can spend more. Credit cards can be used abroad. And the foreign gift ceiling is raised to £300.

Chancellor Mr Roy Jenkins announced the abolition of the three-year-old limit last night, just in time for travel agents to get ready for a holiday boom.

Ending the restrictions was made possible by the balance of payments surplus and the new strength of sterling.

It was speeded by widespread evasion of the rules by holidaying Britons, who are estimated to have salted away £100 million abroad to supplement their holiday spending. Now they can bring this money home — and help Britain's balance of payments.

Travel agents and air and shipping lines welcomed the Chancellor's decision as the best tonic they have had for ten years.

Woman's Own 1970

Holiday?

Sir,—Another Bank Holiday over and I am convinced that the time has come for a change.

At the public counter we began our Easter Slog a week before-hand with double pensions to be paid. On the Thursday before Good Friday we had queues to the door all day.

With no extra help at the counter we are expected to do two days work in one, while the public behave as though we are going to close for about six weeks!

I arrived home exhausted and for what? We were back at the slog on Saturday for another onslaught and the dreaded Tuesday looming ahead. The P &TO can never enjoy any public holiday under present circumstances.

I think its time we followed the lead of the Supermarkets and opened for business all day on Good Friday. Public counters could then close for three days and give us a real holiday.

Either that or let us remain open for the whole holiday and have time off in lieu at some other date.

I for one would no longer have that feeling of dread every time a public holiday looms towards us. I may even be able to go away for a few days as, outside industrial workers do!

R. F. WILSON.
P & TO. Sandwich.

The Post 1970

POTTY REQUIRED

I am taking Lindy, aged two, to Scotland from London, just before Easter. We are travelling by train, and as I shall have to cope single-handed with her folding pushchair, a suitcase, and a small bag with her immediate necessities, I just can't cope with her potty, and I know she won't use the lavatory on the train. Does anybody make a collapsible potty that would fold flat enough to slip into her bag? Yes, the Cindico firm have produced the "Cindiloo" a potty with normal "bowl" and detachable frame with collapsible legs. When travelling, polythene bags are secured within the frame, in place of the bowl, and after use can be fastened and disposed of when convenient.

The Cindiloo costs 25s. complete with inner "bowler hat" and twelve disposable bags. (Spare packs of twelve bags cost 1s. 6d.) Available at baby shops, nursery stores and baby departments.

Woman 1970

Babbacombe
Bay, Devon,
1970.

Thursday

12.00 noon	Swimming Instruction.
2.30 p.m.	Junior Showtime.
4.00 p.m.	Slot Car Race Meeting on the "St. Lambert Raceway".
7.30 p.m.	Holiday Time Revue.
9.30 p.m.	Paper Bouquet Competition in the Sun Lounge.
10.45 p.m.	Town Crier and Glamorous Grandmother Competition in the Ballroom.

Friday

9.15 a.m.	Visit to the Welsh Mountain Zoo, Colwyn Bay—meet in Reception.
10.30 a.m.	Clipper Treasure Hunt.
2.30 p.m.	Clipper Olympics.
7.30 p.m.	Prize-giving Ceremony in the Ballroom.
8.30 p.m.	Join in the laughter and fun of Carnival Night and the Fancy Dress Competition.
11.40 p.m.	The Skipper and Crew say "Au Revoir".
12.00 midnight	Goodnight Shipmates and "Many Happy Returns".

Prestatyn Holiday Camp souvenir programme 1970